A Manual on
BOOKSELLING

What Is a Good Bookseller?

To be a successful bookseller one needs an innate fondness for books, an infinite capacity for pains in handling details, a certain poise and self-confidence which is the basis of selling ability. Beyond these one must cultivate business ability, for successful bookstore management is based fundamentally on the same principles as any other retail business: aggressive merchandising and sound financial control.—FREDERIC G. MELCHER, *The Successful Bookshop* (New York: National Association of Book Publishers, 1926)

A Manual on BOOKSELLING

Second Edition

How To Open and Run Your Own Bookstore

Edited for the
American Booksellers Association by
Charles B. Anderson
and
G. Roysce Smith

Sanford Cobb,
Advisory Editor

American Booksellers Association
New York

First edition published in 1969; second edition in 1974.

First Printing

This edition is specially prepared for distribution to members of the American Booksellers Association, Inc., 800 Second Avenue, New York, N.Y. 10017. A trade edition with identical contents is available from Harmony Books, a division of Crown Publishers, Inc., 419 Park Avenue South, New York, N.Y. 10016. No part of this book may be reproduced or utilized in any form or by any means, electronic or mechanical, including photocopying, recording, or by an information storage and retrieval system, without permission in writing from the Publisher.

Inquiries should be addressed to Harmony Books, a division of Crown Publishers, Inc., 419 Park Avenue South, New York, N.Y. 10016.

ACKNOWLEDGEMENT: Some of these articles originally appeared in slightly different form in *Publishers Weekly.*

Printed in the United States of America.
Published simultaneously in Canada by General Publishing Company Limited.

Book design by Carol Callaway

LIBRARY OF CONGRESS CATALOGING IN PUBLICATION DATA

Anderson, Charles B
  A manual on bookselling.

  Bibliography: p.
  1. Booksellers and bookselling—United States.
2. Booksellers and bookselling—Handbooks, manuals, etc. I. Smith, G. Royce, joint author. II. Title.
Z476.A63 1974   658.8'09'0705730973   74–79783
ISBN 0–517–51646–2
ISBN 0–517–51647–0 (pbk.)

Contents

V. DEPARTMENTS 2: SIDELINES

VI. PROMOTION AND ADVERTISING

VII. A BOOKSELLER'S CONTINUING EDUCATION

List of Figures

Foreword

SANFORD COBB
Former President,
Association of American Publishers, Inc.

Bookselling was once a simple thing—the author was his own book-seller. In Colonial days, when an author had completed a manuscript, he sought out a printer and contracted, at a price, to have a certain number of copies of his book run off. Then he, the author, went about securing his own distribution. Gradually, though, the printer began to keep a few copies in his shop and to sell them on commission. If he was a good printer, he was serving a number of authors, so he soon found himself with a varied stock of books to sell. By a natural process, printers began to exchange their stocks of books with each other and presto—bookshops! Prescient printers also began to learn from experience why particular books appealed to the public and to discover ways of guiding authors with regard to style and manner of presentation. Thus they became, by evolution, editors and publishers.

During the nineteenth century, many important houses combined the facilities of printing, publishing, and bookselling. Even in the early decades of this century, such illustrious names as Doubleday, Scribner's, Putnam's, and Houghton Mifflin come to mind. Today we live in a society so complex that with one or two notable exceptions the functions of publishing, printing, and bookselling have again become separate. And rightly so. But the word "publish" still carries its classical meaning: "to make known," as in "publish glad tidings," and the function of the bookseller includes, as always, the responsibility of providing the bridge between the originator of a thought—the author—and the individual who will benefit from that thought—the reader.

Nowadays there are published each year between twenty and thirty thousand new books that are directed toward the general public, or, to be more precise, that great collection of people with varying special interests who make up the general reading public. Obviously no bookseller can stock so large a quantity of new titles, let alone the 350,000 or more books that remain in print in this country. Nor can any single review medium give them the notices they deserve. But it is the bookseller's responsibility, particularly if he operates what is still fondly known as a "personal" bookshop or, even, book department, to guide his customers as best he can to the books they want and need. It is from this that he gets his greatest satisfaction.

Having been for a wonderfully rich period of his life involved in personal bookselling in an alert, intelligent community, this editor can give personal testimony to the joy of operating what was not only a bookshop, but a meeting place for the readers in the community, a source of information about new and forthcoming books and even, on occasion, a means of introduction to the pleasures and benefits of the printed word.

Bookselling is not easy. In most instances it doesn't provide monetary compensation comparable to other types of retailing, but if it is pursued with enthusiasm, if its practitioners never lose sight of the fact that it is a business and therefore subject to the disciplines of cost control and prudent management, then it can be one of the most rewarding of vocations.

As one who has spent a full and satisfying life with books, not only as bookseller, but as publisher and explorer of new avenues of book distribution, it has been a great personal satisfaction to have a part in preparing this new, enlarged edition of *A Manual on Bookselling: How To Open and Run a Bookstore*.

The work of almost forty individuals, each an expert in his or her field, the *Manual* covers as many aspects of the art of selling books as possible, and will hopefully be found useful by beginners and the experienced alike. To all those contributors, who gave so generously of their time and expertise, the editors are deeply grateful.

One hopes, having lived with the manuscript during its development, that the major point it will make is that it is possible to run a financially successful bookstore or book department. But because so many of the contributors are practicing booksellers, it cannot help but carry another message as well: Running a successful bookshop serves the community in a special way, and booksellers—real booksellers—derive intense satisfaction from their vocation.

I should like to acknowledge the extreme pleasure of having been closely associated in this project with Charles B. Anderson, owner of Anderson's Book Shop, Larchmont, New York, and chairman of the Publications Committee of the ABA, and G. Roysce Smith, executive director of the ABA—veteran booksellers both, and a source of continuing inspiration to their colleagues and friends.

Preface

CHARLES B. ANDERSON
Anderson's Book Shop,
Larchmont, New York

There have been a good many changes on the American bookselling scene since the first edition of this *Manual* was published in 1969. There are more titles by far for a bookseller to cope with, in both hardback and paper, than there were then, making almost mandatory for even the smaller stores some system of inventory control, a subject not covered in the first book. Remainders have become a more important part of the stock-in-trade of almost all stores. Bookstore architects and planners have developed shelving and display fixtures that have made the fixturing of a few years ago almost obsolete. The computer and microfilm have recently found their way into some stores. With the growth and expansion throughout the country of suburban shopping centers, several hundred booksellers have in the past five years set up stores in these locations, and hundreds more are wondering whether they should be tempted. For these and other reasons a revision of the *Manual* was in order.

Actually this is more than a revision. It is a considerably larger and different book. More than half the articles are entirely new, written expressly for this edition. Those articles from the old book that we have retained for the new have had a thoroughgoing revision and updating. When my good friend and former coeditor, the late Joe Duffy, for many years executive director of ABA, worked with me in planning the first edition of the *Manual,* we did not have at hand much material that has since become available as a result of courses taught at the Booksellers School, an educational project sponsored jointly by ABA and the National Association of College Stores. This material accounts for the articles on inventory control, merchandise budgeting, accounting methods, and publicity and advertising. Also covered here are subjects that Joe Duffy and I, for one reason or another, just never got around to including in the first book, such as selling a store, insurance, wholesaling or jobbing, out-of-print books, and reference-book departments. New also is the Glossary of bookseller's terms, which your editors hope will be useful and perhaps interesting for neophyte and veteran booksellers alike.

Thirty-seven booksellers and friends of bookselling have con-
tributed articles for which they have received no payment or reward
other than the satisfaction that must surely come to them of sharing
their expertise with fellow booksellers and of showing them how to run
better stores. On behalf of my coeditors and of the Board of Directors
of ABA I should like to express sincere thanks to all of them.

I want to express my personal thanks to my coeditors, Sanford Cobb
and G. Roysce Smith, both of them former booksellers. San and Roysce
have given hundreds of hours to the planning and production of this
volume and have brought imagination, integrity, and high editorial
competence to the task. It has been a stimulating and rewarding experience to work with them.

Introduction

Bookselling Is a Good Career

JAMES F. ALBRIGHT
Former Regional Manager, Dallas,
Cokesbury Division of Methodist Publishing House

A decision to go into any type of selling is often influenced by the fact that one can get a start at selling with few qualifications beyond the determination to find a job. But if you choose bookselling, it should be because you like books—all books. You must like them well enough to live with them all the time—to think books, talk books, read all kinds of books and book reviews. On the other hand, if you are the type who "simply loves books" and have the idea that bookselling is a leisurely way of life, amid cultural surroundings, where you spend your time reading your favorite tomes and gossiping with literary customers and authors, forget it—and apply for another kind of work.

A successful bookseller needs certain definite qualifications and aptitudes. In addition to an interest in books, he should have a well-grounded interest in the book where accounts of profit and loss are recorded. Anyone planning a bookselling career should be able to read, count, write, and spell ordinary names and words and to copy extraordinary ones correctly. He should have enough preliminary education to have a real knowledge of the alphabet and facility in using it to arrange books, look up references, make lists, and carry out the other simple routines of bookselling. Some of my readers may feel that I offer these criteria with tongue in cheek, but anyone who has had anything to do with hiring young people today knows that they are often lacking in these areas of rudimentary education. The qualities of temperament, character, behavior, intellect, and appearance that are desirable for a career in retail bookselling need not be enlarged upon here. Some background in literature is of course an asset.

How does one get into bookselling? The first step is to get some practical experience. Find a bookshop willing to put you on its staff and give you a chance to work at various duties. There is no telling how long it will take to make a good bookseller of you. Much depends on *your* energy and enthusiasm for the job.

If you are certain that you want books to be a part of your lifeblood, if you know beyond a doubt that dealing in books will give you lasting satisfaction, then you will get genuine rewards out of bookselling. You may not make a lot of money, but as a bookseller your extra dividends will come in the satisfaction of holding in your own hands books— objects that are not merely cloth and type and paper but embody the toil and hope and genius of many minds and lives. As a bookseller, you form a creative alliance with the authors, publishers, designers, typographers, and all the others who have a part in making books. The more the bookseller knows about the work of others in the book trade the better he can perform his own vital task.

The bookseller may also count as part of his profits the satisfaction of handling a commodity *everyone* respects, though, compared with the sales of other "necessities," few buy. Those who are interested in easier money and more lucrative returns may think the bookseller is to be pitied for putting so much talent to work for so little monetary return. But a bookstore can also flourish in its modest way, if the bookseller applies to the selling of books the same degree of enthusiasm that is applied to the sale of other products.

Today's bookshop is a great deal more than a mere collection of books, however rich that collection may be. It is an ordered collection; the very arrangement of the store is an aid to ordered thought. Behind this order is where you, the bookseller, fit in. No matter what type of store, your main work will be to function as an interpreter and guide to the vast storehouse of man's knowledge. Wherever there is a bookshop, there will always be a bookseller; there is no danger that he will someday be replaced by a machine.

All booksellers share one primary purpose—to bring books and people together. And in that purpose they have the support of thinking men such as former President Lyndon B. Johnson, who once told a group in the White House Cabinet Room: "Books are the most effective weapons against intolerance and ignorance." The entire bookselling profession rests upon a knowledge of and interest in books. The book market is the arena where the cultural battles of each generation are fought. Here the ultimate clash of ideas, wise and foolish, social and antisocial, is expressed. The literary art is all-inclusive; new movements in science, painting, music, architecture, politics, and religion go forward with a covering barrage of books.

It is not the bookseller's job to tell the prospective reader what he must read. We already have too much standardization and conformity in our daily routine. But it is the bookseller's task to see that the *right* book is sold to the *right* person. It is his primary goal to see that the readers he encounters find the books they are seeking and need. This is how readers are developed, and this is the foundation of a bookstore's turnover and profit.

Booksellers today are affected by many problems in book distribution. The "romance" of bookselling must yield largely to the "science" of bookselling. Booksellers must step up their promotional activities and develop a firmer grasp on their markets in the face of competition from publishers, book clubs, and others trying to capture the consumer.

The bookseller must work hard, intelligently and unendingly, to present books to every area of his community interested in reading and the development of home libraries for the use of books as sources of needed information. He must attempt to awaken larger and larger numbers to the value of books and the delights of reading. He must go into the market place and compete with television, movies, golf, and hundreds of other diversions that take people away from books.

The craving for knowledge exists in all of us. The desire to seek this knowledge in books can be cultivated in anyone. There are millions of Americans who actually want books but who either do not know they want them or do not know how to use them. If booksellers can reach these millions, they will be instrumental in raising the level of American civilization. Whether booksellers do this for money, for glory, or for love does not matter.

There is no lack of room for a large expansion of retail bookselling. Several years ago it was estimated that half the population of the country had no access to bookstores. The wide distribution of paperback books has made it easier for more people to buy books, but there is no evidence as yet that the book market has been much more than nibbled at.

On the wall of my office hangs a carefully hand-lettered quotation from Clarence Day. The words have been displayed because they express most aptly the spirit behind the task of bookselling.

The World of Books
  Is the most remarkable creation of man,
  Nothing else he builds lasts.
  Monuments fall,
  Nations perish,
  Civilizations grow old and die out
  And after an era of darkness
  New races build others.
  But in the world of books are volumes
  That have seen this happen again and again
  And yet live on
  Still young,

Still as fresh as the day they were written,
Still telling men's hearts
Of the hearts of men centuries dead.

Perhaps you can decide today to become a bookseller.

The New Store

Opening a Bookstore*   1

RON BARNEY
Educational Assistant,
American Booksellers Association, Inc.

What preparations should I make for opening a bookstore?

Learn elementary bookkeeping and something about basic business concepts such as budgeting, turnover, and inventory control. It will be critical to the success or failure of your store that you order books realistically in terms of your sales capacity and, once ordered, keep track of them until they are received, sold, and paid for. Since most of your business will be done in very small quantities per title, it will be essential that you are capable of handling the resulting paper work efficiently.

If it's at all possible, you should also work in someone else's store for a while, even if it's only part-time work during the Christmas season. You can learn about finding and ordering books in any store and, if you seize your chances, involve yourself in other bookselling procedures as well. If you're unable to get previous experience, part of your new store's expenses must go toward paying for your own on-the-job training.

Once you get into the planning stages, you'll need to learn as much as you can about your community so you won't get stuck with a bad location.

What kind of location will I need?

One that will attract enough business to enable you to pay expenses. To give you an idea of how many customers that may be, let's assume you'll be able to run the store all by yourself. How many books will you have to sell to pay your salary?

---

*This article is reproduced from a pamphlet of the same title that is available from: American Booksellers Association, Inc., 800 Second Avenue, New York, N.Y. 10017.—Eᴅ.

Salaries account for between 15 and 17 per cent of most bookstores' net sales. If your salary amounts to 17 per cent and you pay yourself $8,500 a year, you'll need to make net sales of $50,000 a year. If you are open 6 days a week, or 313 days a year, you'll need to make sales averaging $159.74 a day. This sum is the equivalent of selling 128 paperbacks at $1.25—or 23 hardbacks at $6.95—every day.

These two approximations are artificial, of course, but they may give you an idea of the number of buying customers you will need to have. The most profitable bookstores are generally those that are located in busy shopping areas with a lot of foot traffic and those that serve active book buyers such as college people. You will probably have to locate in a population center of at least 25,000 to make a success of a books-only bookstore.

A "books-only" bookstore? Are you suggesting carrying other merchandise?

Yes, especially if you open in a smaller community. Other types of merchandise are usually offered to the retailer at around 50 per cent discount—about 10 per cent more than the discounts for books—allowing a store to operate on a smaller sales total. If you want to locate in a *really* small community, you might consider opening another type of store altogether, one that has a book department. You can increase the number of books you carry as you develop a clientele.

If I can get 50 per cent on other merchandise, what discounts can I expect on my books?

The whole matter of publishers' selling arrangements—discounts, shipping points, billing procedures, returns policies, etc.—is so complicated that the American Booksellers Association, Inc. (ABA), publishes a listing of them that amounts to more than five hundred pages in its *ABA Book Buyer's Handbook* every year. We can only give you the most rudimentary idea of these arrangements here.

Discounts vary with what you order, with where you order from, with how many you order, and sometimes, in seasonal offers, with when you order. If you carry a general selection, though, you can anticipate an average discount of a bit less than 40 per cent on your stock. You may find it useful to think in three main categories of books: *long discount, short discount,* and *mass market.*

Long-discount books are those that carry discounts of 40 per cent or more. Most general hardbacks (trade books) and many, though not all, paperbacks fall into this category. Some publishers offer up to 50 per cent on very large orders of long-discount titles; the usual discount, however, is 40 per cent, and it is available only on orders for a certain minimum number of copies. Single copies are often available from publishers at discounts of 40 per cent or slightly less, when ordered under the Single Copy Order Plan, or SCOP.

Before you go on to short-discount and mass-market books, would you explain SCOP?

It's an industry-wide agreement whereby the bookseller prepays and does the paper work of processing his order, enabling the publisher to process the order at a saving. The publisher passes this saving back to the bookseller as added discount on the book.

There are alternatives to ordering single copies through SCOP. If you order from a major publisher, you'll usually be able to think of enough books from his list to fill out the minimum order necessary for regular discount. Also, if you order specified quantities from a wholesaler, your discount will be 40 per cent or very close to it.

Then there are book wholesalers?

Yes, several types of them. The wholesalers we were referring to just now are those that carry currently popular long-discount titles. They usually offer standardized discounts of 40 per cent or slightly less, making the publishers the primary sources for your larger orders. Also, they tend to carry the faster-moving titles only, making the publishers the only sources for less popular books. Nevertheless, you'll probably want to order from these wholesalers whenever possible. Since they offer much faster service than publishers, you can use them almost as if they were your own warehouse and keep less inventory in reserve. Since they carry wide selections, you can order the titles of several publishers from them at once, consolidating paper work. And since they are more concerned with selling quantity than with selling the titles of a particular publisher, they often may offer information about books that sell well in other stores.

Magazine distributors are the primary sources for books issued by some publishers of inexpensive paperbacks. These publications are called "mass-market" books because they are sold almost anywhere you find a magazine rack, as well as in bookstores. They are sold under one of the two types of discount.

What about those other discount categories? Long-discount books are those that carry 40 per cent or more?

Right. Short-discount books are those that carry discounts of less than 40 per cent, regardless of the quantity of the order. Textbooks and books of a highly technical nature usually have short discounts; most of them must be ordered directly from the publishers. If you carry short-discount books, you will have to subsidize your margin by carrying more profitable merchandise as well or by reducing operating expenses drastically.

Strictly speaking, all books carry either long or short discounts. It is practical, however, to think of mass-market books as a special, separate case.

Publishers offer other paperbacks to booksellers at long discounts when the books are ordered in quantities of 5 to 10 or more. Mass-market books usually carry publisher discounts only when ordered in quantities of 25 to 50 assorted volumes. They are available in smaller quantities from magazine distributors for discounts that usually run between 25 and 35 per cent.

What if I buy a lot of books that won't sell? Will the publishers buy them back from me? You said the ABA Book Buyer's Handbook *listed "returns policies"* ...

Like discounts, returns policies are complicated. Most books are eligible for return only within specified periods of time, generally beginning three months and ending one year after publication. Some publishers accept returns on all books ordered from them; some accept no returns; some accept returns only after granting written permission; and many publishers penalize stores 10 per cent if they do not quote the invoice numbers on which returns were purchased. The maximum credit you will receive—from either publishers or wholesalers—will be what you originally paid minus shipping charges to and from your store.

So you'll have to be careful about returns. You may lose less by cutting the prices of dead titles in a special sale than by going through the expense and paper work of returning them, only to receive partial credit.

Is that why I see so many sale tables in bookstores?

Fortunately, no. Most of the sale books you see have been sold to stores at long discounts on marked-down prices.

The sale books you see most often are *remainders,* titles that have been partially or wholly closed out by their publishers. Specialized dealers buy inventories of publishers' overstock, determine new, lower prices for them, and resell them to bookstores.

Some sale-table items are *reprints* of titles which were originally expensive, but which can be sold at reduced prices because they have proven popular enough to be produced cheaply in massive printings. Some are *special imports,* generally originals produced in huge quantities specifically for sale tables. Both bargain reprints and special imports usually come from the same dealers who sell remainders.

How soon will I have to pay for my books?

You may have to prepay your first stock orders, but prepayment is usually necessary only for books ordered under SCOP. Once you've established credit, most publishers will bill you for regular orders at the time of shipment, some offering a 1 or 2 per cent discount for payment in full before the tenth day of the next month. Invoices dated after the

twenty-fourth of a month are considered as billing in the month following.

How can I establish credit?
Only by applying to individual publishers and wholesalers. If you
give a financial statement to the Association of American Publishers,
Inc., One Park Avenue, New York, N.Y. 10016, the association will help
you by making copies of the statement available to its members. No one
in the publishing industry provides a credit-rating service.

Where can I get publishers' and wholesalers' addresses?
From the *ABA Book Buyer's Handbook*, which is available only to
ABA members; or from the *American Book Trade Directory*, a biennial
publication of the R. R. Bowker Co., 1180 Avenue of the Americas, New
York, N.Y. 10036. Both of these listings also contain the addresses of
remainder dealers and wholesalers.

Can I get catalogs at the same time I request credit?
Probably. But there are other sources of information about what
books are available. All the most widely used bookstore references are
publications of the R. R. Bowker Co., a Xerox Company. Besides the
American Book Trade Directory just mentioned, Bowker references
include notably *Books in Print* and *Subject Guide to Books in Print*,
both published annually; *Paperbound Books in Print*, published trian-
nually; *Forthcoming Books*, published bimonthly; *Publishers' Trade
List Annual; Publishers Weekly* magazine; and other items relating to
the book trade both here and abroad. The Bowker catalog has full
information about these publications. [*See also* Chapter 43, "Trade
Tools for the Bookshop."—ED.]
ABA and the National Association of College Stores (NACS) have
jointly prepared "Tools of the Trade," a cassette tape recording for
self-instruction in the use of major book-finding references. "Tools of
the Trade" is distributed to non-members of ABA by Bowker; it may be
ordered from ABA after you join the association.

What books should I stock?
You may want to choose in part from the books that sell well
elsewhere, for instance, those given in the current best-seller lists, the
ABA Hardbound Basic Book List, and the *ABA Paperbound Basic Book
List*. The ABA lists, revised periodically, include only staple back-list
items. They come free with ABA membership.
Your choice of initial stock should be influenced by an analysis of
the community in which you plan to locate. Such an analysis might
include a study of what other bookstores carry and feature, conversations with local librarians about what is most popular, and consideration

of the people and industries in the area. Your customers will ultimately determine what books you stock, since you probably can't afford to carry many titles that don't sell.

About how much should I spend on my initial stock?
Probably the best way to answer that is to calculate from your net sales for the year. One way of projecting a net sales figure is to base it on the salaries you want to pay.

As we've already noted, salaries account for between 15 and 17 per cent of net sales in most bookstores. If you are your only employee and you pay yourself $8,500 a year at the higher percentage, you'll need to make sales totaling $50,000 a year.

If that seems like a lot, remember that it's sales for the whole year. Total sales should be between three and five times the average retail value of your inventory.

Turnover, the number of times that you sell your average inventory during a given period, is an important index of business health. Bookstores that carry hardbacks should have a turnover of about three. Paperback stores must aim for a turnover of five, since their books have lower retail value and must be sold more frequently in order to produce the same sales figure.

If you do exactly three turns a year, your average inventory at retail, and the retail value of your initial inventory, for sales of $50,000 a year will be one-third of $50,000, or $16,666.66. If you are able to get exactly 40 per cent discount, the cost of this stock will be 60 per cent of $16,666.66, or $10,000.

How much selling space will I need?
Enough to display your inventory effectively so that you can reach your sales goal.

In 1968 an ABA survey showed bookstores making yearly sales of $72.94 per square foot of floor space. With inflation, that figure is low for 1974. If you are able to make sales of $80 a square foot, you'll need 625 square feet of selling space for $50,000 total sales a year.

You might get by on less space, but sales per square foot depend on more than just the area of your store. While it is possible to get your books into a very small area by shelving them all spine out, library style, you'll be able to sell more books if you use additional space to show them off. The exact proportion of space you'll need for display depends on what you stock, the character of your store, and what fixtures you have.

How much will fixtures cost me?
We used to say a minimum of $2 a square foot, but prices are changing. You can easily pay more than $10 a square foot if you buy prefabricated shelves or gondolas and have them installed profession-

ally. If you are able to cut your costs to $4 a square foot, fixtures for 625 square feet will cost $2,500.

What expenses will I have in opening?

Miscellaneous expenses might include the cost of a sales license, legal fees, and the like. You may also have discretionary expenses for such items as a store sign, an adding machine, a cash register, and a grand opening.

And you will certainly have to have money to pay toward salaries and other operating expenses until your store breaks even, that is, until your sales begin paying your operating costs.

How much will I need to pay toward operating costs before I break even?

Some stores pay 75 per cent of their operating expenses after six months and break even before the end of their first year. It is not unusual, however, for a store to take two years to break even, and some take longer.

You'll need an amount equal to the difference between total sales and total expenses during the period between opening and breaking even. The faster you can increase sales and the more minimal you can keep expenses, the sooner you will break even and the smaller your total opening cost will be.

The rate at which your sales grow will depend, among other factors, on where you locate, how appropriate your selection is to your clientele, whether you advertise or not, and even what time of year you open (many stores report that they do as much as 25 per cent of their total year's business in the month preceding Christmas, but as little as 7 per cent in the vacation month of August—it's best to open just before a heavy season). Anything you can do to increase the appeal of your store, remind people that you are there, and foresee community needs will increase your rate of growth and decrease your opening costs.

The level of your operating costs will be somewhat inflexible, since some of your expenses will be fixed.

Most of the percentages we've been using here are from a survey sponsored by ABA in 1968 titled "Success Factors in Book Retailing," copies of which are available from the ABA office. In the survey, twenty-six *profitable* bookstores submitted detailed financial statements to Ernst & Ernst, a New York accounting firm. Ernst & Ernst prepared composite operating ratios from their statements, with results comparable to previous bookstore surveys. [For more information on operating costs, *see* Chapters 2, 10, and 13.—ED.]

Where can I get more information?

There is a wealth of literature available about general business practice. Some of the better titles include D. J. Duncan, C. F. Phillips, and S. C. Hollander's *Modern Retailing Management* (Homewood, Ill.: Richard D. Irwin, Inc.); J. K. Lasser's *How To Run a Small Business* (New York: McGraw-Hill Book Co.); J. N. Myer's *Accounting for Non-Accountants* (New York: Hawthorn Books); C. S. Telchin and S. Helfant's *Planning Your Store for Maximum Sales and Profits,* published by the National Retail Merchants Association (NRMA), 100 West 31 Street, New York, N.Y. 10001; *The Independent Retailer and the Shopping Center,* a copublication of the NRMA and the International Council of Shopping Centers; and *Small Store Planning for Growth* and *Buying and Selling a Small Business,* published by the U.S. Department of Commerce's Small Business Administration.

You may want to attend the Booksellers School, a five-day period of instruction devoted to the techniques and knowledge required to operate a trade, or general, bookstore or book department. The only formal training in bookselling available in the United States, the school is held in two locations, one in the east and one in the west, during late winter of each year. Any employee, owner, or prospective owner of any bookstore may attend, though preference in accepting applications is given to members of ABA and the National Association of College Stores, the school's cosponsors. Information on the next sessions is available from either ABA or NACS.

Once you have decided to go ahead and start your business, it will be to your advantage to join the ABA and receive all its information services. Details of member services are available from the ABA office.

When may I join the ABA?

At any time, even before you open your store. The continued health of the entire book industry rests in the development of new, strong retail outlets for books in response to changing needs. The American Booksellers Association is keenly interested in the establishment of bookstores to fill those needs.

When your plans have crystallized a little further, you may have specific problems we will be able to help you with. If you wish further information, please call on ABA. We will be very happy to be of service to you.

Bookselling is not the easiest business to be in, but we believe it is one of the most satisfying. If you can make a go of it, we want you to have your store. Maybe someday soon you can be making a living from your own business and, at the same time, delighting, instructing, and feeding the soul of a community with yesterday's, today's, and tomorrow's books.

Choosing a Location 2

GORDON W. BRYANT
Former President,
Charles E. Lauriat Co., Inc.,
Boston, Massachusetts

A good location is a primary factor in the success of any retail outlet. Many personal, economic, and social considerations must influence your choice of a business location. Before you sign a lease, take all the time you need to study the area and the particular site. Even if you risk losing what at first glance looks like a prime location, do not be pressured into a hasty, unresolved decision. Be sure you have the right spot for you—and for the book business.

There are personal preferences to be considered fully in choosing a successful location. Where do you prefer to live—and do business? Do you need to be among your friends or near your family? Or do you feel you would like to break away from your close ties and strike out in a territory that is new to you? Perhaps your health or the health of someone in your family requires a certain climate. Perhaps you must stay in a certain area to look out for your property or other interests. Or you may have an opportunity to buy or become a partner in an established bookstore. The type of bookstore you want to open could limit your potential market and, therefore, the number of locations that would be suitable. Do not ignore any of your personal needs. You may have to relinquish some of these personal demands when you finally make your choice, but if you should, you will be aware of the drawbacks and avoid a great deal of unexpected disappointment or even failure.

There are genuine advantages to going into business in a community where you are known. An established reputation is a valuable asset in getting credit. Your knowledge of the community and its people, based upon your own observation and experience over the years, is of immeasurable value in choosing a site. If your home community or an area where you are well known needs a bookstore, the situation is ideal for solving your problems of finding a location.

Types of Locations

A city offers many opportunities for bookselling—the larger the city, the broader the opportunity. If you are planning to open a full-scale general bookstore where the key to success is traffic, both heavy and the right kind, you *must* locate in a city. The large masses of people concentrated in urban areas make it possible for large department and specialty stores to flourish, and these stores stimulate a flow of pedestrian traffic that filters off to the many nearby smaller shops that offer special kinds of merchandise and services.

Urban populations with their many and varied cultural activities buy more books of all kinds than most rural populations. The theaters, opera, art galleries and museums, libraries, and innumerable other cultural institutions concentrated in cities stimulate reading and book buying. There is a place for almost any type of specialized bookstore in a large city. Foreign language books, art books, music books, scientific books, and books of almost any special interest will find a ready market.

There are also certain drawbacks to owning a city bookstore. City locations usually require bigger stores with higher rentals, larger inventories, more staff, more experience, and, of course, more capital. The competition in cities makes the newcomer's task more difficult. He must be prepared to do a better job than the already established competition, offering a more complete selection of stock as well as better and faster service. His security problems will be more acute.

While personal reasons must play a big part in your choice, wanting to live in a certain city is not sufficient reason for opening a bookstore there. Before you decide to locate in a city, make a thorough study of the social and economic advantages and disadvantages of going into the book business there.

Consider the population. Is it growing or has it reached its peak? Is it on the way down? What type of people live in the city? How do they spend their leisure time? What are their occupations? Their incomes? Is their income steady and dependable, or do they have seasonal layoffs? It is better to locate a retail business in a city with a well-balanced variety of industry than in an area that depends on a few large plants. What kind of homes, schools, churches, banks, amusements, and cultural activities does the city have? Are the activities seasonal or year-round? Does the city have aggressive civic organizations? Does the population participate in civic activities? All these factors can help you judge the potential market for books.

Is the city you are considering the trading center for a broad area? Or do its inhabitants shop elsewhere? What stores are located there? Are they popular with the local population? Are they progressive, developing enterprises?

How much competition would you have in the city you are considering? Does this community need another bookshop? Competition is a business stimulant if there is sufficient purchasing power in an area to support a new outlet. A good balance of competition creates a marketplace—a center of trading activity attractive to buyers. But when there are too many stores in an area selling the same merchandise, sales are pulled down in all of them.

What is the probable future of the city? Are its surroundings likely to change from a predominantly agricultural area to an industrial area? Is industry likely to stay there, and grow in number and importance? What is the possibility of new educational facilities, schools and colleges, developing there?

A neighborhood store may be located on the fringes of suburbia, the main street of a small town, or, in large cities, in the various outlying retail districts located along the principal thoroughfares and neighborhood streets.

Since the neighborhood store derives its principal support from the residential area around it, the character of the neighborhood is of major importance, and must be studied carefully. As in your evaluation of the city, once more you must take a good look at the population, the trading area, the trends, and the competition before selecting a neighborhood.

What is the income level of the residents? People with higher spendable incomes are better prospects for book sales. What types of homes are there in the neighborhood? Apartment buildings offer more buying power than single-family dwellings. Better housing usually means more discriminating, better-educated people—more readers and book buyers. Does the neighborhood have a bookstore? Could it support another bookstore? Do the people trade there or do they trade in another area? Is the neighborhood healthy, alive, growing?

The number of retail shops in country homes as an adjunct to the home is increasing steadily. Some of these small businesses are maintained solely as seasonal ventures in vacation areas, others are year-round businesses. These shops are generally far removed from any supporting neighborhood following and must depend on transient trade or mail-order business. The country store is usually a one-man business, and operating costs, such as building and fixtures, are minimal. Expenses must be kept low to offset the restricted sales volume.

Choosing the Site

Having chosen the region, city, and neighborhood where you believe there is a good opportunity for a new bookstore, you are ready to select the site. Take plenty of time to weigh all the possibilities of the locations offered, and do everything you can to get the best location for your needs. There is, of course, a limit to the amount of rent you can pay, but remember—the cheapest site could be the most costly in the long run.

Take a look at the street you are considering. Is it attractive? Are people drawn there on their way to other shops, theaters, or other points of interest? Are the other stores on the street outlets that cater to the same type of people your bookstore would? Choose a location between large or important stores that draw traffic back and forth between them, so that your store will be in the line of traffic. Choose to be among shops that offer complementary lines rather than competitive merchandise. A store on the corner is generally better than a store in the middle of the block, but a middle-of-the-block location may be preferable if it is nearer to the main corner of the area than other corner locations. Consider, too, whether a nearby shopping center offers strong competition.

Is the motor traffic heavy on the street you are considering, making it difficult to cross? Is it a one-way street?

Does one side of the street have noticeably greater pedestrian traffic than the other? Is it warm in winter? Shady in summer? Are the best stores located on one side of the street? Is it the home-going side? The heavy bus-stop side? Close to the subway entrance?

Is there adequate public transportation to the area? Does it come from the better residential areas? Are there adequate parking facilities handy?

In estimating the value of the site for a bookstore, do not consider the volume of the traffic only—get a clear picture of the nature of the traffic. Where are the people coming from? Where are they going? Why are they passing this location? Do the people passing here have the ability and inclination to buy books? Are they in the area to shop, such as women from the nearby residential areas might be, or are they primarily industrial or clerical workers rushing to and from work?

Consider the future of the site. Is the location you are considering in the line of the city's new growth? Be sure it is a section that is improving and not declining. Cities tend to expand along main thoroughfares that lead to better residential sections, pulling the shopping area in that direction.

Are there restrictions in zoning ordinances that might retard your expansion? Are there physical barriers, hills and bridges, that separate this section from the larger part of the area's population? Avoid locations that are adjacent to undesirable businesses or vacant lots (unless they are used for parking). Avoid sites characterized by objectionable noise, odors, smoke, wind, dust.

Check the history of the site. Have buildings in the area remained vacant long? If so, find out why.

An aggressive bookstore is well received in any good shopping center. It lends prestige to the area, and is a good traffic builder. Shopping centers catering to communities populated by families of middle-class business and professional people provide a greater potential book market than areas serving a predominantly lower-income agricultural or industrial population. Areas serving a high concentration of women shoppers are favorable for bookstores.

The large shopping center is a prime location for a full-scale general bookstore. It is a city in itself with a ready market created by well-known, well-advertised department stores. Traffic to the area is strengthened also by all kinds of attractive specialty shops, all conveniently grouped for easy access by today's motorized shopper. [Full discussion of shopping centers will be found in Chapter 3, "Shopping-Center Locations."—ED.]

When you are satisfied with everything else about the location, examine minutely the condition of the store and the building. Have your store planner, contractor, architect, or fixture man, as well as your insurance broker, look it over with you.

Check the store front and window display space. The current trend in store fronts is to open up the front with glass to the greatest extent possible, making the whole interior of the store your window display. Your architect can help you here. Will the landlord provide the new store front if remodeling is necessary? If not, would it be worth doing yourself? Remember, this is the most important display area in your shop. [See Chapter 4, "Using a Store Planner," and Chapter 5, "Bookstore Architecture and Design."—ED.]

How many entrances does the store have? One *wide* entrance allows for better control over possible thievery than a store with two or more entrances. On the other hand, the added accessibility provided by a back door opening onto another street or parking lot may be worth the added risk. If possible, do not have steps in the entrance that could cause accidents. Stores in older buildings usually have the conventional two-window front with a narrow vestibule door. This type of doorway is inefficient and unfashionable by current standards, and, if possible, should be modernized. Here again, your architect is the best judge of what needs to be done and whether the cost of the reconstruction is economically wise for this site at the rental asked.

Study the interior floor plan. A store with good width in proportion to its depth is better than a long, narrow store. Straight-walled rectangular or square shops, free of columns or broken areas, are desirable. This type of layout provides better display areas, better customer control, and more efficient control of pilferage. The visual obstructions created by nooks make them great havens for shoplifters. High ceilings provide extra wall space for storage and display of books, promotion materials, or decorative prints.

Examine the building carefully for fire hazards. The fire insurance rates can be excessively high on old buildings. Check the store carefully for needed repairs. This means a thorough examination of walls, flooring, ceiling, stairways, lighting, heating, and air conditioning. Check the wiring. Is it adequate for the lighting and air conditioning you will need? Rewiring can represent a substantial investment for you if the landlord is unwilling to absorb the costs. Be sure the water supply and toilet facilities are adequate and in good repair. Sprinklers will lower your fire insurance rate, but will your landlord insure you against loss from water damage resulting from leaky sprinklers?

Check the store's basement. A small basement means you will have less storage area and be forced to keep your inventory small or use valuable first-floor space for backup stock. A large basement gives you the room you need for seasonal buildups of stock. If your stock moves fast in your salesroom, you will need a fairly large storage area, unless, of course, you have a handy resource for quick delivery or reorders. Be sure that your receiving and shipping facilities are easily accessible to truckers.

And one final caution—is the space you are considering adaptable for future expansion?

Setting Up the Budget

Up to this point in your planning, you have done a great deal of thinking about your location, developed a general idea of the lines you want to carry, and formed a general image of your store. Before you sign your lease, buy your stock and fixtures, and make all the other necessary arrangements to set up shop, you must formulate a clear and precise budget picture.

Try to arrive at a fair estimate of what your minimum sales should be. Your talks with various landlords in the area, other shopkeepers on the street, and experienced booksellers in other towns should be helpful in estimating this figure. When you are satisfied that you have come up with a realistic estimate of a sales budget, break it down according to percentages for cost of goods sold, salaries and wages, rent, utilities, and other operating costs. Fill in the expenses that are fixed or controllable (utilities, advertising, insurance, interest, taxes, etc.). Your completed budget will show what you can afford to pay for your two most important variables—rent and salaries. Typical bookstore operating ratios for profitable stores are available from the American Booksellers Association (the 1968 Ernst & Ernst survey); these figures can be valuable guides in making up a budget such as the one shown in Table 2.1.

TABLE 2.1

TYPICAL BUDGET
(Based on Estimated Annual Sales of $50,000)

Sales	100.0%	$50,000
Cost of Goods Sold	63.0	31,500
Salaries (including owner) } principal variables {	20.0	10,000
Rent	6.0	3,000
Interest, Dues, Taxes, Donations	1.1	550
Advertising	2.0	1,000
Depreciation	0.7	350
Utilities	0.5	250
Printing and Stationery	0.9	450
Shipping Materials	0.8	400
Insurance	0.6	300
Maintenance	0.3	150
Miscellaneous	0.3	150
Incoming Postage	1.5	750
Total Expense	34.7	17,350
Profit	2.3%	$ 1,150

The rent you pay for a location and its relation to your estimated sales is a major factor in determining whether you could run a profitable bookstore there. No matter how rosy a picture your landlord may paint, do not sign a lease hastily. *Be sure you can afford the rental.* The best location could be of little value if it costs more than you can afford to pay. The recommended rent for a bookstore with annual sales of under $50,000 is 6 per cent of total sales. For an exceptional location that provides heavy customer traffic for long hours, day and night, you might stretch your rent budget to 8 per cent of total sales, or even a little more.

If you feel certain you can make a go of a book business in the location you are considering, try to get at least a five-year lease, with option to renew for another five years. A ten-year lease may be an even better deal. The longer the term of the lease, the better advantage you have in negotiating the rent.

If you have reservations about the location, the neighborhood, or bookselling, it would be better to sign a one- or two-year lease, even if this means paying more rent. But in negotiating a short-term lease, try to get an option to renew at about the same rental for another three to seven years.

Percentage rent agreements have become quite common in recent years. In a percentage agreement, a minimum is set to cover the landlord's costs and extra rent is assessed in proportion to sales over the agreed-upon minimum. Such an agreement offers the advantage of maintaining a lower rent if your business should drop. If you should enjoy good business, you would share your good fortune with your landlord; if business should go sour, you would limit your losses. In a percentage lease agreement the landlord can often be persuaded to reduce the percentage rent as the store's sales go up. The landlord thus provides an incentive to keep sales climbing and still obtains a reasonable share of the revenue of increased business.

If you are negotiating for space in a wholly owned shopping center, try to get the landlord to give you exclusive rights to sell books in the center—that is, exclusive rights among the smaller independent shops. Large department stores and chains usually cannot be so restricted in what they can sell.

Even though you may have had a great deal of experience negotiating leases, bring a lawyer into the talks when you are about ready to agree to terms—if you haven't done so already. The peace of mind he can bring you will be well worth his fee. A lawyer can help you secure added concessions from the landlord. And, more important, because of his knowledge of leases he can steer you away from a disadvantageous agreement.

Here are a few tips on negotiating with the landlord. Get to know him, so you can better understand how he is thinking. Be calm, friendly, but persistent. Know when to listen—and when to change the subject. And, of course, get the best deal you can.

Figure 2.1 provides a useful checklist for guidance in choosing your location.

FIGURE 2.1   CHECKLIST FOR GUIDANCE IN SELECTING A SITE*

POINTS UPON WHICH SITE IS CHOSEN	ANSWER (Give yes or no, numerical, or qualitative answer)	RATING			
		Excellent	Good	Fair	Poor
Competition					
Number of independent stores of same kind					
Same block					
Same side of street					
Across the street					
Number of chain stores					
Same block					
Same side of street					
Across the street					
Kind of stores next door					
Number of vacancies					
Same side of street					
Across the street					
Next door					
Traffic Flow					
Sex of pedestrians					
Age of pedestrians					

*Based on a checklist in *Selecting a Store Location* (U.S. Department of Commerce Economic Series, No. 56 [Washington, D.C., 1946]), pp. 21-22, o.p.

FIGURE 2.1 *(Continued)*

POINTS UPON WHICH SITE IS CHOSEN	ANSWER (Give yes or no, numerical, or qualitative answer)	RATING			
		Excel-lent	Good	Fair	Poor
Traffic Flow (Continued)					
Destination of pedestrians					
Number of passers-by					
Automobile traffic count					
Peak hours of traffic flow					
Transportation					
Transfer point					
Highway					
Kind (streetcar, bus, subway, automobile)					
Parking Facilities					
Side of street					
Store					
Frontage (in feet)					
Depth (in feet)					
Shape of building (must permit efficient operation)					
Condition					
Heat (type)					
Light					
Display space					
Back entrance					
Front entrance					
Display windows					
Rent and Lease					
Corner Location (If not, what is it?)					
Unfavorable Site Characteristics					
Fire hazards					
Cemetery					
Hospital					
Heavy industry					
Relief office					
Undertaking establishment					
Vacant lot—unless it can be used for parking					
Garages					
Playground					
Smoke, dust, disagreeable odors, etc.					
Poor sidewalks and pavement					
Old and worn-out neighboring structures					
Number of Professional Men in Block					
Medical doctors					
Dentists					
Lawyers					
Veterinarians					
Others					
History of Site					

Shopping-Center Locations   3

GERALD N. BATTLE
Retail Store Marketing, Department Manager,
Cokesbury Division of Methodist Publishing House,
Nashville, Tennessee

Whether a shopping-center location figures in your immediate plans or
not, it is to your advantage to know something about shopping centers,
how they operate, general lease terms, and other pertinent details. If
your town or city has a medium-to-large shopping center and you do
not locate in it, one or more of your competitors will.

A modern shopping center by definition is a complex of retail
establishments offering a variety of goods and services, brought together in a common location to share both the expenses and benefits
resulting from such a concentration of business. Most shopping centers
are put together by developer-landlords, the best of whom exercise
extreme care in the selection of tenants and in the design, maintenance,
and promotion of the center. Basically, a shopping center attempts to
guarantee traffic to the tenants.

There are three major types of shopping centers:

1. The *strip shopping center* is a one-story, straight-line structure
with several small businesses under one roof. Usually oriented to trade
from a restricted and very localized area, strip shopping centers do not
contain major department store branches or other large single-unit
traffic generators. A typical strip center will contain a drugstore, food
store, hairdressing salon, and several other small shops of various kinds.
It will sometimes, though rarely, offer opportunity for a bookstore.

2. The *cluster shopping center* derives its name from the fact that
it consists of a number of buildings of various sizes, usually connected
by walkways that are sometimes covered. There may be an open courtyard between buildings, with street access on the periphery of the
cluster, or there may be street access between the buildings themselves. Both designs have advantages. With street access between the

buildings, cars can park at the door of each store. In the courtyard design, shoppers are encouraged to a greater degree to stroll between buildings. The cluster shopping center will always be medium or large in size and often will contain an office tower. The cluster type enables the developer to locate complementary shops in the same area to the advantage of all. This can be a very good location for a bookstore.

3. The *mall shopping center* locates all business under one roof in an enclosed pedestrian mall to create an arcade effect, with parking areas surrounding the mall. Most malls consist of two stories, an upper and lower level. Individual study can determine whether the upper or lower level is the more desirable. Rarely are there two identical centers; and the design, the skill of traffic handling, and the wisdom exercised by the developer in choosing and locating tenants can be the determining factors. Mall shopping centers are invariably medium-to-large or huge in size. In examining a large number of such malls, I have never seen a small one, nor do I recall ever seeing one without at least one outlet for books. Most have two or more. They provide a good location for a bookstore.

All of the medium-to-large shopping centers have "anchors," large stores which have developed a following and which generate traffic on their own. Branches of large, well-established department stores are generally thought of as the most desirable anchors. Every medium-to-large shopping center must have at least two. The larger, more successful centers will have three or four and occasionally, but rarely, five.

Higher-priced restaurants help generate evening traffic. Restaurants with moderate-to-medium prices are a must in every shopping center and few centers are without them. A major Sears Roebuck store is an excellent asset to any shopping center because it generates a high volume of business, and you can be sure intensive research was done to establish the desirability of the location. Few retailers do as careful a research job as Sears.

The rental cost of desirable shopping-center locations will be high. Rates vary from center to center and depend on desirability, but you will have to be prepared to pay from a minimum of $5 per square foot to $9 per square foot or more, plus other costs and a percentage of sales. Some careful arithmetic will tell you the minimum number of square feet you will need to create the volume you must achieve to reach the break-even point. When you calculate the break-even point to obtain a profitable return on investment, then you can calculate what you must do beyond that figure.

Add-ons are those charges that a tenant must pay in addition to basic rent per square foot. Some typical add-ons are:

- *Merchants' Association fees,* usually based on so many cents per square foot. Twenty cents per square foot on an annual basis would not be unusual. Thus if you are occupying 2,000 square feet, a Merchants' Association fee of 20¢ per square foot would cost you $400 a year beyond your base rent.
- *Maintenance of parking area.* An assessment for the upkeep of the parking lot is another very common add-on. This will usually also be based on square footage and can be from 20¢ to 25¢, adding another $400 to $500 per year for 2,000 square feet.
- There is usually a *tax base year* cited in the lease. Tax increases beyond those paid during the base year are passed on to tenants on a prorated basis according to amount of space occupied.

These add-ons are the most common, but another additional cost of doing business in shopping centers is the percentage levied by the landlord on the gross sales of each tenant. Percentages vary and are usually negotiable—depending on your bargaining skill, how badly the landlord wants you as a tenant, and other matters. It would not be unusual to be asked to pay 5 per cent to 5½ per cent of gross sales over a certain figure. A not unusual example would be 5 per cent of gross sales over $200,000, where the tenant is paying $5 per square foot for 2,000 square feet. Most bookstores will not want to pay more than 5 per cent, and 5½ per cent should be considered tops.

In going into a new shopping center you will sometimes find two basic types of rental opportunity available. In other instances you may be offered only one or the other. In a *bare-walls lease* the landlord turns a shell over to the tenant. This means three walls and a roof with power available and water piped to the shell. Everything else is a leasehold expense for the tenant, including all interior finishing, front treatment, air conditioning, and heating (except in rare instances when this is a part of the landlord's expense). There may be an allowance of so many dollars per front foot for a store front. In some cases there may be a construction allowance, although the latter seems not to be frequently offered in recent shopping-center developments.

In a *lock-and-key job* the whole space is presumed ready to accept, with the exception of interior painting. In this case the walls are primed and taped, ready for a final coat of paint. A lock-and-key job does not include floor covering, which is in all cases at the expense of the tenant. If you have an option, the lock-and-key offer is to your advantage. While you sacrifice a degree of control over the treatment of your space, this is largely a matter of décor and rarely changes the functioning ability of a store. There is considerable advantage in not having to make a capital expenditure in leasehold expense along with the demands on your time such an operation will entail. You're better off to pay a higher rent, and avoid the need to invest capital in leasehold expenses.

Where to locate within a shopping center is a matter for individual study. Each shopping center is different and has a different kind of mix. The kind of store you are running and other things will affect your decision. Even the direction the shopping center faces has a bearing on the best location. There are no realistic guidelines to lay down in this area. Each center requires individual and careful analysis.

It may sound as if shopping-center locations are too costly for the individual bookstore owner, who would have one unit or possibly two units. In some instances, this is the case, but for the bookstore owner who can get into a good shopping center and who has the financial resources to manage it, there are adequate rewards. A good shopping center promotes itself vigorously with special campaigns throughout the year. The bookstore owner is assured of traffic, and he knows that every advertising dollar he spends will be reinforced and backed up by the advertising dollars spent by his neighbors and by the promotions the center itself puts on. His place of business is physically well-maintained and attractive, and the surroundings are designed to attract and accommodate customers in a way no other location he might choose could be expected to equal. There is always adequate parking for his customers, himself, and his employees. It is easier to attract employees —and especially part-time or seasonal employees—to a shopping center than to a center-city location or most other locations. If the arithmetic works, a shopping-center location comes as close to assuring success as any site can.

Shopping patterns have changed significantly in recent years. Increasingly the shopping center has taken on a new dimension in many communities. Booksellers cannot afford to overlook the potential a good shopping center offers the individual bookstore. It will be a mistake for the personal store to leave shopping centers to the chains. The individual store that's good enough can do well in a good shopping center.

Using a Store Planner

4

KEN WHITE
President, Ken White Associates, Inc.;
President, Institute of Store Planners

Bookselling has undergone great changes in the past several decades. The advent of mass-market and trade paperbacks, the burgeoning of the remainder book, and the growth of the number of hardbound titles have all had an effect on the bookselling business. The changing pattern of retail merchandising has also had its effect on methods of selling books. With the appearance of air-conditioned malls and shopping centers in the early 1960's, the traditional bookstore has taken a new form, responding to a new concept of retailing.

Some of the chains that have emerged, including Pickwick Book Shops, B. Dalton, Bookseller, and Walden Book Company Stores, have proven to investors that it is possible to run a multi-store operation successfully in the shopping center and free-standing environment. We can look forward to a number of new national and regional chain bookstores opening during the next decade.

Chain stores, however, have their limitations. They acquire a stereotyped look, based on a specific formula that is repeated coast to coast. Moreover, such stores find it difficult to improve their appearance if they are locked into a long-term lease.

These stores need not replace privately owned, independent bookstores, if the independents will develop concepts unique to their particular communities, keep abreast of their market, and seek to innovate when it becomes necessary. Success for the independent bookseller lies in creating a unique bookselling concept that runs *counter* to that of the shopping center.

An important aspect of independent bookselling is the creation of a personality for the bookstore. This may be drawn from the locale or may be an extension of the owner's personality. It must, however, appeal to the type of customer most likely to be attracted into the store.

This is where the store planner makes his contribution. The planner's expertise can be a major factor in the development of a merchandising philosophy and concept that is completely right for a specific location and market.

This article will review the functions of a store planner and indicate many of the ways in which he can assist in the creation of a new bookstore or the remodeling and redesigning of an established one. For the names of store planners in your area who are experienced in bookstore planning, consult the Institute of Store Planners, P.O. Box 538, Grand Central Station, New York, N.Y. 10017

Great Bookstores Don't Just Happen

Really fine bookshops are the result of a specific set of procedures that begin with the individual owner, who must give as much thought as possible to the market, the various locations available, and the ways in which he thinks his store can truly be different from the competition. It is helpful for the owner of a store, or one who is planning to start a store and has a particular space in mind, to put his ideas down on paper, as either a layout or a written statement. These data, together with a checklist of store fixtures and features, can then be reviewed with the store planner, either in his office, at the site, or elsewhere. These conversations are often recorded to form minutes or notes that are distributed to the planning staff so that everyone concerned with the project is kept informed.

From this information, several block plans are drawn. These plans take into account the legal requirements and plot in the various ideas, concepts, and alternatives that have been discussed. A store-fixture and traffic-circulation arrangement is evolved. The block plan is thus revised and supplemented with sketches, elevations, or models (as the particular circumstance and funding warrant). These documents would include recommendations for equipment, lighting, energy systems, furnishings, graphics, and décor, and a statement of probable cost should be presented at the same time.

The legal implications of building a bookstore are amazing, and the advice of a planner will help to avoid costly pitfalls. The planner will not only advise the bookseller on the costs required to make his concept a reality, he can also offer considerable assistance to the attorney who draws the lease.

Additional time and money can be saved because the planner knows about the over-all mechanical systems required by the store, insuring proper heating, ventilation and air-conditioning equipment, as well as sufficient lighting. Proper security is another essential factor.

The use of checklists is a great aid. They serve as a reminder of the hundreds of items required for the operation of a bookstore. They can also be used to assign responsibility as to who will accomplish the work. The owner? The general contractor? The fixture contractor? Or the store planner? The planner will have such lists for your inspection.

The store planner can assist in analyzing the contractor bids received and furnish the necessary data concerning finishes and color to the successful bidder. He can check and review shop drawings and make periodic observations of the progress of the work during construction. Often he will be asked to certify payments to the contractors and issue a report of the contractors' compliance with the contract documents.

In projecting a new bookstore, it is essential to differentiate between planning and design.

Planning is the professional activity that identifies the way in which a retail store will work. The bookstore planner is skilled in designing retail stores, preparing plans and specifications, and observing construction. He is not an architect, but works closely with architects who are, on occasion, closely acquainted with the practical requirements of retailing. [Some architects who specialize in bookstores are equipped to offer many of the functions of a store planner.—ED.] The store planner is equipped to create bookstores that will attract customers and get maximum sales from every square foot of space, while permitting comfortable movement of both customers and merchandise.

Design is the professional aspect of store planning concerned with implementing the visual merchandise concept. The difference between the chain-store supermarket look and the warm and wonderful browsing store lies in the environment created by the careful design of décor and sales fixtures. Store fixtures are an integral part of the design concept, but before they and other functional elements can be selected, however, the planner and the owner will need to undertake some basic analyses and agree on over-all objectives.

Planning Procedures

First, of course, is site selection. Assuming the site has been selected, the next step is to determine the store's *ambiance.* Will it be formal or informal? How can it best serve the neighborhood or part of the country in which it is to be located? Will books be the only stock in trade or will there be sidelines such as greeting cards, gifts, or regional handicrafts? Will the store perhaps be combined with another enterprise, such as a print gallery, or, as has happened in several places, with a tearoom or a restaurant?

Then comes merchandise planning, a twofold process involving analysis of merchandising records and possible achievements, leading to attainment of merchandising goals. Studies of department areas and locations, turnover, and similar factors are helpful in determining requirements for lineal footage, including space for forward and reserve stock. This type of planning, used as a guide in deciding the size and layout of a new store, can also be used to determine if a modernization program for an older store is indicated.

Another important early step in planning is to determine sales methods. One or more of the following methods may be used in the same store:

Self-selection. Merchandise is often displayed on fixtures to encourage the shopper to touch, examine, and select titles without pressure by sales personnel. Salesmen are present to give service when asked to do so, however. The cash-and-wrap desk is often located within the department, so that the customer has a second opportunity to browse and buy. This method sells more merchandise and permits personnel to give assistance to more customers.

Self-service. Merchandise is on open display so that the shopper selects items from the gondolas or wall units without sales help. Very often, he must enter the area through a gate and exit via a checkout counter, and thus has little chance to "take a second look." Signing is essential, since the shopper is on his own. Bookstores in high-pilferage areas do not use this method.

Over-counter selling. Merchandise is shown to the shopper by a salesperson stationed behind a showcase or counter. Since the shopper is being served, he may not feel free to handle the goods as he does when self-selection or self-service methods are used. Rare books, special editions, and gift items lend themselves to this method.

Then the planner and the owner may develop a sales-space matrix. This is a chart showing the proposed square feet of floor space and the proposed merchandise for each department. If the project is the remodeling or relocation of an existing bookstore, it is possible either to start with existing figures and work forward—or, as in the case of planning a new store, to start with the estimated total future volume, which is then broken down into suitable sales areas, based on assumed departmental volume, etc. Even a thoroughly experienced retailer may need expert guidance in order to plan such a project realistically.

Finally, before proceeding to the details of design, there must be a circulation plan. The planner and owner will agree on a fixture plan showing expected customer movement throughout the sales areas. This is the basis for the location of fixtures, displays, sales counters, cash-and-wrap desks, and other facilities to assure maximum merchandise exposure to the maximum number of shoppers. A good plan will avoid traffic congestion, provide easy access to cash-and-wrap facilities, and assist in preventing pilferage.

Design Details

Only now is it time to select the fixtures and decide on the lighting and other functional design elements.

There are numerous kinds of sales fixtures, but they fall into several general categories:

Sales tables are enclosed units, usually 2 feet 6 inches to 3 feet in height. The top is used for merchandise display, a built-up construction may be added to increase display space, and forward stock (storage) can be accommodated on lower shelves.

Gondolas are center-floor units, low-based, with adjustable and sometimes removable shelves or brackets, often convertible for the display of hanging merchandise (posters, frames, etc.). In general, the gondola displays up to four times as much merchandise as the showcase, and the shopper can easily see and touch the items.

Showcases have glass-enclosed top sections for merchandise display and bottom sections for reserve stock. Usually 3 feet to 3 feet 2 inches high, they are used chiefly for over-counter selling by sales personnel.

Wall cases. In the self-selection wall case, the base is usually deeper than the upper shelves, to provide a place for large books. Wall cases are designed for hardbound or softbound books, or for conversion from one to the other.

In the early 1960's, the bookselling industry made wide use of two systems that were in many instances visually disturbing, though highly effective. These were wire racks and pegboards. Though versatile, these two items too frequently have detracted from the central idea and atmosphere of a bookstore.

Today's bookseller has access to new systems that are specially designed to meet both construction and merchandising requirements. These systems may consist of entire fabricated walls that may be rapidly installed on an existing structural surface—meeting fire requirements—and at the same time are flexible in the presentation of paperback or hardcover books of any size. Planners know of these systems because it is their job to know. In a similar fashion, there are standard sales tables, a variety of types of service desks, and other products that have been specifically designed with the bookseller in mind. In each case, these systems can be modified with decorative treatment to create a special environment determined by the store owner and the planner.

Still another device is the use of the raised platform, also referred to as a *podium*. The major advantage of the podium concept is that it tends to build layers of perimeters and eliminate gondolas. It provides a clear view of the selling area from all parts of the bookstore and remarkably free access to shelves and tables. The concept makes a very positive contribution to security—and it works.

Many major cities have requirements for fireproof certifiability when fixtures are permanently attached to the wall.

Along with fixtures, lighting is of major importance. There are three major types of illumination, which are used either alone or in combination for effective bookstore lighting:

Incandescent lighting, with clear or frosted lamps familiar to every householder, reflector lamps, and other types, is suitable for general lighting and is by far the best for spot lighting.

Fluorescent lighting, with fixtures and tubes that provide continuous strips of light, ranging in length from eight to ninety-six inches, supplies three times as much light per watt as incandescent lighting does, and may be recessed or exposed. It also generates less heat and thereby helps to minimize air-conditioning and total energy cost.

Track light, similar to incandescent lighting but capable of being adjusted in any length or shape, is appropriate for use when false ceilings are eliminated and the underlying structure is exposed.

The planner normally receives a standard fee based on either a percentage of the total cost or hours or areas involved. Every legitimate planner will furnish an estimate of these charges prior to commencing with the work. The figure generally lies between 10 and 15 per cent, depending on the planner and the complexity of the job.

In general, whether a percentage is charged or some other method is used to determine the planner's compensation, the fee for a $25,000 job will probably run to about $3,000; a $50,000 job about $6,000; and a $100,000 job about $12,000.

The creation of an innovative bookstore and its successful operation is a challenge for anyone who loves books and seeks a retailing career.

The philosopher Erasmus said, "When I get a little money, I buy books; and if any is left, I buy food and clothes." There are many people who value books as dearly as the food that physically sustains them. A carefully planned bookstore can feed that hunger.

Bookstore Design: An Architect's View

5

DANFORTH W. TOAN

B. Arch.; AIA; Partner, Warner Burns Toan Lunde;
Adjunct Professor in Design, Columbia University School
of Architecture

The bookstore is a unique problem in retail design in that the product, the book, is both an object (merchandise) and an abstraction (cultural heritage). Nevertheless, it is merchandise, and with certain important distinctions the architect who designs a bookstore should adhere to five basic retailing requirements: (1) make it appropriate, (2) make it economic, (3) make it work, (4) make it attractive, and (5) make it sell. How do we go about it?

1. *Make It Appropriate*

The most significant element in designing a bookstore is the bookseller himself, not the designer-architect. The bookseller's decisions will have far greater impact on the ultimate economic success of the venture than those of the architect.

What is the appropriate location? Will there be an adequate market? How large will the store be? How will adjacent stores help ensure the kind of high traffic volume on which the store will be highly dependent? What shall the inventory include in addition to books (hardbacks, paperbacks, games, posters, greeting cards and stationery, *objets d'art*, records, and so on) and in what proportions?

How is this kind of data collected? Economic surveys and analyses that define socio-economic dispersions of a region and market penetration of a shopping district are frequently available. The bookseller's own research will uncover both the competition (other bookstores, general merchandise stores with book departments, and so on) and the local shopping patterns. Other judgments are also required. What will the locale become ten years hence, a period that may be only half the term of the lease? Are there developing factors that might make an in-town location more attractive than the huge, remote shopping center an hour away in outer suburbia?

The expected clientele is of great importance. Does the average income, level of education, and employment base indicate sufficient numbers of potential customers with enough interest and disposable income to support the enterprise? From these questions the bookseller begins to formulate his merchandise plan, which will project for the designer an image of the kind of operation under consideration.

The more clearly the client is able to define his decisions regarding location, size, market, the breadth of stock carried, and the merchandising plan, the better able will the designer-architect be to develop a handsome, efficient shop.

2. *Make It Economic*

Certainly a successful bookstore must be outfitted within a realistic budget that will not put undue strain on the anticipated profitability. Annual rent for larger stores is assumed to be in the order of 6 to 10 per cent of anticipated gross sales (smaller stores should strive for 6 per cent or less) with alterations costing perhaps between 2 and 3 percent of gross sales over the period of amortization.

As a rule of thumb a reasonable investment for store alterations might be somewhat less than the annual rent. This rule is subject to wide possible variations due to hours of operation, clientele, traffic volume, exposure, and rent itself. Published estimates of gross annual sales per square foot in various categories of merchandise are always suspect, but it *is* a known fact that bookstores tend to fall at the high end of the scale. Banks, airlines, jewelers, famous department stores, high fashion boutiques, and bookstores have traditionally been the shops best able to afford the very high rentals of New York City's famous Fifth Avenue shopping strip—six bookstores between Forty-second and Fifty-seventh Streets.

Hence the bookseller should say to himself, "If the rent is $X per square foot of gross area, can I expect to make a gross income ten to sixteen times that for each square foot? If so, I should be prepared to spend very roughly $Y per square foot to renovate the area." (This would be somewhat fewer renovation dollars if the rent is high, somewhat more renovation dollars if the rent is low.) Variations of construction costs and rent levels may be significant. In any event, construction costs over the life of a ten-year project are not major, especially with depreciation allowances. Money spent now on a sound project should prove to be a worth-while investment.

The lease should be examined carefully to see what will be provided by the landlord to the tenant. There may be a wide variation both in services (lighting, heat and/or air conditioning, etc.) and in construction (finished ceilings, floors, store front including doors, etc.). These can have a profound effect on the cost of construction work.

3. *Make It Work*

Having established a construction budget for the project, it is time to retain an architect or interior designer. Selection of the appropriate professional is an art in itself since the requirements are extensive. The designer must be talented; knowledgeable, preferably (but not necessarily) with previous experience in designing bookstores or other retail commercial work; familiar with costs in the area; capable of collaborating in converting a merchandising plan into a physical one; and possessing enough imagination to transform space into an attractive environment in which to browse and buy.

Should you choose *an architect or an interior designer?* The architect usually has thorough knowledge of all aspects of a project from design concepts, architectural and structural matters, mechanical/electrical systems, and appropriate contract documents down to code requirements and building permits, as well as costs. However, the breadth of the architect's training may not include experience with interiors and the fixtures from which the merchandise is to be sold. The interior designer's principal concern lies in the planning of interior shapes, surfaces, furnishing, and fittings. A project requiring major construction, considerable mechanical and electrical engineering work, particularly in a competitive bid situation involving code interpretation and building permits and eventual supervision of the construction work itself, would usually call for an architect. A less complex undertaking, involving general construction work limited to partition changes, floor, wall, and ceiling finishes, and fixturing layout, will call for an interior designer.

The right professional will undoubtedly be worth his fee, although it may at first seem high (12 to 20 per cent of construction and fixturing costs, for all services). However, his fee may largely be saved through his knowledge of design, his imagination and construction know-how, and his handling of competitive bidding. Finally, the real economy lies in the efficiency and attractiveness of the physical result.

The selection of a professional must also depend on the ability of client and designer to work together. The designer should be given a point of departure for his skills in the creative use of space and physical organization and the sensitive use of color, texture, and light. This will produce the sought-after *ambiance* while dealing simultaneously and realistically with the more technical and complex aspects of the project and the client's individual requirements.

For the bookseller doing less than $100,000, there may be a question of whether to retain a designer or simply to go to the "fixture manufacturer." One pays for what one gets in any situation, and while the supplier may not charge specifically for design, it is one of his hidden costs. Then, since he is a sole source, you lose the enormous advantages of competitive bidding on purchased items while obtaining a standard, out-of-the-catalog result. Moreover, important aspects of the project may lie beyond the supplier's field. Do explore both alternatives before making the decision.

The layout. The store plan should create hierarchies of the merchandise depending on the need for more or less exposure. Thus one might, for example, arrange merchandise in the order shown in Table 5.1.

TABLE 5.1

TYPICAL ORDER OF MERCHANDISE EXPOSURE

Most Exposure	Large art or historical-survey books Hardbacks Best-sellers	High rate of $ return
Less Exposure	Special or technical publications—cooking, sports, gardening, sex, hobbies, "how to," tax, business, technical, etc.	Special interest
Special Exposure	Gifts, games, art objects, prints, posters, records, accessories	Gifts
Least Exposure	Children's books, paperbacks, fine books, service areas for stationery, etc.	Buyer's choice

Once the disposition of merchandise is determined and appropriate areas assigned to handle the volume of merchandise anticipated in each, traffic patterns may be developed that will promote maximum exposure without inconvenience to the shopper. This problem can usually be solved by a system for the main aisles that carries the customer through the store without his being forced to retrace his steps, but with a number of side trips also available. The joy of discovery is important to real book buyers. Encourage serendipity!

Special attention is required at the cash-and-wrapping desk, which must control both arrival and departure of each shopper in a natural and casual manner, handle sales efficiently, and in normal times deal with almost all of the store's business. (In periods such as the Christmas rush, supplementary service and/or wrapping desks cut down the congestion.) Placing the cash desk to the right of the exit on leaving the store follows United States traffic conventions and saves confusion.

The store plan also includes the manager's office and the stockroom. These tend to be placed where space allows. Stockroom size should be as small as is consistent with carrying the inventory needed to support the volume of sales estimated, and with handling deliveries. These areas should not be allowed to become non-productive, hard to supervise and in danger of becoming catchalls.

In considering store layout, the seller tends to "overfixture," and the designer to "underfixture." Narrow aisles crowd up easily, discourage browsing, are almost impossible to light, and provide poor access to the lower shelves. Leonard Schwartz, when head of the McGraw-Hill Book Company stores, stated that 90 per cent of the customers seek the same 10 per cent of the titles, while 10 per cent of the customers seek 90 per cent of the titles. Therefore the high-demand, high-traffic areas of the store should not be overcrowded. He also states that "the breadth of the inventory is the magnet to attract customers; the depth of the inventory determines profit and loss." Books that are less in demand may thus be shelved compactly and efficiently. There is a strong tendency for the bookstore owner to insist on more display capacity than is needed, which results in overcrowding and makes shopping a less pleasurable experience.

A significant aside. Increasing losses due to shoplifting are naturally a matter of great concern to all merchants and must be carefully considered in the planning. Concave mirrors and TV cameras are deterrents, while having the manager's office elevated in the supermarket tradition may have some merit. A service desk with good visibility in the center of the floor gives a degree of inconspicuous supervision. Keeping the shelving below eye level (five feet six inches) and avoiding alcoves, multiple floors, and high obstructions that hinder the staff's general overview make general surveillance easier.

4. *Make It Attractive*

The bookstore's design must convey simultaneously a wide range of impressions: art and amusement, fact and fantasy, how-to-succeed and do-it-yourself, scholarly work and popular favorites. Whether the approach is serious with scholarly overtones of a wealthy man's private library or popular, flashy, and loud, the customer's expectations are strongly influenced by the basic visual character. Therefore, it seems reasonable that elements of both extremes should be combined: lively color with dark warm surfaces; soft, quiet carpeting with occasional rough textures; subdued lighting with brilliant accents. And the exterior of the store should establish and reflect the interior insofar as possible.

The show window. Nothing quite stimulates interest in the printed word as well as the sight of someone else reading. That is why we like to arrange the bookstore window so that a portion of the customers will be there—browsing. The fixtures are visible from the street and yet sell within the store, thereby making the customers participants. A broad, vinyl-covered counter approximately twenty-eight feet long in the window of the Smithsonian Museum Bookshop is twenty-eight inches deep and stands on chromium pipe legs so that it appears almost to float. Oversized books are laid out along it for easy inspection and there are almost always a few browsers there.

On entering the store, the customer should feel he is in the right place—a stimulating environment that will fulfill his shopping wants. The visual impact derives from the range of possibilities confronting him, at first bewildering, but gradually sorted out. This accessibility, variety, and choice in a warm and inviting setting exhilarates the shopper and makes selecting and buying a book an experience rather than merely a transaction.

The store's perimeter, established by its walls, looks best covered with books to at least an eight-foot height, through the use of modular shelves. The jackets are posters, graphically illustrating the content of the books. We have often used very dark walls and washed the wall with light so that the jackets float against the negative background like tessera of stained glass. Bright backgrounds are also useful for other effects, but pastel and light walls that may compete with the jackets and show dirt should be avoided. Expensive wall finishes behind book displays are generally a waste of effort and money.

Floor coverings are also an important design feature. If the store opens directly from a sidewalk (rather than enclosed mall), the entrance area might be covered with a durable material such as quarry tile, slate tile (quarter inch thick), or any of a variety of small tiles, which come in a variety of shapes (the small round ones are attractive). They are impervious to dirty and wet feet and give a rich appearance.

Carpet is ideal within much of the store. It is warm, rich in color and texture, easy to clean, and in the new indoor-outdoor synthetic versions, can be surprisingly inexpensive, attractive, and durable. We have used "carpet graphics"—bold supergraphic patterns of contrasting colors—to delineate large areas or circulation paths to simplify future replacement of worn sections.

A few concessions to comfort and a friendly atmosphere are also of value. While it may not be desirable to turn your store into a reading room, scattering several chairs appropriately about the store conveys a genuine feeling of concern for the customers' comfort and adds a note of warmth.

Lighting. "Space is reflected light." This statement by architect Louis Kahn is a constant theme of the profession and can probably be traced back at least to Vitruvius. Inelegantly put, we see that which is lit; hence designers have great concern about lighting as a primary tool in revealing the interior environment. They speak in painter's terms of "washing" a wall, "highlighting" an area, "bringing out" a plane or leaving another underlit. They also speak the technical language of foot-candles, lumens per square foot, downlights, recessed fixtures, fluorescent or incandescent, light span, duplex outlets, conduits and raceways.

The Society of Illuminating Engineers, influenced over the years by the electrical utilities and manufacturers of light bulbs and fixtures, has been advocating ever-higher light levels, to the point of absurdity. The cost in energy and dollars is doubled. You pay for the light and you pay for the air conditioning required to get rid of the heat the light produces. Current recommended light levels for bookstores are about 100 foot-candles, whereas 50 to 60 foot-candles is quite adequate with occasional contrasting pools of greater brightness. Over-all and uniform lighting produces a flat, impersonal atmosphere lacking in shadows and warmth—probably not what you need or want for your store.

Incandescent fixtures are very inefficient as a light source when compared with fluorescent. However, they should be used, sparingly and selectively, to produce brilliance and sparkle. In any event, sophisticated and expensive fixtures are to be avoided, especially if they require special, hard-to-get lamps with a short life expectancy.

Fixtures. The fixturing of bookstores is a high art, for the arrangement and design of the fixtures shapes the configuration of the interior.

Consider the book itself: a solid, usually disproportionately thin for its height and width, in a maddening array of sizes, normally required to stand upright—fastened together only along one edge of the length, subject to failure through shear and torsion, highly damageable, required to be displayed by the spine or cover.

Libraries have an efficient solution: the bookstack or bookcase. Four to five feet from upright to upright, it displays the book spine out on multiple shelves seven feet high with relatively narrow aisles, thirty to thirty-six inches wide. This is great for a large catalogued collection of one of a kind, but obviously is not designed for selling. In contrast, tables do a good job poorly—they display the books quite grandly but are highly inefficient in the use of floor area. Ideally, the bookstore fixture would combine the best aspects of both, exposing the covers face out, slightly sloped so the eye can scan all with a minimum of bending; the shelves above sloping back, terminating at the bottom in broader, table-like platforms that can be piled with the larger books. Such a fixture, though it gives optimum display, is expensive and space-consuming.

A compromise is a vertical stack with narrow shelves, five feet six inches high (to carry a reasonable amount of stock that can be well lighted), tilted back about 5 degrees to increase the visual exposure while preventing books from falling off.

Shelving in any logical system, such as subject matter, size, or saleability, will unavoidably be subject to change. One is often tempted to opt for *flexibility,* one of the most expensive words in the mother tongue. The various adjustable hardware systems are costly and, by observation and from expert testimony, are seldom changed after the first setting. If a few shelves have to be moved, it may be best simply to call in a carpenter.

If the job is sufficiently large to warrant it, the store fixtures can be custom designed, bid for competitively, and bought at or near the cost of stock catalog items of similar quality. While this involves extra work and responsibility for client and designer, the result can help enormously to reinforce the full image and character of the store. Chains of stores find this the best way to go.

Some suggestions about fixtures:

- Fixturing costs can run very high—as much as twice the cost of general construction.
- End-supported shelves permit modular uprights. If these are spaced more than three feet apart, watch the shelf design or they will sag.
- Knife brackets may slice into the merchandise.
- Steel shelves, cantilevered from the rear, can give you a marvelously continuous shelf, but with consequent loss in variability of heights within that length.
- For paperbacks, you'll have trouble finding anything better than the wire racks, fixed and revolving, but at times it's worth trying.
- Wood shelves one inch thick (actual thickness, five-eighths of an inch) will start to sag if over three feet in length.

5. *Make It Sell*

The emphasis on bookstore design should not, of course, result in an artistic success and a merchandising failure. On the contrary, it is axiomatic that good design will stimulate trade and contribute substantially to a store's success. And no role is more important to this success than that of signs and graphics.

In this age of anonymity, identification is important; for the merchant this is doubly true. Innumerable studies of shoppers' patterns have shown that loyalty to purveyor and product may often be very strong. It is important for the individual bookseller to fix that pattern as firmly as possible on the buyer, especially since the general public does not always distinguish among stores that of necessity carry a considerable inventory of identical products. Identity must be established by location, the selection of merchandise offered, the service, and the recognizable visual image. Important to this last are signs and other graphics.

While there are specialists in graphic design, your architect or interior designer will probably be anxious to help you in this area so as to ensure that all elements in the design are carefully interrelated.

First, a logotype must be designed, including lettering style, colors, and possibly a related symbol. Elements of this will be used for:

- *Exterior sign.* In most cases this should be an illuminated sign (since you are likely to be open at night), well designed, neat, and informative. The exterior treatment, the character and color of the lettering, will carry through into the interior.
- *Interior signs.* Subject identification signs are essential for the shopper to find his way around without need of constant direction. These signs can cause problems unless they are mounted on the wall. If hung from the ceiling, they often produce visual confusion by competing with light fixtures *et al.* Signs are frequently mounted on the ends or at the center of a fixture, although those in the Smithsonian bookstore simply replace a displayed book on the top shelf.

We designers love to use color identification whenever possible, but beware, unless the user is thoroughly grounded in the color code known as the Munsell system, he usually loses interest after red, yellow, and blue. Furthermore, such systems lack flexibility. A recognizable color (or colors) for the entire store is a much more powerful and successful method than attempts to identify subjects by means of a complex color scheme.

The store motif may even be reproduced on shopping bags, which offer a fine opportunity to spread the word. Today, they have become the all-purpose carryall, partially replacing handbag, briefcase, and other superfluous forms of luggage. A plastic bag with a good, striking color and graphics, perhaps shaped as a tote bag, shoulder bag, or attaché case, may cost a few cents more but may result in literally hundreds of distinguished people touting the store around the city. Transparent areas in the bag make it possible to check the contents easily.

How does one deal with the delightful ambiguities of the book as both merchandise and cultural heritage, popular taste and scholarship, the ephemeral and the permanent? This is an intriguing challenge to any architect or designer.

Making the Move to a New Store   **6**

ELLSWORTH YOUNG
Former owner, Phillips Book Store,
Cambridge, Massachusetts

If you are nicely located and business is good, changing to a new location, whatever the reason may be, is apt to be very disturbing. Having been through this experience—moving from what we considered an ideal location to one that offered certain problems and involved hazards, possibly we can offer some comments and suggestions that will be reassuring and helpful.

Planning To Move

In the first place, there are actually some advantages to replanning and moving into a new place, as well as a number of obvious disadvantages. The book business has changed considerably in recent years, and stores designed and built some years ago are no longer as useful as they should be today. When you stop to consider it, you are not running the same store that you did ten or fifteen years ago. Book-buying habits have changed; paperbacks and remainders are a more important part of bookselling today. Your own operation and emphasis have probably changed a good deal, and in spite of spasmodic readjustment of layout and fixtures, you are handicapped by equipment so old that it has already been written off in your accounting. New techniques and materials, new and better equipment, and a more suitable and more coordinated store layout can actually help you run a better store and make more money, if you are forced to take the plunge, or if you decide it is necessary to make a change.

With better planning and new materials, total expenditure for new fixturing can be kept down, in spite of the considerable advance in building costs during recent years. Undoubtedly, better use of space, updated layout and fixtures, and better display of books can in the long run pay for all costs and bring in larger profits.

If you plan to move, you will need to find a suitable new location, and an architect will be very helpful to you in making the decision; therefore it is probably well to select your architect, if possible, before you decide on a new location. Naturally, it is better if he has had experience with bookstores, but we feel that he should at least have had some previous work in retail-store planning. [See Chapter 4, "Using a Store Planner," and Chapter 5, "Bookstore Design."—ED.]

In making a decision, rent, size of store, as well as suitability of space and customer traffic, will need to be weighed. [See Chapter 2, "Choosing a Location."—ED.] Finding and arranging for a new store involves legal problems, and a local attorney can offer helpful advice with respect to landlords, rents, etc., and can check over the lease before you sign. Perhaps he can secure better phrasing of the lease to protect your interests. At least he can explain the terms of the lease to you.

This can be a time of discouragement and frustration. Obviously not everything about a new location will be to your liking. You will need to put your emphasis, in making your choice, on the things that seem most important. You can then plan and work to offset some of the seeming disadvantages. In our case, we took a less desirable location (from the point of view of customer traffic), with higher overhead, than we had had previously. However, we did get more space, and much better organized space, and were able to update our layout to fit our changed and changing operation. Happily, business increases exceeded our expectations, after the first few difficult months of transition. Perhaps it is as well to be somewhat pessimistic in such matters, for then you will undoubtedly plan more carefully and work harder to make your bookstore a success.

You are fortunate if you are already established in your community before you move into a new store, no matter where the new store is. You already know your market; you have a clientele that is in the habit of coming to you for books. Nevertheless, you should try to estimate the effect of your new location and your new layout on the volume of business you will be doing and the type of books you will be selling. These factors can then be taken into consideration when planning the new arrangement of stock—the allotment of space to certain types of books (children's books, technical books, paperbacks, etc.).

Visiting other bookstores and other retail stores and studying the model bookstore at each ABA Convention will help to crystallize your ideas on the type of shelving, fixtures, style and color of outdoor sign, etc., that you will eventually want. You will not only find things that look good to you, but you will discover things that you want to be sure to avoid. Such visits may help you to select an architect if you have not already done so. Be sure to see stores designed by the architect you choose, note the features that you like or ones that would need changing to fit into your store. Talk with the people connected with the stores you visit. We found two complaints were typical when discussing architects and planning. Avoid these errors:

- Expecting the new store to come out complete and perfect, with no changes needed. Plan as carefully as you can, but you will certainly need to make changes here and there after opening.
- Trying half measures. The resulting job will be unsatisfactory, and you will not get a unified, attractive, and efficient layout. The appearance of the new part will clash with the old and there will be operational problems, too. In planning and redoing a store, it is best if all parts of the whole are considered and the interrelation of these parts planned for.

Prior to moving day, a good deal of layout planning needs to be done with the new store's fixture diagram. This architect's drawing should indicate approximate book capacities of each fixture or section of shelving. The diagram, together with a tabulation of volume counts for subject groups in the old store, will provide most of the information needed for marking up the new layout. Careful consideration is given at this time to the amount of browsing likely for various subjects, the advisability or need of flat display, grouping related subjects so they are shelved near each other, and the amount of space available in different fixtures (i.e., which section or sections a certain fixture can accommodate best). For areas that are less accessible, such as a balcony, books can be selected that will be least affected by this disadvantage.

This will also be a time, unfortunately or fortunately, for some rethinking about your store equipment, supplies, and services. Your new store may require a change in bags and wrapping paper—at least you will want to consider it. Perhaps you may want to add sidelines, or reduce them. If you have been on a cash business you may decide to undertake charge accounts. As if you have not already had enough expense, you may feel that some of your old equipment does not fit properly into your new store—perhaps it is an inadequate and ancient cash register that needs replacing, or a desk, or a typewriter, or chairs. As you know, new fixtures make old equipment look even older.

Before store plans are made, you should discuss your ideas of stock arrangement, work areas, and other points with the architect. He will need to provide proper display and shelving for special types of books, for example, art books, bargains or remainders, oversize pictorial books, and paperbacks. Enough space will need to be allotted for work areas and for storage. You should decide which types of books should be placed in the front of the store, along the side walls, in the rear, or in center areas. Related subjects or types of books should be shelved as near each other as much as possible, a customer convenience that increases sales. Some books need or benefit greatly by flat display; others are sold mostly on call or have less jacket appeal and can be placed less prominently, with spines out. Probably the architect will want you to count the books in your old store (titles and volumes), breaking this down by subject groups. He can thus get a picture of your total book stock and its various parts and make a more satisfactory arrangement of stock and space allotment.

Many changes are necessary, or should be considered when moving to a new store. Planning ahead on these will avoid headaches. For example, will you use the same telephone setup in the new store? If you change from a simple single phone and extension to several phones with push-button controls and an intercommunication system, your telephone number will of necessity be changed. Your old number will still be in the directory until the new issue, unless you can arrange otherwise. Plan to order new printed supplies (letterheads, special-order notification cards, order forms, etc.), and have these ready with the new address at the time you open. The outside sign, if you plan to use one, should be designed, approved, and constructed well in advance. This sort of planning can take more time than you imagine, and it is very helpful to have your sign up before you open in a new location. We did not allow enough time for some of these items, and found that unexpected delays were troublesome and costly.

Methods of Moving

In our experience (we moved some 50,000 volumes twice in sixteen years), the actual moving of the book stock, equipment, and so forth is not so big a job as one might imagine. Even with a large stock, you need not be out of business more than two days. Every day you are closed, particularly if you have competitors, adds to the cost of moving, so it is best to find ways of reducing this time.

For the first move we made, we hired only a moving van and a driver, and provided and instructed our own crew (mostly college boys). Uniform box shelving was set up around the walls of the van and books were carried on and off the van on plywood trays—two piles of books, in order, on each tray. The books came off the shelves in order, section by section, and were placed in the new store on the proper shelving, ready for the reopening. All books went into preplanned locations and were kept in strict alphabetical order.

This scheme worked well. However, we did it a little differently the second time. We still had the uniform boxes (about three feet long and ten or twelve inches deep—used in the stock room of the old store), and these were again filled with books, in order. (We made no attempt to package the books, for either move, as this would have wasted a great deal of time.) The books were merely inserted in a single row (in some cases two rows), spine out, in the boxes. About six or eight full boxes were placed on a dolly and rolled up a ramp into the truck. When the van was filled with dollies and books, it went to the new store and disgorged its load. The labeled and numbered boxes were put in front of the proper sections for shelving. Our staff members supervised the loading of the books in boxes. They were kept in order and thus, when they were unloaded, could be put into their proper places in the new store. The moving men were instructed by one of our people as to where to leave the boxes in various parts of the store. This plan worked well and after two days the most active 90 per cent of our stock was in its proper place, organized and ready for customer calls.

Picking a mover who will do a good job and save you money is not easy. On the move we made in 1964 we saved at least several hundred dollars by getting a reliable, but small, mover who would work with us. He gave us less sales talk than the other estimator, and a good performance. The mover we selected said he could do the job with five or six men, while the other man planned to use about fifteen men in his razzle-dazzle program. We decided we could not properly supervise and keep that many men busy.

After the Move

After you have moved into the new store there will be an extended period of ironing out details, modifying fixtures, changing arrangements, adding additional small units. One must see a new store in actual operation to find out what should be moved or altered. Many of these things cannot be anticipated when looking at preliminary drawings. Probably it is well to make arrangements with a local carpenter-mechanic who can help you with repairs and alterations as needed. Having someone of this sort handy will mean that you will get some of the things done that you know should be done.

In spite of careful preplanning, this adjustment will take more time and probably more money than you expected, depending on how particular you are, or what type of store you picture. The cheering part of this is that your new store should become more and more functional and attractive to you and to your customers as the changes are made. Naturally, if you can make your customers and your staff happier, it is going to improve your business.

Change begets change. Try to remember, while you are busy with a multitude of other things related to the new store, that your staff may get unhappy, concerned, or restless. Some of them may like the old store better—they may not like the changes you are making, which you think are updating your business. You will have an informational and selling job to do with your staff members. Explain what is going on and why. Get their ideas on areas that are of special interest to them. Outline the advantages of the new setup, show how service can be improved and work organized better. In addition, it is probably a good time to go over your salary schedule and consider adjustments planned or due soon.

You also need to discuss the new store with customers and explain some of the changes and improvements. Some will still say they prefer the old store. You and your staff will need to win them over by improved service, and explanations of advantages. Others will, of course, be loud in their praise. In any case, you will need to step up your advertising and consider other ways of promoting the new store. If you move to an entirely different location, you especially need to inform the public and train old customers to come to the location. If it is not in so good a flow of traffic, you will want to consider adding other services (perhaps charge accounts), additional lines, and the like, to offset the disadvantage. Perhaps you have some ideas for promotion that you never got around to using. This is the time to use them if they seem sound.

Your advertising can feature the growth of the store, an anniversary, the increased stock, ease of browsing. Perhaps you can also arrange with the local newspaper for a picture or pictures with a news story about the new store. An open house can be planned to notify people of your new location. This, by the way, does not need to be done as an official open house until you and the store are ready for it— possibly some weeks after you open, when most of the alterations and changes have been made. Perhaps a series of advertisements on the local FM station or in the local newspaper will seem desirable. You may want to advertise in media different from those you have used in the past, for you can reach new customers this way and you will need new customers and increased sales to help pay for all the improvements!

When it is all done, you and your staff should be tired but happy, with a more attractive and more functional store, a better stock of books better displayed, and an increasing number of customers buying many more volumes.

Selling Your Store 7

JAMES B. KOBAK
President, James B. Kobak, Inc.,
Publishing Consultants

ANNOTATED FOR STORE BUYERS
BY G. ROYSCE SMITH

The subject of selling a business which one has owned and operated for many years is one which few people like to think about. There is so much of *you* in the business that it is hard to conceive of someone else running it. Selling a bookstore especially brings out these emotions, because it is so personal.

Not to consider the intelligent disposition of your business, however, is sheer folly. For most people this is the largest single asset they own—and for many, the only property of real value. Since it is so important, the best results can be obtained only through careful planning. It is something you will do only once in a lifetime, and you had better be sure you do it right.

When To Sell

Any businessman periodically reviews his situation to determine his best long-term plan. At some point in these reviews the idea of an eventual sale is bound to come up, even in terms of three or five years later.

Normally, adopting a plan for selling should be done long before most people think it is necessary. The right time is when things are going well, profits are high, there is growth, and you are having the time of your life.

Reason? Because this is when the business is worth most. When you start getting tired, it is probably too late. And there is nothing like an enthusiastic salesman, which you are when things are going well.

The last thing you should do is put the decision off—and off—and off. You are the best one to sell your store. When you get too old, or too

45

ill, or have passed away, your wife, your executor, your lawyer, your bank—no one else can do it as well, or obtain as good a price.*

And if you still want to remain as active as before, you can almost always find a buyer who would like you to run the store and give you a portion of the profits while you do.

The best approach is to start planning for selling some years ahead of time.

Why? Simply because most of us most of the time do not run our businesses as well as we know how. We often do things because we enjoy doing them our own way, even if we know it may not be the best way. If you are considering selling your business in the future, the time to get it in shape for a sale is now. Businesses are bought for their earnings—and let's make sure the earnings are as strong as they can be when the time comes. Some things that can be done now are:

- Make sure that the accounting records are clear, helpful, and accurate. If you have not had a good accountant, now is the time to get things in shape. Good records are helpful for a buyer to understand exactly what has been happening in your store. Not only that, they indicate that you have been operating the store in a business-like way.
- If any personal expenses have crept into the business—if your favorite uncle is on the payroll, but not really contributing much—now is the time to recognize and reorganize. You don't want earnings depressed in future years for non-business expenses.
- Get rid of all those obsolete books that you bought by mistake several years ago when you were new in the business. Make sure to write them off so that they do not affect future earnings.
- Close up departments which have been consistent losers but which you enjoy so much that you could never really face up to the red ink.
- Make sure returns are made to publishers on time so that you don't end up with more obsolete inventory.
- Review the charge customers and be a little more hardhearted about giving credit—and about collecting.

In other words, run the store in the most business-like way you can for the next few years, even though you may not enjoy it as much.†

---

*Buyer, beware, if the owner has lost interest in his shop or contact with his customers. A sure sign is when sales have peaked and are declining.—G.R.S.

†These six points are exactly what a prospective buyer should look for: business-like records; an absence of essentially personal expenses; a clean and essentially saleable inventory; a lack of slow-moving sections that might reflect the owner's rather than the customers' interests; records showing timely, systematic returns; and an up-to-date accounts receivable.—G.R.S.

Why and to Whom

Obviously not all businesses should be sold. If you have been able to get your children involved and to train them to take over when you retire, there may be no reason to sell. This, of course, does not happen often. And sometimes even when it does happen, the best way for making the transition is through a sale between members of the family. In this way retirement income can be developed for the older generation and operating control for the younger.

But for most, a sale comes into the picture at some point. The reasons for selling are readily apparent:

- The owner has reached the stage physically or emotionally where he no longer wants to carry on.
- The owner would like to realize the fruits of his many years of labor.
- It is unwise for most families to have all their assets in one basket.
- Competition, or some other outside force, has depressed the business to the extent that the assets of the owner are insufficient to make a comeback.

Difficult to reach though the decision may be, there are times for almost everyone when the need to plan to sell a business becomes overwhelming.*

There are a number of factors to be considered besides price alone in determining to whom to sell. For instance:

- If you get a better price from one party than another, be sure that he is able to meet the payments.
- If you get a better price because of an installment sale over a number of years, make sure that it is really more than getting cash today —and investing it—might be.
- If you are being paid partly out of future earnings, be sure the buyer is capable of running the business to create those earnings.
- You spent years building the business. Be sure that you sell to someone who will carry it on well. Part of you will always be in the store.

The types of people you might consider in selling your business are infinite, but normally they fall into such areas as: family members, employees, competitors, or chain operators.

Sometimes public companies will be involved. The method of dealing with each of these is different. And usually the method of payment will be different, too.

Remember that you are *selling* your business. This means that it is wise to bring all the techniques of selling to this task just as you would

---

*Only the final item—"competition, or some other outside force"—need concern the buyer, who must be certain that he recognizes any such detrimental external factor and is able to determine that he can cope with them better than the present owner.—G.R.S.

for a sale of Christmas books. Go about developing a list of potential buyers in an organized, structured way.

Sure, visit your lawyer, banker, accountant, insurance man, and other advisers to see if they have any suggestions. But this is the most important sale you will ever have. Do more!

Try the ABA for suggestions. Advertise locally, in *Publishers Weekly,* and in other logical places. You can do all this without revealing to your customers or competitors that you are thinking of selling, and it probably won't hurt even if they do know.

The whole idea is to make the best sale you can.

Even if you decide to sell to employees, it is good to contact some outsiders in addition. You might find the prices they could pay are so far beyond those which the employees can afford that you could not turn the deal down.

What should you tell the buyer? Everything!*

There is no use trying to fool a prospective purchaser. He is going to find out just about everything involving the store, whether you tell him or not. And if you have told him, your credibility is that much better.

Besides, it has often been said that a good deal has to be good for both parties, or it isn't good for either. This happens to be true. If one side is trying to take advantage of the other, the chances are that there never will be a transaction at all.

The best way to acquaint a purchaser with your business is by developing a booklet describing it. In financial circles this is known as a prospectus. It should contain such things as:

> Ownership
> History and description of the business
> Any information you may have about key
>   customers
> Competition
> Key employees, their duties and salaries
> Fringe benefits
> Description of the geographic area in which you
>   operate
> Any unusual events that may have occurred in
>   recent years and the effect they had on the
>   business
> Potential of the area in which you operate
> Balance sheet at the most recent possible date
> Profit and loss statement for at least three years

---

*Buyer, be sure he does!—G.R.S.

This whole affair can normally be confined to twenty pages or so. But it gives a potential purchaser a bird's-eye view of the entire situation and gives both you and the buyer a common basis of fact from which to work.*

If there is real estate included with the business, it is helpful to know the fair market value. Often an appraisal is called for. The real estate, of course, represents a value above that of the business itself. The same would be true of other non-operating assets, if there are any.

In addition to the normal profit and loss statement as prepared on an accounting basis, it should be amplified to adjust for unusual items. For instance, if there was a theft or a fire, these do not represent ordinary operations and the costs, with annotations, should be added back to profits to show more realistic results. The number and nature of such unusual items are limitless.

To give a realistic picture of operations, it is also helpful to include normal salary figures for the owners if they are active in the business. Sometimes they pay themselves either too much or too little. Often, personal expenses are included that have nothing to do with the business. These should be adjusted for.†

How To Compute the Value

It is, of course, difficult to negotiate a good sale unless you are familiar with the going values that are paid for stores in your neighborhood. Unfortunately there are no real rules of thumb for the value of any business, no matter how much you hear to the contrary. While many people will idly say that a bookstore is worth its annual volume —or five times its before-tax profits—it just isn't necessarily so. The whole situation is much more complex.

Values of businesses depend, first, on historic earnings. But beyond that must be considered the quality of the management, the competition, changes that can be made, the potential both short- and long-term, excess assets that exist above those necessary to run the store, the eagerness of the buyer, the eagerness of the seller, the method of making the purchase—and almost everything else.

---

*In looking over the items offered in the prospectus by the seller, the buyer should, of course, pay most attention to the balance sheet and the profit and loss statement, but every item deserves close scrutiny. Remember that a change in management usually is accompanied by some attrition of key customers and key employees. It is not unusual to find an older key employee, who has long since ceased to carry a fair share of the work load, making unusual demands because of seniority or actively working against a new owner through misplaced loyalty to the old owner.—G.R.S.

†As is pointed out elsewhere, too often owners show no salary on their profit and loss statement. If they are active in the business and particularly if they manage it and do the buying, a realistic sum —say 8 per cent of net sales—*must* be assigned to expenses as their salary before a reasonable net profit can be determined.—G.R.S.

To get some idea, however, make some calculations along the lines of the examples in Tables 7.1 and 7.2. Suppose you have a balance sheet and profit and loss statement like this:

TABLE 7.1
BALANCE SHEET

Cash	$10,000
Accounts receivable net of bad debts	25,000
Inventory	25,000
Other assets	5,000
Land and building at cost less depreciation	20,000
	$85,000

Accounts payable	$30,000
Mortgage payable	10,000
Owners' equity	45,000
	$85,000

TABLE 7.2
PROFIT AND LOSS STATEMENT

	1973	1972	1971
Net sales	$120,000	$110,000	$105,000
Cost of goods sold	70,000	65,000	60,000
Gross Profit	50,000	45,000	45,000
Operating expenses	28,000	25,000	30,000
Net profit before taxes	$ 22,000	$ 20,000	$ 15,000

As discussed before, the profit should be adjusted to reflect as closely as possible the actual operations of the business (Table 7.3). In this case let us assume:

TABLE 7.3
ADJUSTED STATEMENT

	1973	1972	1971
Net profit before taxes	$22,000	$20,000	$15,000
Loss from fire in storeroom			8,000
To adjust owner's salary to $12,000		(3,000)	(4,000)
Net profit before taxes, after adjustments	$22,000	$17,000	$19,000

To get some idea of the value of the business based on its earnings, consult with your banker, accountant, or other local person who is knowledgeable about prices in your area. Let us assume, for this purpose only, that they say it is about six times earnings before taxes. The calculation goes like this:

Average earnings for three years:	$ 19,300
	× 6
	$115,800
Add the value of the land and building if owned by the bookseller, per appraisal:	30,000
	$145,800

Thus the value of the company might be somewhere in the $150,000 range. This gives you a rough guide for talking with potential buyers.

Specialists Who May Help

You are in the business of selling books, not of selling businesses. This is one of the most technical and complex things anyone can do in today's economic world. Before you finish you will find that there are legal implications, accounting implications, and tax implications, as well as simple business and emotional implications.

While you may not have much trouble reaching an agreement with the buyer about price, you will find that "it ain't what you do, it's the way you do it." Sometimes there are tax methods where the buyer pays less and the seller gets more. These are obviously beyond the scope of this article.*

The plain fact is that you cannot do without an attorney who is skilled in corporate law, an accountant, and a tax man (who may be one of the first two). Normally, too, it is helpful from the standpoint of both the buyer and the seller to have a third party help with the negotiations. When sticky points come up he can be more objective than the principals. If he is experienced in helping to make deals, he can dream up creative solutions to what may appear to be impossible problems.†

This third party may be an attorney, an accountant, a banker, a business broker, or any other trusted and experienced businessman. This is highly skilled and highly technical work that normally commands fees larger than the normal work they do for you.

---

*The example of a tax situation in which the seller gets more regardless of what the buyer pays is when the terms of sale list a sum paid for good will. The buyer should know that in practical terms there is no way to buy or sell good will. Yet many potential buyers come to the ABA office and ask, "How much should I pay for good will?" The answer is "Nothing," for good will has no tax advantage or resale value for the buyer, and he cannot depreciate it. However, it does represent a tax advantage to the seller to show in a sales agreement that a part of the money he is being paid is for "good will" rather than capital gains. The question is this: "Is the total of what I'm getting worth the total of what I am paying?"—G.R.S.

†The buyer will also want *his own* attorney and accountant as well as a possible third party.—G.R.S.

It is helpful to be sure that there is an understanding with your advisers as to what their rates are to be, and on what basis fees are to be paid.

You may or may not require the services of a broker. There are lots of people who do this type of work. They may actually call themselves brokers, or they may be attorneys or accountants who are involved in such affairs. For actual brokerage work a percentage of the selling price is normally paid. Five per cent on the first million dollars is normally quoted, but special arrangements can often be made.

If you are approached by a business broker whom you do not know, be sure to check his reputation and exactly what role he expects to play. Some of these brokers do what is known as "fishing," telling sellers that they have buyers and vice versa until they can make a match. And if they introduce you to the eventual buyer you may owe a fee without knowing what you got into.

This is not to imply that good brokers cannot be helpful and in many cases make the difference between accomplishing a transaction or not.

I wish there were no such word as "negotiate." It has an unpleasant, gamelike connotation.

You are there to *sell*—and this may be the biggest and most important sale you ever make. Forget sparring with the opposition and put on your sales hat.

First step in selling—as in anything else—is to find out as much as you can about the buyer. Why does he want to buy; what does he think he can do with the store; what are his means; how good a businessman is he; what do you know about his immediate family; and so forth. Then gear your conversation to what will appeal to him. If he is a good purchaser, he will be doing the same in connection with you, and a pleasant negotiation will take place.*

Coming to grips with the need to sell your business is not easy. It can be traumatic at times. And the actual work involved in making the sale can be terribly time-consuming and nerve-racking.

When you reach the point where you feel that is the step which will be necessary, do it in an organized and planned manner. Not only will you get a better price for the store, but the wear and tear on you and your family will be that much less.

---

*Buyer, this article is a very fair summary of what a seller should offer a buyer. It also tells you exactly what you should expect of the seller. In turn, you must be frank and fair as well. In the long run, the best deal is the one made in an atmosphere of mutual trust, which is not to say that you must not take every opportunity to ascertain the trustworthiness of every party to the agreement. And the other parties will do the same about you.—G.R.S.

Operation
and Financing

How To Become a Bookseller

8

G. ROYSCE SMITH
Executive Director,
American Booksellers Association, Inc.

The very first letter I found awaiting me when I came to work for ABA in 1971 was from a young aspiring bookseller.

> *I would like to know what are the qualifications to become a salesclerk? I do know a couple: you have to get along with people, you must not force any customer to buy a book, when kids are fooling around and messing the place you must be very polite with kicking them out.*
>
> *Please tell me how old you must be, how tall must you be, must you have a good personality? Please send me a sample application form. Thank you for your time.*
>
> Yours truly,
> PAM S.

Here, on my first day of a job designed to help educate booksellers, I had obviously run into the first child in all the world who wanted to grow up to be a bookseller. What would I say to her? I picked up my pencil, and it poured right out.

> DEAR MISS S.:
> *Thank you for your letter of October 28, 1971, asking about the qualifications for becoming a clerk in a bookstore.*
>
> *There are no standard qualifications for becoming a salesclerk. Each store has its own standards.*
>
> *You are correct in thinking that you have to get along with people, although some of America's greatest booksellers have been notorious grouches. They were so grouchy, indeed, that when they got older they somehow become lovable "characters." However, it's better for most of us to get along with people the amiable way.*
>
> *You are correct, too, in thinking it is wrong to force a customer to buy a book. Nothing will lose you customers faster than selling them a book*

which you know they will not like. If you want to develop regular custom-
ers, you must care about them.

Every store has its own policies about the forcible ejection of unruly
patrons, whatever their age. Not all stores are polite about it.

A salesclerk must be old enough to meet the age requirements of her
state. There are seldom requirements as to height. An offensive personality
is strictly bad news.

Most employers want to know where you live, how old you are, your
social security number, your past employment record, your education,
what kind of work you want, and what references, business and personal,
you can offer.

I hope you decide to become a bookseller.

I could have gone on writing Pam indefinitely, and I should like to think of this article as an extension of that letter I began on my first day.

People who work in bookstores today don't particularly care for being called clerks. Perhaps we should call them booksellers. This isn't too farfetched an idea if they have had the proper training. What shall we call them until then? Apprentices? Not a good word over here. Floor staff? That sounds better, and it's more descriptive. After all, good bookstore personnel must be more than salesmen.

Whatever the name they are called by, their jobs should be carefully described *in writing,* both for their edification and for that of their supervisor. Once one starts to write out what a job consists of, one begins to realize why it is so hard to find a good bookstore staff.

A bookstore-owner friend of mine recently found that the labor market in his college community had become glutted with B.A.'s, M.A.'s, and even Ph.D.'s for whom there simply were no jobs. Aha, he thought! Here was his chance to put in his master plan: a really qualified person as the head of every section of the store, someone recently out of college who was tuned in to the needs and demands of college students, someone who knew what was important in his field. As chance would have it, he only had two old-timers left on the staff. He was surrounded by bright, eager young people who were really going to help him fulfill all the dreams he ever had about a bookstore.

Mechanically, things went along just fine. You never saw such interest being taken in books, books, books. Slowly, however, he began to notice that fewer of his older customers were around the store as much. He got calls from customers claiming his pride-and-joys were being rude. Friends stopped him on the street to ask why his staff had quit giving service. Others said that when they asked for a book they were simply told, "It's in the philosophy section over there."

He brought these complaints to his weekly hour-long staff meetings, which had been designed in part to replace the job descriptions that he had not written for this new group. From these meetings and through discussions of their constantly modifying roles in the store, he hoped to evolve a new kind of bookstore personnel. At the end of the year, he and his staff would be equipped to write job descriptions such as no one had ever written before. Until then they could fly loose.

It wasn't working. He knew it. What was wrong? Why, with such brilliance around him, were things going wrong with his customer relations? The staff itself could find no grounds for the complaints in their behavior. Perhaps he had not heard what Kurt Vonnegut had said about the younger generation: brighter than previous generations without necessarily being more competent.

Competence was what he had to give them and had not.

Toward the end of the year, he asked each of them for his job description, writing down what he thought he did on a daily, weekly, and monthly basis. Then my friend would, in consultation with each of them, rewrite their job descriptions.

What he got was something else entirely. If you want a revelation of De Millean proportions, get the people who work for you to write down what it is they do. You will probably find, as he did, that they will nearly all be concerned with self. He certainly found his staff almost totally unconcerned with others, particularly customers.

There were very few references to customers at all. Here are the only comments that consisted of more than a word or two:

"Customer service includes helping customers to find and order books or listening to them complain because they can't find a book. It includes long explanations about procedures and directions, few of which are listened to."

"The remainder of my time," said another, "is spent straightening shelves and tables. I also try to spend time each day talking to customers and most important to fellow employees."

Customers, one gathers, are people who spend their time complaining or not listening when they are being told what to do. Conversationally, they are of secondary importance to one's fellow employees, which is probably true if one's encounters with customers are limited to "long explanations about procedures."

Since customer service had been a recurring topic of discussion at his weekly meetings, my friend was stunned at the absence of any real feeling for it in these job descriptions. He brought the whole problem up again at the next meeting.

After some minutes of the usual protestations that they did not have an aversion to giving service, one of the group asked, "Just how much service are we expected to give?" And another followed: "Why don't our customers realize that this is a self-service store?"

There was the answer—in the real generation gap, not the celluloid one. He had not realized that this generation has grown up in the postwar world of self-service. For them, *total* self-service is a real concept. It is valid.

Their contemporaries, they reported, resented being led to a book by the hand. They wanted to find it, and if they had to ask for help it would only be to find out in which general area the book would most likely be kept. Dubious, my friend thought about this. It is possibly true, he thought, that in America an individual can live through his life without getting any personal service, once he has been delivered.

If you need food, you go to a supermarket. If you need clothes, appliances, paint, scissors, Band-Aids, dishes, fertilizer, or almost anything else, you can find it in a discount store filled with aisles and aisles of merchandise tended, one assumes, by invisible presences. You can check your own antifreeze and radio tubes, buy stamps from a machine, or get hotel reservations from a computer. Presumably, we will eventually come to the state Walker Percy predicts for us by 1989 in *Love in the Ruins:* Everything that quits working is simply abandoned where it stands because no one wants to be anything so menial as a serviceman.

So, as I would tell Pam, when you open your own store, even if there is only one employee, a part-timer who sweeps the sidewalks, for example, write down his duties. It doesn't have to be any more detailed than you want it to be: "The duties of a sidewalk-sweeper shall be to sweep the sidewalk at 8:15 A.M. weekdays, using the broom that will be found in the broom closet to the left rear of the stockroom."

Then when you do get big enough to have some floor staff you want to turn into booksellers, perhaps you will include these things in what you tell them in your written job descriptions:

- Books don't just take care of themselves. They have to be straightened and dusted every day—sometimes more than once—so that they will look pleasing to our customers.
- We need to be aware of what is selling so that it can be replaced to keep the next customer happy.
- We need to know what customer bought the book that needs to be replaced so that we can suggest a similar book to him the next time he comes in—if we didn't do so when he was in this time.
- We need to be alert to the customer's desire for assistance without hovering or bending his ear when he is trying to browse.
- We need to know how our customer hears about the books he buys, and to be familiar with the same book reviews that he reads in the printed media, listens to on the radio, or watches on TV.
- We need to read, but even more we need to learn how to do what our customers do—browse. But we must do it better.
- We need to know the tools of the trade so that we can help our customer when he has a problem.
- We need to know our store policies so that we don't promise a customer something and then fail to fulfill the promise.

These may seem very simple, basic things, but it is the basic things that we need to write down and remember. Otherwise we can fool ourselves into thinking we know them and are doing them. By writing them out, we assign an importance to them.

In the world of retailing, there are four basic elements: inventory, staff, paper work, and customers. In the list above, the recurring element in each item is "customer," because he's the reason for the other three. He's the reason we're in business, though it's easy enough to say you want to become a bookseller simply because you love books. Just remember this one more thing to tell yourself, as well as your staff:

We need to love books, all right, but even more we need to love attention to detail, attention to the needs of the people we serve, and attention to service.

Hiring and Training Personnel

9

BARRY R. MARK
Former Assistant to the General Manager,
Doubleday Book Shops, New York City

In spite of a growing trend toward self-service in bookshops, salesclerks are still as important a part of the bookshop as the books. The traditional bookshop, where the salesclerk assists the customer in making his selection, cannot function without adequate well-trained personnel. I do not wish to imply that books cannot be sold (or for that matter are not sold) through supermarkets and other self-service outlets, where the clerk merely wraps the customer's selection and collects the money. But I am restricting this discussion to the store that offers the more complete service.

Hiring New Help

What type of applicant is it desirable to attract? The answer is simple—the kind of person who will make customers feel welcome in the shop and satisfied when they leave, looking forward to a return visit. Even a well-stocked, well-designed, and immaculate store, full of intelligent book people, can be an unpleasant place to shop if the salesclerks are poorly groomed or inattentive to the customers.

Letters to the editor and other current comments on the decline of service in retail stores repeatedly cite lack of courtesy—not lack of knowledge—as the main complaint. When a salesclerk is inattentive or discourteous, the stage is set for a customer complaint about lack of information, poor selection, or anything else that may strike him, including the color of the walls.

Only after it has been decided that the applicant for a bookselling job has the right personality should his knowledge of literature and his ability to learn more about the book business be considered. It would be ideal to have a sales force entirely composed of clerks who could readily respond to customers' inquiries for the most obscure titles. "Yes, I know the book. The title is *A Kayak Trip Up the Amazon,* written by Admiral Perry, and published in Australia in 1884 by Kangaroo Press. It has a red cover, is 5¼ X 8½ inches and sells for $250."

The book trade includes numbers of people with long years of experience and vast knowledge of books. But it is frequently necessary to hire someone whose book knowledge may be limited, compared with that of these experts. He should recognize the name Dickens and know that the Dewey Decimal System is related neither to naval warfare nor to the new mathematics. For the job of salesclerk, it will be easier to teach the book business to an inexperienced but personable employee than to try to change the ways of an experienced bookseller who may feel he knows more than the customers and everyone else in the shop —including you. Individuals have a surprising and gratifying ability to acquire a general knowledge of basic stock and the current books—if they have the desire to learn. The right people will learn about books in the shop.

Now that we have an idea of the type of person who should be hired, let us discuss some of the more formal aspects of hiring. Every applicant should be asked to fill out an application form. The formal application has a number of advantages: It provides a personal history of the applicant before the interview; it is a record of the applicant's references; if the applicant is hired, the application becomes a permanent record for the files; and it may also furnish information for a file of applicants for future openings in the shop.

Don't miss the opportunity, in the first interview, to find out as much as possible about the prospective employee. An inexperienced interviewer may make the mistake of doing more of the talking than the applicant. The applicant should be encouraged to talk, using every opportunity to "bring him out" and discover if this is the type of person one would want in the shop. An owner or manager doing his own hiring is able to select the new employee to meet *his* needs. If someone other than the manager or owner interviews applicants—a personnel department, for example—it is vital that a person be hired suitable for the situation he will work in, not someone who would get along only with the people in the personnel department.

Where can good bookstore personnel be found? Bookstore personnel may be recruited from a number of diverse areas. The local college is a particularly good source of part-time personnel for both selling and stock work. Men and women over forty-five, often turned away from other industries because of age or health (pension, insurance, and medical plans in many companies discourage the employment of persons over forty-five), make excellent permanent employees in bookstores. In suburban areas, housewives, especially mothers of school-age children, are eager to work on a part-time basis and often make exceptional booksellers.

The nature of the merchandise—books—gives the bookstore an advantage over other retail establishments in recruiting personnel. The woman who would not dream of telling her friends she sells lingerie is more than likely to be proud to tell them she sells books. For this reason alone, it is far better to give the applicant an accurate and complete picture of the job than to have a disappointed and disgruntled clerk after the first few days of work.

The lady who "just loves books" and is much impressed by the surroundings of the bookstore might be shocked to learn that the books must be dusted, that the job is eight hours a day of standing and walking, that inventories must be taken, and that customers are often difficult to please, as well as some of the other wearing and less glamorous aspects of bookselling. The satisfactions of bookselling strongly overcome these less appealing aspects of the job, and these should also be emphasized, of course.

The first interview should also include a complete rundown on hours of work, salary, and insurance coverage. Many misunderstandings can arise from a lack of complete information in these areas. It should not be assumed that the applicant will expect to work forty hours a week, if that is what is required. Many industries work only thirty-seven or thirty-five hours. It is vital to be clear about the exact salary the job pays and when a raise may be expected. Insurance coverage is now offered employees in most businesses, and it should be made clear whether this coverage is paid for by the employee or the employer, or whether it is shared. A pamphlet outlining the coverage or a copy of the policy should be given the new clerk. [*See* Chapter 16, "Insurance and Protection."—ED.]

Training New Employees

Most people fear the unknown more than they fear a particular problem. The more information given a new employee about his job, the easier it will be to train him. Every new employee, regardless of his background or experience, must be trained in the essentials of the specific operation. The training can be formal or informal, depending upon the size of the shop and the number of new employees to be trained at a particular time.

The first step in training the new employee is to introduce him to the entire staff. The basic rules of the shop, whether official policy or the result of long-standing custom, should then be outlined in detail. The most simple information, a matter of course to the initiated, is unknown to the newcomer. And failure to go through this essential introductory phase could mean a bad beginning for the new employee.

The formal training program for new employees of large organizations include many areas that are not applicable to smaller operations. But the following checklist, culled from standard programs, provides the six key points to cover:

1. Exact responsibilities on the selling floor.
2. Understanding of classifications of books, where they are displayed, and the method of restocking.
3. Use of reference works, *Books in Print, Subject Guide to Books in Print,* and others.
4. Understanding the mechanics of all types of sales, with particular emphasis on use of the cash register.
5. Who the supervisor is and what types of problem should be turned over to the supervisor.
6. Policy on salary reviews, fringe benefits, and similar personnel policies.

A thorough check of the new employee's work should be made regularly in the first weeks following the initial training program. It is better for the new salesperson and his supervisor to correct mistakes immediately than weeks later. Incorrectly prepared sales slips can result in the loss of packages. Mistakes on the cash register may result in cash shortages and inaccurate sales records. These as well as other areas of minor errors should be cleared up before anything more serious results.

Many companies have found that suggestion awards are profitable for both the company and the employee. Even a small or medium-sized retailer can benefit from the workable ideas of an intelligent, interested employee. Many excellent, money-saving ideas are submitted by employees, and granting cash awards for good ideas is money well spent. While there may not be a formal suggestion award program, if an award is made the entire staff should be informed about it and others encouraged to participate.

No one has devised a method of detecting dishonest employees before they are hired. And at one time or another in every large organization a long-term trusted employee has been caught stealing from the company. A total awareness of the problem is the first step in protecting a business against internal dishonesty. It should be completely understood by the employees that steps will be taken to prefer criminal charges against any employee caught stealing. Larger shops may wish to investigate the possibilities of bonding all employees and thus protecting the company.

Proper use of the cash register is a valuable guarantee against employee dishonesty. It should be a rigid requirement that each sale be rung up immediately and the money placed in the cash register no matter how many customers are waiting for attention. If personal observation is not always feasible, it may be desirable to hire a shopping service such as Willmark, Dale, or Merit to send shoppers into the shop to report on employees' courtesy, efficiency, and honesty. Staff members should be informed that they are being checked, and shopping reports, good or bad, should be discussed with the clerk concerned.

Invoices and freight bills should be spot-checked from time to time to make certain that the merchandise was received. If an employee is authorized to sign checks or pay out petty cash, these records should, of course, be checked regularly. The employees concerned should be aware of this supervision.

Personnel Records and Costs

The laws governing employment in retail shops are many and varied. They range from the regulation of the number of hours a female employee may work to stipulations on the withholding of federal and state taxes. Complete and accurate records must therefore be kept of each employee's hours of work, wages paid, and amounts withheld from wages for taxes. Government tax forms for Social Security and Unemployment Insurance must be filed periodically. Since requirements vary from state to state, it may be necessary to secure guidance in preparing these reports.

From the first day of his employment, each employee should have an employment record showing his address, telephone number, starting wage, and other basic information. Any raises should be recorded so that the employee's salary history is available at a glance. Samples of the employment history cards used by Doubleday Book Shops are available upon request to Doubleday & Company, 277 Park Avenue, New York, N.Y. 10017.

While personnel expenses are a bookstore's second largest overhead cost (after cost of goods sold), they are frequently not analyzed as carefully as they should be. In some larger retail operations there is a constant battle between the operating head on the selling floor, who never has enough clerks, and the personnel department or operating manager, who is convinced that there are so many clerks in the department that they must be tripping over each other. This contest is generally resolved by a fairly accurate appraisal of the number of salesclerks required.

In the owner-managed smaller shop, the owner must study his personnel requirements more carefully since he doesn't have the benefit of two points of view. It is not possible, under every circumstance, to have sufficient staff to wait on everyone immediately (if business is good, that is), just as it is also not possible to stock every title that may be requested.

Analysis of personnel costs may be approached in a number of ways. To get an idea of the number of salesclerks needed at various times, sales may be estimated by day and by hour, adjusting the schedule of full- or part-time salesclerks to cover peak hours. A record should also be kept of the number of salesclerks employed at various times of the year. The best way to record this information is in terms of actual hours worked. This figure is easier to analyze than a combination of the work schedules of full- and part-time clerks and is a fairly simple record to maintain since it is information used for salary records. A record of the total number of hours worked will allow accurate estimates of staff time from one year to the next, during the same periods; but changes in salary could distort the actual dollar cost.

The standard figure for personnel costs for various stores is *total salaries as a per cent of sales.* This is derived by dividing total salaries, including commissions and vacation pay, but not payroll taxes, by total net sales. Recent department store figures on total-salaries per cent ranged from 16 to 18 per cent. This figure should not be confused with *selling* salary as a per cent of sales, which will run lower since it does not include managerial, clerical, or accounting salaries.

Bookkeeping Basics **10**

G. ROYSCE SMITH
Executive Director,
American Booksellers Association, Inc.

Bookkeeping is the recording of the events that affect the financial condition of a business. *Accounting* is the analysis, verification, and reporting of these events with the goal of improving that financial condition. Lack of proper records or an inability to understand the ones that do exist is a major contributing factor in 84 per cent of small-business failures, according to the U.S. Department of Commerce.

The records a business needs will vary with its size. Size will also govern whether a business needs and can afford a bookkeeper and/or an accountant.

In the space allotted here, we can only describe the basic records a store needs to keep and what should be done with them. Further study may be done in *Accounting for Non-Accountants* by J. N. Myer (New York: Hawthorn Books) or *Accounting Essentials* by N. Paul Harmon and Neal Margolis (New York: John Wiley & Sons), or any number of other books. Or you may want to take a night course in basic accounting at a local community college or business school, although few booksellers will feel compelled to go that far.

Whether you like it or not, there are people other than your friends, to whom a casual answer is sufficient, who will want to know exactly how your business is doing. The many tax collectors—federal, state, and local—may make arbitrary assessments if you can't support your figures with concrete evidence from day-to-day records. You will also need records to satisfy your banker. Banks do not lend money or extend existing loans on guesswork.

But most of all, records provide the information that will make the running of your store a pleasure. Lost time, forgetfulness, carelessness, and many other past mistakes will disappear. You will know when you did your business, when and where money was spent on inventory and expense items, and why you met your sales goal without showing additional profits.

Records must be kept of (1) what you sell, (2) what you buy for sale, and (3) what you spend to keep the business operating. Let's examine the types of records that have been developed to accomplish this task.

You must know what you sell for cash and for credit and what you accept from customers for return.

When the customer pays the full amount of his purchase at the time of sale, the transaction is known as a *cash sale*. At the time of the cash sale, a record of cash received must be made, either in the form of a receipt (sales slip) or by being rung on a cash register. Some stores do both.

The sales slip or the register tape must show (1) the date, (2) the amount received, and (3) the sales tax.

If a prenumbered sales slip is used, it may easily be designed to serve for more than the single purpose of recording cash sales. The same form may be used to record credit sales, customer returns, money received on account, and money paid out simply by providing appropriate boxes to be checked on the form. If the title of the book sold is written on the sales slip, this can be used for inventory control as well. The consolidation of many forms into one is highly desirable.

When the customer pays nothing or less than the full price at the time of purchase, it is a *charge sale*. A charge sale creates an account receivable and must be kept separate from cash sales. While it is not essential to create a sales slip for a cash sale if you have a cash register, a sales slip must be made for each charge transaction even if a cash register is also used. When customers make partial payment for an item, both cash and charge documents are needed.

While date, amount, and sales tax are sufficient information on a cash transaction, a charge sale requires the following additional information: the name and address of the customer, salesclerk's identification number or initials, the quantity and description of each item, and the customer's signature. At the end of each day, charge sales should be totaled and posted to an accounts receivable ledger. The charge sales slip is filed under the customer's name as a record of amount owed and at some point posted to the individual customer's account.

The procedure for handling credit sales through the major credit card companies is, of course, prescribed by them.

Sales returns and allowances result when a customer is dissatisfied with a purchase and the seller agrees that his complaint is justified. If the initial transaction was for cash, pay the customer cash in return, if that is your policy, and make out a sales slip, being sure not only to check the merchandise-return box but writing "refund" or "allowance" clearly across the slip. If the initial transaction was a charge, check the merchandise-return box and write "credit" across the slip.

The Chart of Accounts

To this point, most of what we have said is logical to most laymen with a rudimentary grasp of business. We have been talking about the records that everyone who has ever made a purchase has seen and handled. These records are but the beginning of record-keeping. They must be organized. This is done by entering them in books, or book-keeping. It is here that things begin to get complicated for the uninitiated. There are any number of bookkeeping and accounting systems. You may buy one ready-made at the office-supply store, or you may hire an accountant to devise one specifically to fit your needs. Unless you know approximately what your needs are, however, you may find yourself running through several accountants (and their fees) before you find the right one.

Similarly, you may also need a bookkeeper to record documents in the books. But both bookkeepers and accountants cost money, and you should know what each does and whether you need one, the other, or both. These matters will be discussed at the end of this chapter.

It is impossible for us to devise a bookkeeping system for everyone here. We can only describe the elements of some basic systems. Hopefully this should give you guidance in choosing or devising a system for your own use.

First, we need to know the difference between a journal and a ledger. A *journal* is a chronological record of business transactions, a primary working tool. Journals are also called "books of original entry." A *ledger* is a summary of accounts. An *account* is a bookkeeping device used to record increases and decreases in assets, liabilities, or owner's equity as a result of a business transaction. *Assets* are the things with money value that a business owns, such as cash, money due from creditors, inventory, buildings, land, fixtures, equipment, and supplies. *Liabilities* are what the business owes, such as bank loans and money owed to publishers or other suppliers. *Owner's equity,* also called "capital," "net worth," and "proprietorship," is the difference between assets and liabilities.

Before a journal or a ledger may be used, it is necessary to set up a *chart of accounts.* There are five major categories of accounts: the three which we have just described—Assets, Liabilities, and Owner's Equity—plus Income and Expense. The first three categories are ultimately summarized on the *balance sheet,* which is a statement of net worth at a specific time. Income and expense accounts are summarized finally on the *profit and loss statement,* which tells you whether you are operating at a profit or a loss. The balance sheet, which states your position, is what your banker wants to see; and the Internal Revenue Service wants to see your profit and loss statement, which states activity.

Within each of these major categories, there will be many accounts. It is helpful to write a description of the kinds of transactions that are to be entered against each account for reference purposes and to ensure accuracy. Then the accounts should be arranged in proper sequence and numbered. The span of numbers should be great enough to allow the addition of new accounts as the business grows. It will probably be necessary for you to consult a professional accountant or bookkeeper to set up a chart of accounts that will suit your situation. Generally speaking, cash and quickly negotiable assets are listed before assets, which are difficult to convert to cash, and current liabilities for which funds must be available in a comparatively short time are listed before long-term obligations. A sample chart of accounts is given in Figure 10.1.

Bookkeeping Procedures

Once you have your chart of accounts, you are ready to consider what kind or kinds of journals and ledgers you will need.

There can be more than one kind of journal or ledger. A very small business, however, may well use only one of each. If only one journal is kept, it is called the *general journal.* If supplementary journals, such as the cash journal, purchase journal, cash receipts journal, cash disbursements journal, or payroll journal, are kept, the general journal is used to record openings, closings, corrections, and unusual entries that cannot be recorded in the special types of journals.

The general journal consists basically of a column for the date, a second column for the name of the account affected, a third for entering the posting reference in the ledger, a fourth column is headed Debit, and a fifth is Credit.

It is absolutely essential to an understanding of bookkeeping to remember that in general journals, "debit" and "credit" refer only to the position of the columns on the accounting form. If a transaction causes an account to increase, the category of the account (asset account, liability account, expense account, etc.) determines whether the increase is recorded in the left (debit) column or right (credit) column. This concept in bookkeeping is perhaps the most difficult for the layman to understand.

It may help to remember that every transaction affects at least two accounts. Every entry in a debit column in an account causes a corresponding entry in the credit amount of one *or more* other accounts. A single transaction may affect many accounts, but for that transaction the total debits and the total credits must be equal.

FIGURE 10.1—SAMPLE BALANCE SHEET ACCOUNTS (1-500)*

Account No.

ASSETS (1-300)

Cash (1-50)
Petty Cash (Cash on Hand)	11
Cash in Bank—General (Regular Bank Account)	21
Cash in Bank—Payroll (Payroll Bank Account)	31

Receivables from Others (51-100)
Accounts Receivable—Customers	51
Accounts Receivable—Others	81

Inventories (101-150)
Inventory—Goods for Sale	101
Inventory—Supplies	121

Prepaid Expenses (151-200)
Prepaid Advertising	151
Prepaid Insurance	161
Prepaid Interest	171
Prepaid Rent	181

Property and Equipment (201-250)
Land	201
Buildings	211
Buildings—Allowance for Depreciation	212
Automobiles and Trucks	216
Automobiles and Trucks—Allowance for Depreciation	217
Furniture and Office Equipment	221
Furniture and Office Equipment—Allowance for Depreciation	222
Leasehold Improvements—Rented Property Improvements	246
Leasehold Improvements—Allowance for Amortization	247

Miscellaneous Assets (251-300)
Business Starting Costs	251
Deposits (Advance Payments)	261

LIABILITIES (301-450)

Notes and Amounts Payable to Others (301-350)
Notes Payable—Short-term	301
Accounts Payable (Bills Payable)	311
Sales Tax Payable	321
FICA Tax Withheld	331
Federal Income Taxes Withheld	332
State Income Taxes Withheld	333

Expenses Owed to Others (351-400)
Accrued Wages (Wages Owed)	351
Accrued Federal Unemployment Taxes (Owed)	371
Accrued State Unemployment Taxes (Owed)	372
Accrued Real Estate Taxes (Owed)	381
Accrued Inventory Taxes (Owed)	382
Accrued Federal Income Taxes (Owed)	391
Accrued State Income Taxes (Owed)	392

*This is, once again, a *sample* chart of accounts. It is not to be applied without thought to any store. It is too complicated for the small store and too incomplete for the large store. There are other ways of numbering accounts as well. In any case, every chart of accounts should be designed to best serve the individual case at hand.

FIGURE 10.1 (*Continued*)

Long-term Obligations (401–450)
    Notes Payable—Long-term 401
    Mortgages Payable 411
Owner's Equity (451–500)
    Capital Investment (Investment in Business)* 451
    Capital Stock (Stock Issued)† 461
    Drawings (Cash Used Personally)* 481
    Retained Earnings (Profit Not Spent) 491

PROFIT OR LOSS STATEMENT ACCOUNTS (501–800)

Sales and Other Income (501–550)
    Sales of Merchandise 501
    Sales Returns and Allowances 502
    Cash Discounts Allowed (Customer Discounts) 503
    Service Charges 511
    Rental Library Income 521
    Miscellaneous Income 541
Cost of Goods Sold (551–600)
    Cost of Merchandise Sold 551
    Freight on Purchases 561
Operating Expense Accounts (601–799)
    Wages and Salaries 601
    Rentals 611
    Advertising 621
    Taxes (except Federal Income Taxes) 631
    Interest 641
    Supplies 651
    Dues and Subscriptions 661
    Repairs 671
    Travel and Entertainment 691
    Outgoing Postage to Customers 701
    Outgoing Postage—Returns to Publishers 702
    Telephone and Telegraph 703
    Group Insurance 711
    Workman's Compensation Insurance 712
    Bad Debts 721
    Heat, light, and power 731
    Depreciation 741
    Professional Services 751
    Miscellaneous Expense 761
Federal Income Tax 800

*Sole owners and partners only.
†Corporations only.

Accounting convention holds that the following transactions be entered in the debit (left) column: (1) each increase in an asset; (2) each decrease in a liability; (3) each withdrawal of capital; (4) each decrease in a source of income; and (5) each increase in an expense. Conversely, the following transactions are entered in the credit (right) column: (1)

each decrease in an asset; (2) each increase in a liability; (3) each addition to investment in the business; (4) each increase in a source of income; and (5) each decrease in an expense.

Or it may be easier to grasp as stated in Table 10.1.

TABLE 10.1
EXAMPLES OF DEBIT AND CREDIT ENTRY

Category of Account	Increases are recorded as:	Decreases are recorded as:
Asset Accounts	Debit (*left*)	Credit (*right*)
Liability Accounts	Credit (*right*)	Debit (*left*)
Owner's Equity Accounts	Credit (*right*)	Debit (*left*)
Income Accounts	Credit (*right*)	Debit (*left*)
Expense Accounts	Debit (*left*)	Credit (*right*)

Therefore, in recording transactions in the general journal, a single transaction will take at least three lines—one for the account debited, one for the account credited, and a third for an explanation. For example, let's record the cash receipts from one day's sales:

Date	Name of Account	P.R.	Debit	Credit
Sept. 12	Cash		200.00	
	Sales			200.00

We have shown the increase in the cash account (an asset account) by an entry in the debit column. The other account affected is sales (an income account), and its increase is shown by an entry in the credit column.

The posting reference (P.R.), or folio, column is filled when the bookkeeper posts the journal to the ledger. The account number to which the entry was posted is entered here. This is also a quick check on whether all journal entries have been posted to the ledger.

The general journal is adequate for recording *all* the activities of a small business or one with relatively few transactions during an accounting period. Larger businesses or businesses having a large number of transactions of a similar nature may find that they need supplementary journals. The advantages of using supplementary journals are that they reduce the size of the general journal, simplify the posting operation, allow more than one person to work on the books at the same time, and permit ready access to summary information by logical grouping of similar accounts.

We have named the commonly used supplementary journals earlier. Now, let's examine them briefly.

The *sales journal* is a summary of sales on credit, or non-cash sales. It may be a record of individual transactions, or if a prenumbered sales book is used in which one copy of every transaction is kept permanently in numerical order, it may be simply a record of the beginning and ending ticket numbers with the total increase in accounts receivable for the day.

The *cash receipts journal* is a summary of cash showing the source from which the cash came. A typical cash receipts journal may, like the sales journal, take two forms. It can be simply a record of the total increase in cash received for the day with columns for breakdowns into amounts received from cash sales, from payments on accounts, and from sundry sources. Or it may be a more detailed breakdown by individual accounts.

The *purchase journal* is used to record purchases of merchandise on account. Purchases of non-merchandise on account are entered in the general journal. Typical information recorded in the purchase journal includes the date, the invoice number, the name of the seller, the date paid, the check number by which it was paid, and the amount of the invoice.

Whenever a firm makes a payment in currency or by check for any reason at all, the transaction may be recorded in a *cash disbursement journal.* The information recorded includes the check number, the payee, date written, gross amount, cash discount taken, net amount, and a distribution to the accounts affected.

Some very small businesses operate without a general journal, and use only a cash receipts journal and a cash disbursements journal. They keep a file of duplicate sales slips instead of a sales journal and an open invoice file instead of a purchase journal. Such a system, while seemingly simple, requires that the cash receipts and the cash disbursements journals be more complex than those described here and limits the user's ability to retrieve or analyze information. A *payroll journal* or register may also be kept. Simple forms, available at office supply stores or from your bank, enable you to write the payroll check, payroll journal, and the employee earnings records all at the same time. They relieve you of duplicate work and are highly recommended.

The entries in the various journals do not bring together in one place all the information about one account. The journals are posted to ledgers, which are groups of accounts. Ledgers may be bound or loose-leaf books, or may be groups of ledger sheets or cards filed in a tray or cabinet. Each page or card of a ledger is concerned with one and only one account. *Posting to the ledger* is copying the journal entries on the correct account page in the ledger. The *account balance* is the difference between the debits (left side) and credits (right side) in the ledger. If the larger total is in the debit column, the account shows a *debit balance.* If the larger total is in the credit column, the account shows a *credit balance.*

If the firm has many customer charge accounts or buys merchandise for resale from many sources, it is advisable to have two subsidiary ledgers for summarizing the accounts of each individual customer (*accounts receivable ledger*) and each individual supplier (*accounts payable ledger*).

At the end of the accounting period and when all the accounts have been balanced, the balances are listed on a *trial balance* work sheet and summed. The debit balance and the credit balance should be equal or else the error that created the imbalance must be tracked down and corrected. If an amount has been incorrectly journalized or posted as a debit or a credit or if an incorrect account title has been entered in the journal, a line is drawn through the incorrect entry, title, or amount and the correct entry is written above it or in the proper column. However, when an amount has been posted to the wrong account in the ledger, a *correcting entry* must be made in the journal to document the correction.

At the point of preparing the trial balance work sheet, we must know whether we need to be on a cash or an accrual basis of accounting. If we show on our statements only cash actually received or spent during an accounting period, we are on the *cash basis.* If we show all business transactions that have occurred during an accounting period regardless of whether cash was received or spent, we are on the *accrual basis.* The accrual accounting system takes notice of unrecorded liabilities (such as that portion of a salary which is due an employee if the end of the accounting period falls between paydays), the apportionment of prepaid expense (such as supplies that will be used in more than one accounting period), and the apportionment of income (such as special orders for which customers have paid in advance). Most businesses operate on an accrual basis or a modified accrual basis.

When all adjusting entries have been made on the work sheet and the debit and credit columns in the trial balance and the adjustment columns are balanced, respectively, the next step is preparing the balance sheet and the profit and loss statement. The trial balance amounts are combined with the adjustment amounts and are properly transferred. Asset accounts, liability accounts, and owner's equity accounts are transferred to the balance sheet. Income and expense accounts are transferred to the profit and loss statement.

After the financial statements have been prepared and before entries from the next accounting period may be made, the books must be closed. *Closing the books* consists of making *closing entries* in the journal, posting them to the ledger, *ruling and balancing* the ledger accounts, and preparing a *postclosing trial balance.* Making closing entries requires that all balances in the income accounts be added to the owner's equity account, that all balances in the expense accounts be deducted from the owner's equity account, and that the balance of the owner's drawing account be deducted from the owner's equity account. In effect, these entries bring the income, expense, and drawing accounts to zero and increase (or decrease) the equity account by the amount of the net income (or net loss).

After these closing entries are posted to the ledger, the balance of each account is figured and lines are ruled beneath the entries to separate them from the entries of the next account period. The postclosing trial balance is simply comparing the totals of the debit balances and the credit balances from the ledger and seeing that they are equal.

This, in its simplest terms, is a description of the complete accounting cycle. Now you must decide which tasks need doing in your store and who will do them. Your banker and your attorney can advise you. How much of the process can you or a member of your family master? How much time can you spend on it? Do you need a full- or a part-time bookkeeper? How much of an accountant's time must you buy?

When you consider whether you or your family or a bookkeeper will do certain things, remember what things have to be done. Here is a list of the work someone must do:

- Start and keep an accounting system for the accurate and timely recording of your store's cash receipts, disbursements, sales, and operating expenses.
- Periodically prepare the following:
    a) Statement of assets and liabilities as of a given date (balance sheet).
    b) Statement of results of operations for a given time period (profit and loss statement).
    c) Statement of changes in financial position.
    d) Listings of customers owing you money as of a given date.
    e) Listings of suppliers to whom you owe money as of a given date.
    f) Optional financial information as may be needed.
- Prepare state and federal tax returns.
- Prepare Social Security, withholding, personal property, and other tax returns.

Any of these things that you can't do can be done by a bookkeeper. An accountant could do these things, but the expense would be staggering. Accountants are generally used for auditing, professional tax assistance, and consultation on a variety of subjects.

Whatever way you go in constructing and maintaining your bookkeeping system, remember that both too many and too few records are expensive. Keep only the records you really need, but keep them complete and up-to-date.

Please remember that what we have discussed in this chapter are the possible elements of a double-entry bookkeeping system. Your system may be a simpler, single-entry one that you may buy ready-made at an office-supply house. We have tried here to acquaint you with most of the terms and principles of relatively sophisticated systems so that you may have more (rather than less) knowledge when you talk to accountants about your actual needs.

Inventory Control   **11**

MARJORIE J. GOODMAN
Manager, University Bookstore,
University of California
at Riverside, California

Inventory control is simply a method of keeping track of anything that is accumulated to fulfill future demand. This can refer to people, services, or, as in this case, things such as merchandise offered for sale in retail stores.

Published material available concerning inventory and inventory control reveals that one of the reasons for small-business failure is *lack of records.* Without records a manager cannot be aware of historical experience except as his memory can serve with accuracy. Lack of records may lead to costly buying errors—buying too much or too little, duplicating what is already in sufficient supply, or replenishing stocks of items that should never have been reordered.

In Dun & Bradstreet's words:

> *The objectives of inventory control are to keep the inventory in a definite relationship with net sales and with net working capital, the conversion of inventory into cash in the shortest possible time, the minimizing of losses through obsolescence, depreciation, and expenses resulting from carrying excessive inventory, and the development of records to give a constant aging of inventory items similar to an aging of receivables. . . . Products in the inventory that have not been moved for a relatively long period generally prove to be an unprofitable investment; they may eventually be sold at a loss or scrapped because of a change in design or in the line of products, because the items were not suitable or actually needed, or because the goods had been damaged or allowed to deteriorate. An aging of inventory items when closely followed and used furnishes the information to forestall such losses. **

*From *Small Business Bibliography* (Small Business Administration, No. 75 [Washington, D.C., July, 1965]).

Information gathered from established inventory control records can be used to reduce the dollar investment in inventory while at the same time maintaining the level of customer service; or it can be used to gain better service at no increase in investment; or it can be used to achieve better service from a lower investment of dollars. Inventory control can also reduce the costs of ordering, storing, and handling.

Inventory control in retail bookstores ranges from no control except personal scrutiny (commonly termed "eyeball control"), through dependence upon a publisher's representative to do the work, to fully computerized systems. Whatever else it may be, effective stock control for books is more than a simple counting procedure of what is on hand. It should provide information, but it will not supply answers. Inventory records do not replace managerial or buyer judgment; records assist by indicating trends; they make planning possible, and they provide for systematic merchandise planning and budgeting. Another reason for control is the complexity of detail with which retailers must cope every day. Accurate recall would be impossible without good records.

A basic question is how much record-keeping is needed? The completeness of stock records (controls) will be limited by the ability of a business to pay for the cost, and should be further restricted by the worth of such records in producing a more efficient operation now, or as an investment in anticipated growth. The complexity of the system will also be dependent on: (1) number of titles to be controlled, (2) sales volume, (3) kind of equipment and number of staff available, (4) amount of information detail desired, and (5) projected growth of all factors.

A past president of the Booksellers Association of Great Britain and Ireland, Thomas Joy, has said: "The real problem with books is bad stock resulting in too low a turnover." Since turnover is one of the measures of efficiency in a business operation and expresses the relationship of what has been bought to what has been sold, it can be assumed that a good control system will aid in buying merchandise that will sell, or "turn," rapidly. On the other hand, a good control system should also help prevent out-of-stock situations that result in lost sales and a diminished image because of customer disappointment.

There is no single preferred method. Some inventory control methods are simple, some are extremely complex. It is no great problem to devise simple, effective manual systems. There are prepackaged systems available, including sophisticated electronic data-processing programs. Other methods utilize records as simple as handwritten index cards. There are specially designed record cards professionally printed, revolving wheel files, visible index files of various sorts, and other patented equipment.

Knowledge of the particular store—some assessment of what is needed and desired as well as what can be afforded—is the basis of decision. In all discussions of the importance of good records, it should be emphasized that records are working for people, not people working constantly just to keep records. Many stores already spend too much time with paper work and records, and not enough time on the sales floor selling to the customer. Paperback books possibly create the prime example of this because of their relatively low unit of sale. Increased sales volume, rapid turnover, and the lowest possible wage cost are the answers to profit.

Adequate records should produce a better operation by preventing loss of sales through being out-of-stock. Records should also eliminate slow and non-moving titles that serve to clutter the book department, unnoticeably changing the store image from a well-arranged display to one overcrowded with shopworn books.

Six Measurements of a Good Control System

1. *Efficiency.*—Synonyms for efficiency could be speed and accuracy. Can any bookstore employee, including part-time, briefly trained personnel, help maintain the records with a minimum of explanation, and do it correctly?
2. *Permanence.*—Will the system serve indefinitely? Are the materials used appropriate, easily obtainable at a minimum cost with a reasonable life span under constant handling? (Example: paper records versus heavier card stock.)
3. *Flexibility.*—Will the system grow with added titles? Is it cumbersome to add or delete titles? (Some filing systems, especially as they become full, are difficult to rearrange when additions are made.)
4. *Economy.*—Remember, it's not the initial cost, but the upkeep!
5. *Aesthetic Aspects.*—Some methods utilizing the books themselves (e.g., labels or clips) may damage covers or pages or intrude on the good appearance of the store (cards protruding above the trimmed edges of the book, etc.). Furthermore, it is possible to interfere with customer convenience by contrived methods that may get in the customer's way or even fall off when books are examined.
6. *Personal Suitability.*—Is there aversion to doing inventory work on the sales floor, with its constant interruptions? Is it wiser to develop a system capable of maintenance in the privacy of an office? Might it be necessary or desirable to work on the records away from the store site? (Conversely, if those keeping the controls current must be on the sales floor, can a system be devised that can be used there? Certainly it cannot be an overly heavy file, bulky boxes, etc.)

Is there one best way? The answer is No. Each bookseller must judge what he wishes to accomplish and what the business is capable of supporting based on volume of sales and available staff.

Stock control, simplified, consists of knowing what is purchased and what is sold. Basically all bookstore inventory control systems for knowing what is sold fall into one of two major categories: Stock position through *count of inventory on hand,* and stock position through *recording sales.*

Rephrasing this, it is simple to discover what has been purchased by examining the files of purchase orders or other records to which this information may have been transferred. It is not as simple to know what has been removed from stock through daily sales activities. One must either frequently count and check for missing stock, or have a method of capturing information on what is being sold.

Count of Inventory on Hand

There are a number of ways to record inventory on hand, including publishers' lists and store lists.

1. *Publishers' Lists.*—Obviously this is inexpensive since publishers can generally provide an up-to-date order list on which periodic counts can be recorded, or even provide a sales representative who will periodically do the actual work in-store. Disadvantages of the listings include inadequate work space on the forms, inconvenient size, small print, and unsuitable arrangement of the list if it does not follow the store's arrangement of stock. This sort of record does not provide a way to record purchases or other actions affecting stock; thus, it is merely a count and a reminder.

2. *Store Lists.*—The other way to survey inventory on hand is to prepare a store listing tailored to the individual store needs. These may be in as many formats as there are people devising them! Some are simple ruled notebook-filler sheets capable of listing a number of titles on one page. They may be individual record cards in a file (all sizes are in use, *see* Figure 11.1), sometimes refined by use of specific card colors for certain subject categories, seasons of the year, frequency of inventory needed, and so on. Various stores utilize visible card files or multiple-ring notebooks (*see* Figure 11.2), as well as Keysort cards, revolving wheel indexes, punched cards for use with automated equipment, or random information retrieval systems employing special equipment. (The last item is sometimes found in use by municipal police departments for local records and might be available on a shared-time basis from other local sources.)

Store lists are variously filed by author, title, or publisher, or in the same order as stock is placed on the fixtures, depending on individual needs or whim. They are sometimes produced in duplicate for cross-

SALES RECORD

	On Hand	Rec'd	Sold	On Hand	Rec'd	Sold	On Hand	Rec'd	Sold	Hand	On Rec'd	Sold
Jan.												
Feb.												
Mar.												
April												
May												
June												
July												
Aug.												
Sept.												
Oct.												
Nov.												
Dec.												
Total												

FIGURE 11.1. STORE-LIST CARD FOR INVENTORY CONTROL.—This record form, both sides of which are shown, is on ordinary 3″ × 5″ index card stock. It is one example of unit control (one card per title). (*Actual size.*)

Author .... No...........................

Title .... Price.........................

Publisher .... Subj.........................

Recommended by ....

Indicate Short Discount Here ☐

B-82   5M   2-67   5553⁵

Author   Publisher

Title

Section   Price

FIGURE 11.2. VISIBLE RECORD FORMS.—The upper example is obtainable as a lined (but unimprinted) commercial form, punched for multiple-ring notebooks. The forms are inserted by dropping down one ring each time, thereby leaving the author's name visible. The bottom card is designed for special file drawers. In this system, the lower portion of the card is visible. (*Both: actual size.*)

DATE	STOCK	ORDER	REMARKS	DATE	STOCK	ORDER	REMARKS

Publisher   Price

Author   Title

reference filing. Store lists have the advantage of being capable of preparation to suit any logical arrangement. They contain only the store's active, selling titles. They may be designed to maintain the complete record of purchases, inventory counts, and returns of overstock, and may be annotated to show location of reserve and active stock and any other information of use to the store. The disadvantage is the obvious expenditure of time and money for initial preparation and upkeep. It is a truism that a record not kept current is no information at all.

These store and publisher listings are, in brief, methods of control involving inventory of stock on hand through frequent counts to discover what is becoming in low supply or what is actually sold out. For some stores with a large number of active titles and high labor costs, this may be defeatingly slow, repetitive, and expensive.

Recording Sales

There are also ways to capture inventory by recording sales, including control by individual books sold, and control by title.

1. *Control by Individual Books Sold.*—Some stores are able to make a note of titles sold as they move across the checkout counter. The briefest memorandum is generally sufficient for a knowledgeable buyer. During peak periods of the year, however, the system is frequently abandoned with recognition that a complete inventory will be taken as soon as possible to recapture all shortages and out-of-stock situations.

Another common method is to insert into each book a slip or card such as the "Looreen" cards, which are available from certain publishers and which contain necessary reorder information about the book. (*See* Figure 11.3.) This is pulled at the cash register at the time of sale. Some stores are now using adhesive labels with unique code numbers for this purpose. These numbers are recorded on special register tapes for further mechanical processing. Such cash registers are no longer prohibitively expensive. A few have reported using a portable tape recorder at the checkout to capture information.

It is well to reemphasize that inventory control differs from reminders of stock position. Individual cards pulled from books at the checkout give information on what is being sold. This is not total control. For complete inventory control, a record showing the *history* of sales activity of a title, including a record of purchases, is needed. Only then is there information sufficient to reveal whether titles should be ordered in increased or decreased quantities, marked down, returned or phased out. If data cannot be kept on one single record, then all existing useful information must be accumulated on another master record. This is part of the consideration in choosing the system to be utilized.

CASHIER: REMOVE WHEN SOLD.

HOOK OVER CENTER PAGES AS BOOKMARK

PUBLISHER:

BOOK NO.:

TITLE:

AUTHOR:

SUBJECT:

IMPORTANT:
THE EFFECTIVENESS OF THE LOOREEN INVENTORY CONTROL SYSTEM DEPENDS UPON THE CAREFUL HANDLING OF EACH CARD.
AFTER REMOVAL FROM THE BOOK, THIS CARD SHOULD BE PUT IN A SAFE PLACE (PREFERABLY THE CASH REGISTER)—UNTIL AN ACCUMULATION CAN BE TURNED OVER TO THE DEPT. MANAGER. THANK YOU.

Distributed by Harper & Row, Publishers

1 XXX | 2 XXX | 3 XXX | 4 XXX
5 XXX | 6 XXX | 7 XXX | 8 XXX
9 XXX | 10 XXX | 11 XXX | 12 XXX

Cashier will remove this card for Inventory Control purposes

Author

Title

Publisher

Source

If you find this card, please return it to:

Spartan Bookstore
San Jose State College
San Jose, California 95114

FIGURE 11.3. BOOK-INSERT ("LOOREEN") CARDS.—A card is hooked into each book to be controlled, and is removed at point of sale. The card can be forwarded to one of the major wholesalers, who will return it to the bookstore inside the cover of the replacement copy of the book. The card may be used also for in-store control—that is, a card is written out and held until arrival of a book, then is hooked into, and shelved along with, the book. Two types are shown. (*Both: actual size.*)

A card inserted into books has to be sorted in some way to become useful information and a reordering tool. Some stores, in order to avoid the labor of hand-sorting, utilize "sort" cards characterized by a series of punched holes around all margins of the card. (*See* Figure 11.4.) These perforations are numbered, so that punching out certain numbers completely with a special punch creates a method of manually sorting cards.

Sorting the cards that have been collected from books sold during the day may be accomplished by inserting a special needle through a particular number on the margin. All cards in the pack with that same number punched out will drop freely from the needle during the process, automatically sorting for whatever that number represented without the necessity of prearranging or alphabetizing the pack of cards beforehand. This type of card is obtainable in several sizes and is made by several manufacturers (Keysort by Royal McBee, Unisort Analysis Card by Todd Division of Burroughs, etc.). More than one arrangement can be coded on each card by utilizing all margins; thus cards can be alphabetized and sorted by publisher, by subject, by title, and so on, depending on how the store has set up its coding system initially. The system is sometimes called the "poor man's IBM."

Some stores that have started on this system report that it becomes uneconomical and time-consuming when used with as many as 2,000 titles. Devoted users argue the point.

It follows that if a shop intends to pursue a system of placing in every book any sort of record that must be pulled at the cash register, it may well be a punch card for use with a mechanized data-processing system. These key-punched cards can be run through equipment that will automatically sort and list by various arrangements. This sort of mechanical processing, not involving a computer, is not too expensive in many communities where the necessary data-processing-machine time is available. To gain a history of sales experience including purchases there would have to be a further step into a program utilizing the memory of computers. Then data could be accumulated on all transactions and purchase orders created automatically when needed, not to mention other possible documents and analyses. The feasibility of electronic data-processing in retail bookselling is a separate subject. As a rule of thumb it would not be unfair to say that the retail bookseller with sales of under $500,000 annually probably does not need such a sophisticated system.

To recapitulate: The advantages of a system employing a record in every book that can be pulled to capture information on sales are:

- Elimination of labor costs of frequent counts of inventory on hand just to discover what has apparently sold since the last count was taken.

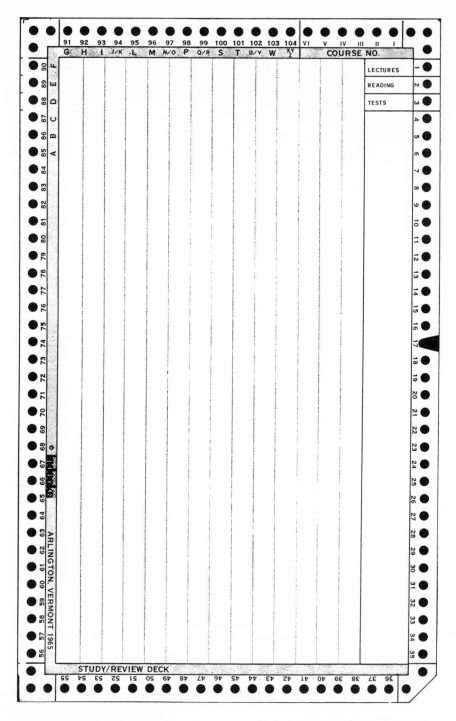

FIGURE 11.4. "SORT" CARD.—The card above, with holes punched around the border, is for use with a special needle, a system sometimes referred to as the "poor man's IBM." (*Reduced size.*)

- Rapid (daily) capture of information to detect trends or sudden runs on certain titles.
- Possibility of changed attitude of clerical help from "stock checkers" to positive sales people.

These are disadvantages:

- If numerous titles are carried, it is no small task to stuff every book with a proper card.
- In an active store, stock needed on the sales floor may be held up in the back rooms until stock cards are prepared. Stock cards awaiting arrival of books can take up sizeable files in themselves!
- Unless there is a consistent system of a card in *every* book, it is difficult for clerks, especially part-time or intermittent help, to remember to pull the sale card unless it is visible.
- Control cards that are visible are sometimes unsightly; cards that are loose sometimes fall out; certain pamphlet-type publications do not lend themselves to loose cards unless they are clipped in. '
- Individual cards in books do not constitute inventory control in themselves, but are sales information that requires further posting to a master record.

2. *Control by Title.*—The final general method of controlling book stock is by *title* rather than individual books. This has been left to last as it is neither an inventory from a list or master record nor a record captured at the cash register at the time of sale.

Briefly the system consists of preparing only one identifying card for each book title, and placing this card behind the stack of books in the sales fixture. This works well where almost all titles have full cover face out. By implication it is best suited to paperback fixtures, although that need not eliminate use in some other areas of the store where certain titles are carried in depth. The system is sometimes referred to as the "greeting-card system" since this is the way card manufacturers generally have developed reorder controls for the pockets of their fixtures.

The store can be patrolled once or more daily, since it takes but little time, and cards pulled when exposed by sale of the last copy, or more efficiently, when books are getting low in that particular pocket. The same card is used again in the reorder process. One card suffices whether there are one or one hundred books of the same title. Some stores attach special holders at the back of the fixture pockets and label this holder with the author and title of the book so any customer or clerk can readily see what is missing from that space. Information on these cards, in addition to purchase order dates and quantities and inventory dates and counts, may include information on location of back stock or any other desirable information.

The advantages of the greeting-card system are simplicity (one card acts as the total control), economy (only one card per title), and easy visibility on the sales floor. The disadvantage is that it does not work where most titles are spine out. Moreover it will not create a complete record or listing available for use in an office area. The system also tends to create a rigidity in stock arrangement if the card holder is fixed to the shelf or pocket. Titles should sometimes be rotated to encourage sales, and empty pockets should not be left empty. Retailers do not sell and customers cannot buy from empty spaces.

There are other, sometimes unusual, ways of dealing with inventory records. A perfectly logical possibility for a small store is to use the store purchase order. By careful arrangement on the orders themselves and subsequent accurate filing, these can be used as a control through posting of regular inventory counts.

At least one bookstore was reported to use at its cash desk a microfilm camera such as grocers utilize in photographing checks. The camera is aimed downward and the clerk runs the book under it for a picture of the author's name, book title, and publisher. In a lighter vein, another small store took a Polaroid shot of all sections of all fixtures every week!

A question frequently asked, in addition to what kind of inventory control is best, is how often should inventory be counted? The answer is, probably once a week. Start with this assumption and experience will reveal areas needing more or less attention. It is useful to have special lists or cards (hot lists) for the current or fad titles that need to be surveyed every day if sales are not to be missed.

The stock control and reorder systems that have been generally described do not provide a record of titles on hand at any given moment. This would constitute a perpetual inventory, and is not generally feasible in retail bookselling. Knowledge of what is on hand usually resides in the memory of store personnel and must be supported by reasonable arrangement of stock on the sales floor. In the last analysis, even with advanced data-processing systems, the only way anyone can be sure that a particular book is on the shelf is to *go out and look!*

The exact format of the control form has not been described in detail; there is no standardization in this type of record among even the best-operated stores. Sample forms may vary from tiny slips or the smallest wheel cards or file boxes to sheets 11 × 8½ inches. Some stores keep as many as three records on every title, each filed differently for a specific use. Some basic items of information that are common to well-run stores are: author, title, publisher (and source, if different), price, edition, purchase dates and quantities, and inventory dates and counts.

Other details utilized all or in part by various stores are: publisher's book code, subject category, stock location, back-stock location, purchase order number, invoice number and date, discount, back order or other status information, and more recently, the ISBN (International Standard Book Number).

Before adding an additional item of information the bookseller should ask himself how often it will be needed and if, after all, it could be managed by exception. That is, when information is needed it is researched in the file of purchase orders and invoices. A good rule is to create a separate record only for those items needed constantly or frequently, and to research items needed only exceptionally.

Keep in mind that the purpose of records is to prevent chaos and lost sales through too frequent out-of-stock situations. The occasional missing title and sale are not going to make or break a book operation. Arbitrary decisions, departures, and an occasional lost record are inevitable. Most booksellers could achieve greater increases in sales by timely attention to new releases or talking with a knowledgeable customer, planning special promotions, and being on the sales floor to sell than by perfecting records.

The key words in keeping stock controls are: *information for prompt reordering, historical data for prevention of waste.* Perfection and perpetual inventory are not among the reasons. There is no *one* best way to control inventory. It requires much study and analysis of the individual operation. Only the bookseller can be the proper judge of what he wants and needs and what his business is able to do.

Practical Details for Improving Profits   **12**

ELIOT LEONARD
*President, Pickwick Book Shops,
Hollywood, California*

What makes a successful bookseller? Success means a lot of things—a smooth operation with satisfied customers, happy suppliers and employees, good community relations, reasonable return on investment of money and time, and most important, a good profit and loss statement at the end of the year.

Profit is a timeworn subject in retailing. The most important factor in the year-end result is the way a store is managed. A bookseller must know how details related to merchandising and managing a store affect and determine his profit or loss—and how to make his operation more profitable.

You cannot reap profits just because you love books, nor just because you love to read, nor because it is a fun hobby, nor even because you work hard. But your operation can be profitable if you pay attention to the *practical details.* Success in bookselling requires lots of hard work and time, constant supervision, and good management procedures and routines—that are followed.

Very rarely does "the roof fall in," nor is a store often affected by a catastrophe that would put it "on the ropes," or put it out of business. Mainly, the little things we do, or fail to do, in three areas—*sales, purchases,* and *expenses*—make the difference between success and failure. The two words "practical details" are the key to successful bookselling.

Out of hundreds of details, let's look at some of the most important in the three areas we have mentioned: (1) selling details, (2) buying details, and (3) operating details. We'll trace the possible effect on a very simple profit and loss statement for a bookstore doing a volume of $100,000.

1. *Selling Details*

Sales are influenced by good merchandising in the store. We can build or lose volume by the way we display, promote, and price our books.

a) Impulse Sales.—A good percentage of all books sold are spur-of-the-moment customer purchases, or what we call "impulse sales"—really impulse "purchases." New titles, best-sellers, humor and novelty titles, a road atlas, dictionary or almanac, seasonal or movie tie-ins, all should be put in front of customer eyes from time to time. Seasonal gift items should be given more prominent display when their holiday and special-occasion time approaches. Dictionaries for graduation; sports titles for Father's Day; special children's titles for Easter; cookbooks and other home crafts for Mother's Day; new editions of handbooks, almanacs, dictionaries, and travel guides—all have their right times for special display spots.

Good locations for impulse items are in main aisles or around the cash register or checkout counters. It is surprising how frequently these books need to be replaced as they sell. In today's world self-selection is a way of retailing life. Visual display has all but taken the place of suggestion selling in most stores.

It is important not to use good display space for slow or dead books. The best titles should be put in good locations and in the window. Impulse is related to something within the customer and the sight of a title often is a reminder to an individual to pick up the book, and an impulse purchase often results. We build sales by selling more of what's selling.

Our $100,000-volume store could add $1,000 a year via impulse sales. It is not too much to expect—one or two more sales per day = 1 per cent increase.

b) Arrangement.—Sales are frequently lost because titles in stock cannot be found. No bookseller will have every book that's asked for in stock, but knowing the stock that is on hand will help the situation and save sales. There must be a system of layout, by subject, to make it as easy as possible for customers and clerks to locate titles. Signs should be neat, clean, and customer-oriented. Books should be alphabetized by author or title within subject categories as much as possible.

No customer should be told "we do not have it" until a second salesperson or the buyer is queried.

By paying proper attention to arrangement and double-checking, our $100,000 store could save one sale a day—add $500 a year to volume = ½ per cent of sales.

c) *Serving the Customer.*—In this area there are dozens of factors that affect sales and direct volume up or down depending on how they are handled. Here are a few:

- Offer to special-order books for customers. This is one of the best ways to build a loyal clientele.
- If the last copy is in the window, or stockroom, get it!
- Don't make promises that cannot be kept. Especially about when a wanted title may be expected to be received or how long it will take to get it to the customer.
- Don't succumb to the temptation of telling a customer a title is already on order when it isn't. The face saved today will in all probability be lost tomorrow!
- Answer all correspondence—including complaint letters—promptly.
- Have a reasonably lenient returns or exchange policy. I do not know of anything that loses more customers and sales than a tough returns policy.
- Be flexible with policies. Don't let the customer leave the store angry.
- Train store personnel to say "hello" and "thank you" and to be cheerful. Nothing turns people off like a bored salesclerk.
- If there are two editions, offer to provide the less expensive one.

By paying attention to correct, courteous customer service, our $100,000 store could add $1,000 to its current volume = 1 per cent a year.

In just the three selling areas that are covered above we added $2,500 a year to our present volume. At the end of this article, we'll see what effect this could have on the bottom line of our profit and loss statement.

2. *Buying Details*

Careful attention to buying details will save money. The most important detail in this area is knowing the publishers' discount schedules. Most general trade titles should not be ordered directly from publishers at less than 40 per cent trade discount. For most publishers, this requires an order of three or five books. Use the *ABA Book Buyer's Handbook* to learn each publisher's discounts.

Why accept 20 or 33⅓ per cent discount when it might be possible to raise an order to three or five and earn 40 per cent trade discount? On one $25 retail order, this can make a difference of $5 additional gross profit. At times it pays to hold an order for a day or two or even longer so that it can be combined with orders for other titles from the same publisher. For example—if three $5 books are ordered at 20 per cent discount, the cost is $12. If two more $5 books are added to the order, it will carry a 40 per cent discount, and the cost for all five books is $15. Therefore, the cost of each book drops from $4 to $3, *doubling* gross profit from $1 to $2 each, and when the five books are sold net profit will have more than double. It might appear that more books were not needed from a publisher at this time. Unless there is a pressing inventory problem, some may be ordered anyway, at no risk. A gimmick used by some stores is to have a list of two or three low cost ($1 or $2) items—by publisher—to add to orders. For example—if the order is for three $5 books at 20 per cent discount, two $2 books may be added to the order earning 40 per cent discount, and the cost of *all five* is $11.40, instead of $12 for three books. *More books cost less.* Even if the two extra books are not sold, the gross profit on the original order of three books is now $6 instead of $3. The two $2 books can even be marked down or donated and still provide more money.

Just adjusting one order per week can save $250 a year in our $100,000 store.

Other *saving* details related to buying stock for the store include:

• Add special orders to stock orders whenever possible. Why pay $4.80 for a $6 book if it can be bought for $3.60? And always check the special orders for clues to adding titles to the inventory. Eliminating a single-book shipment saves 10¢ postage every time. (First pound costs double the added pounds in the package.)
• Buy needed stock from local wholesalers when it is sold out—even if it is at lower discount. Saved sales at any discount still mean more dollar profit.
• Call suppliers long distance to get books faster if they are needed. The first saved sale usually pays for the extra expense.
• Pay attention to publishers' special discount offers, being conservative when replenishing stock if an offer is coming, and buying heavier at the special discount.
• Know those publishers who allow the combining of older titles with new books, and order more basic books at the time new lists are offered.

These are all practical details. There are others more obvious, like watching reviews, having customer request sheets, knowing what is in inventory (stock control), and so on. But it is amazing how some stores do not adjust the timing of their buying to take advantage of discount.

Our sample $100,000 store could add $1,000, or 1 per cent, to gross profits by paying attention to all buying details.

3. *Operating Details*

Cost-cutting through attention to operating detail can make a store manager a real hero. A store can grow or go out of business according to the way it is managed.

Every bookseller should be familiar with the list of operating expenses on a profit and loss statement: rent, advertising, telephone, supplies, insurance, etc., plus the largest expense—payroll. Some expenses are fixed, some are controllable. Attention to the controllable factors can save money—like watching the use of supplies, telephones, etc. Rent, a big expense, is not controllable once the lease is signed.

The big expense—payroll—which is often a half to two-thirds of all expense dollars, is highly controllable. Too big a payroll in relation to sales is one of the most frequent reasons for unprofitable businesses. Let's look at this profit factor in management.

Assume a $100,000 volume, with expenses amounting to 36 per cent of sales, one half or 18 per cent of which is salaries—$18,000. The staff, besides the manager, consists of two employees that cost $8,000 and one part-timer at $2,000. The manager drew the remaining $8,000 during the year as pay.

Another bookstore, with about the same volume, scheduled its three employees so that it operated with about twenty hours less assistance during each week—saving about the time of a part-timer or $2,000 a year. Therefore it brought its expenses down to 34 per cent or $34,000—and the owner's profit was $2,000 more than in the first store.

The larger the store, the more payroll savings are possible. Some stores *are* overpopulated—or have people on their staff who are nonproductive.

Is there control of what goes out of the back door as well as the front? Every time that back door opens, merchandise is accessible to outsiders. Does the receiving clerk count the packages that arrive, and check each one against a bill of lading?

There are dozens of such "managing" items that affect cost. For others, see the checklist in Figure 13.1, Chapter 13.

Let us now summarize the results of paying attention to all the practical success factors we have mentioned.

The store that is good *only* on selling details would add $2,500 to selling volume, and about $1,000 of that would reach the profit line.

For the store that is proficient in buying details *only*, gross margin becomes 41 per cent instead of 40 per cent, and that adds $1,000 to the profit line.

In the store proficient in operating details *only*, expenses go down from 36 per cent to 34 per cent, adding $2,000 to the profit line.

But the store that is proficient in all areas has sales that are up $2,500, an additional 1 per cent of gross profit on those sales, and expenses are down by 2 per cent. His profit, on larger volume, goes from 4 per cent to 7 per cent—a 75 per cent increase.

Attention to these details is what makes a business profitable.

Financing the Bookstore by Merchandise Budgeting   13

G. ROYSCE SMITH

Executive Director,
American Booksellers Association, Inc.

I

A bookstore is for sale, and the owner provides the buyer with some financial information—a monthly sales record, a profit and loss statement, but no balance sheet. Is this adequate information on which to base a financial decision? In this particular case, which is an actual one, it is. Let's look at the facts the owner provided (Tables 13.1 and 13.2).

TABLE 13.1

SALES RECORD BY MONTH

Month	Last Year	This Year
January	$ 1,097	$ 2,786
February	1,861	2,231
March	1,411	2,837
April	1,427	2,521
May	1,659	2,617
June	1,750	1,977
July	1,583	2,580
August	1,467	2,385
September	1,872	3,045
October	2,450	3,985
November	2,508	4,080
December	5,908	9,610
Total	$25,002	$40,654

How do we analyze this information? The sales record isn't too bad. Sales show a healthy increase throughout the second year. But a financial report does not end with sales. The sales record only states the volume on which the net profit is based. The profit and loss statement is a better guide, for all the sales in the world are meaningless unless

TABLE 13.2

PROFIT AND LOSS STATEMENT

Gross sales	$40,654.00
Less sales tax	893.39
Net sales	$39,760.61
Gross profit (@ 35% av. disc.)	$13,916.21
Less expenses	3,464.52
Net profit	$10,451.69

Itemized Expenses

Property and business taxes	$ 101.84
Rent @ $75/mo.	900.00
Insurance	44.20
Incoming postage	1,576.42
Outgoing postage (est.)	170.00
Dues	27.50
Bank service charges	96.36
Reference books	50.00
Telephone	145.00
Electricity	203.20
Miscellaneous	150.00
	$ 3,464.52

Beginning inventory, 1/1, at cost	$12,366.00
Purchases, 1/1–12/31, at cost	29,248.37

they produce a profit to enable the business to continue and grow. The profit and loss statement at hand does not make a very pretty picture.

The first noticeable feature of this profit and loss statement is that it was prepared by an amateur, which is demonstrated by the fact that expenses do not include either salaries or professional fees. Nor is the method of determining gross profit calculated to inspire confidence.

Gross profit is not gross sales less sales tax multiplied by an imaginary average discount ("av. disc."). It is the difference between net sales (sales after sales tax) and the cost of these sales. Cost of sales is determined by exact rather than imaginary figures: To the cost of beginning inventory are added purchases during the period, inbound shipping charges, markdowns, and shrinkage, and from the sum of these figures are deducted cash discounts taken for prompt payment on purchases and the cost of the ending inventory. The resulting figure is the actual cost of sale. Subtracting this from net sales gives gross profit. [The budgeting terms used here are fully defined in Chapter 14, "Budgeting Terms Used by Booksellers," by the same author.—ED.]

Net profit is gross profit less expenses. Expenses do not include incoming postage as the statement under examination would have us believe. Cost of delivery to the store, markdowns, and shrinkage are all inherent factors in the buying and selling of goods and are part of the cost of goods sold. Controllable expenses fall into two major categories: First, salaries and wages, and secondly, services and supplies purchased. Interest, taxes, and depreciation are less controllable items of expense. It is noteworthy that this financial statement omits all reference to salaries and wages and to supplies with the exception of reference books. The only expenses listed are services. There is no reference to interest or depreciation, and there are no state or federal taxes noted.

Therefore, the net profit figure of $10,451.69 is entirely imaginary. No business can run without paid help. If the owner is the help, he must assign himself a reasonable salary before he can consider his expense ledger complete.

Even if he had only paid himself the minimum wage in his state at the time ($1.65 per hour), plus time-and-a-half for one eight-hour day over the normal forty hours, he would have paid himself $4,461.60 for the year. That would have applied if he only worked eight hours a day, six days a week, and if no one else helped him or relieved him for lunch. If his wife came in to work, then her time should also have been charged.

The sum of $4,461.60 is the absolute minimum that the store owner should charge to salary expense. To be honest with himself and with his business, he should charge more. Otherwise, he is fooling himself (and only himself) into thinking his business is healthier than it is.

Given the figures at hand, this is as far as we can go in considering profit in this instance. A complete discussion of the effects of day-to-day operations on expenses will be found in Chapter 12, "Practical Details for Improving Profits," and Chapter 15, "How To Make a Profit in Bookselling."

Expense is not the only factor affecting profit. Turnover plays an important role in the total profitability picture, for it affects the bookseller's return on his investment. Turnover is the number of times the average inventory for a given period is replaced to produce total sales for the period.

Now let us look at this particular store's inventory. On January 1, there was an inventory of $19,000 *at retail* on hand if we increase the figure of $12,366 *at cost* to allow for the average 35 per cent discount estimated by the proprietor. During the next twelve months, an additional $45,000 in stock at retail was received. (Purchases at cost adjusted to reflect 35 per cent average discount.) Sales for the period came to $40,600. Turnover for the period, assuming an average retail inventory of $22,750, was 1.8, a completely unacceptable figure. The cost of the increased inventory must be considered an expense until it is turned into cash by being sold.

Turnover has been called the best yardstick for measuring the success of a business. Some booksellers, who think they are in the business only for aesthetic considerations, ignore turnover and wonder why they never show a profit. Attention to turnover can be taken to extremes; but viewed realistically, it can be a valuable tool by which a retailer may gauge his performance.

Assume that a store is doing an annual volume of $100,000 at retail, and shows a net profit after expenses (*including salaries*) of $3,500, or 3.5 per cent. Turnover, even without any change in sales, can seriously affect the health of this operation. This $100,000 store operating on an average inventory of $50,000 retail is getting only two turns a year. The investment in a $50,000 inventory, assuming a clear 40 per cent discount for purposes of illustration, would be $30,000 at cost. The net profit of $3,500 represents an 11.7 per cent return on the $30,000 investment. But if the store were to do the same $100,000 volume on a $25,000 retail inventory ($15,000 cost), the return of $3,500 on the investment would be 23.3 per cent.

On the decreased inventory the store would be operating with fresh, current stock. Profits should increase because the owner would not constantly have to borrow money on which he must pay interest; his inventory taxes would be lower; he would need to have less stockroom space and could give more space to the selling area; he would spend less money on markdowns because his stock would not stay around long enough to get shopworn; he would be able to control this smaller inventory more easily, and pilferage should decrease; and most importantly, he would find a new sense of confidence and well-being, which would allow him to think more of making sales than of disposing of dead stock.

On the other hand, demanding too high a rate of turnover of inventory can create serious stock problems. Basic titles will not always be on hand, new, fast-moving titles will be in short supply, and the store will not have a representative stock within the fields it has chosen to cover. Consequently, the buyer who goes too far in trying to increase turnover will find he is producing a negative effect. It is necessary to have the right amount and kind of stock to generate the desired sales. Too low an inventory results in lost sales, and customers who are repeatedly disappointed go to other booksellers.

The "right" turnover varies in every business. The right turnover for floor coverings is considered to be two turns a year. For millinery, eight to ten. For books, the consensus is that bookstores should aim for between three and five turns a year. Paperback stores should aim for the higher figure, for the lower the price of the item being sold, the higher the turnover should be. Scholarly bookstores will usually have to be content with the lower figure. But any store whose turns fall below two will be in serious trouble.

How can you spot the causes for bad turnover in your store? The store we have had under consideration demonstrated one cause right in his expense column. The $170 outgoing-postage figure for a six-month period suggests that no returns have been made. The buyer has been unwilling to face up to correcting the mistakes that have created his abnormally high inventory either by making returns where possible or taking markdowns where necessary.

Where should he look for the stock that is not moving, which must be returned or marked down? First and most obviously are last season's new books which did not catch on or which didn't sell as well as expected. Returning these titles should have begun the day after Christmas. Some of these books can be sold at 50 per cent off in the store, and that is cheaper than making returns.

Aside from new titles, we should look at other categories of books. Perhaps the Western Americana section has slowed down. Maybe there has been a shift in emphasis in the cookbook section. Are there too many kinds of Bibles? Are customers favoring paperback children's books over your extensive selection of cloth?

Do you really know how many copies of a title you need to have on hand? A two-month supply when two weeks' will do can sabotage turnover. Or are you not carrying enough of a fast-moving title? Turnover is controlling fast- as well as slow-moving titles. Inventory controls will keep stocks down and sales and turnover up.

Peak selling seasons require properly timed buying. Turnover will nose-dive if you bring Christmas merchandise in on September 1. On the other hand, if you don't get it in until December 1, you will not have books on hand for the beginning of the selling season. If merchandise arrives too late for any promotion through the fault of the shipper, it should be promptly returned.

How can you use a budget to improve turnover? Any budget at all will help accomplish this. A very simple budgeting rule will help. *Remember that if you want to get four turns a year, the stock you have on hand at the beginning of any month should not exceed the sales you plan to make during the next three months.*

Turnover can be improved by the wise buying of new titles. Nothing is easier to say or harder to accomplish. If you do not think you have a customer for a book, don't buy it. We all know that there are far too many books being published today. The editor of a publishing house has his own reasons for each title he selects for publication. You must have your own reasons for stocking a title. Even so, do not buy an inordinate

1. Do I give valuable space to slow sellers or merchandise past its selling peak?

2. Am I slow to take my medicine on a dog, either by return or markdown?

3. Will I buy more of an item than I really need in a reasonable length of time to take advantage of a price concession or a higher discount?

4. Do I fail to get books to the selling floor within twenty-four hours of receipt?

5. Do I find it easy to ignore the fact that overstocks reduce turnover and increase markdowns and shopworn merchandise?

6. Do I buy up to the hilt so that there is no cash in the bank for sleepers?

7. Do I buy with my total season's sale in mind rather than the first month's?

8. Do I keep an old sideline or gift-book line when I take on a new one?

9. Do I buy merchandise which I think just *might* sell?

10. Do I spread myself too thin by offering too many titles in too many subject classifications?

11. Do I buy for best discount and poor turnover from publishers rather than for a fair discount and excellent turnover?

12. Do I reorder basic stock on past rather than current performance?

13. Do I think I can be everything to everybody?

14. Do I buy from publishers equally rather than concentrating on those who give the best terms and service?

15. Do I take in merchandise after the cancellation date that I have put on my order?

16. Do I mark an item or line down without trying it in a different location or with a different display?

17. Do I often buy books that are outside the price lines which sell best in my store?

18. Do I guess at how long a book has been in stock rather than aging it at the time of receipt?

19. Do I think that fast-turning items will take care of themselves?

20. Do I think all the classifications in my store should have the same rate of turnover?

21. Do I carry an extensive array of titles purely for prestige?

*Compiled by G. Roysce Smith. The correct answer to each question is "No."

FIGURE 13.1 *(Continued)*

22. Do I carry duplicate items by carrying competing lines?

23. Do I take seasonal merchandise in too far ahead of the selling season without extended dating for payment?

24. Do I keep promotional merchandise (i.e., remainders) too long after the promotion has passed?

25. Do I work without a buying plan?

26. Do I think it would be good to have a better system for following up on orders, but find that I don't have time to work on it?

27. Do I accept the publishers' representatives' stock counts and suggested orders without question?

28. Do I think that turnover is, in itself, a sought-after objective?

29. Do I stock up from the publisher to take advantage of a discount break or an advertising allowance when I would be saving money by relying on my jobber?

amount, particularly if you are within range of a good wholesaler. Certainly you should not buy the entire amount you expect to sell on your initial purchase. Your salesman, if you have one, will disagree with this statement because that is his job. Your job is to manage your resources so that you will be in business when next he calls. For twenty-nine questions to ask yourself if you want to improve turnover, see Figure 13.1.

II

Turnover is not all science. There are a lot of subjective decisions that affect it and one of these is what a store stocks. A more objective decision is *when,* for this can be controlled by a merchandise budget. Let's consider *what* first.

When a store is just opening, it analyzes its community. Then it tries to get together a stock that is "representative" for that community.

Beginning booksellers (and some who have been in the business long enough to know better) are inclined to think that there ought to be one single list that will make them and all other booksellers instantly successful. The truth is—there is no such list.

The only person who can tell you what a truly representative stock will be for your bookstore is you.

A representative stock on Nantucket will certainly not be representative in Salt Lake City, just as what may be representative in the store down the block may not be representative for you, even though it might have common elements. A representative stock reflects the personality of a community as it is filtered through the personality and sensibility of the bookstore buyer.

All buyers, being human, bring to their work some degree of subjectivity and an even greater degree of subtlety as well. The best buyers are the ones who recognize and allow for the differences between their own personalities and those of their communities and realize that the personalities of both are constantly changing.

When we keep sales records by title or record lost sales or analyze our special orders, we are looking for the ways in which we may respond to such changes.

Stock with good turnover is a flexible stock. A flexible buyer can respond to these changes as they occur, and a flexible stock will result. There is a scientific tool to help him do that. It is called "merchandise budget."

Robert Frost used to say that, for him, writing what he called "free verse" was like playing tennis with the net down. Working with a merchandise budget is putting the net up in the game of retailing. It makes the game worth playing.

Let's construct our merchandise budget as if we were just opening a new store.

We have studied traffic, we have a good idea who our customers will be and what they will want to buy, we have counted the number of people in our community and know their average income. We think we stand a good chance of having a healthy first year. We think that we will do $100,000. We are going to open on July 1. We want to make a budget for the first six months. Our first step is to estimate expected sales by month for this six-month period (Table 13.3).

These figures, then, are our *planned sales.* How did we arrive at these figures? Well, July isn't the best month in the year for any bookstore outside a summer-resort area, and we aren't as ready to go into business as we thought and have not really ordered enough stock to give the new business a big initial push. In August, there is back-to-school

TABLE 13.3

PLANNED SALES

July	$ 3,000
August	4,000
September	7,000
October	10,000
November	9,000
December	25,000
Total	$58,000

business and people tend to get caught up on books they've bought for summer reading. In September, we are back at work in earnest, and new books are coming out again. In October, we plan a remainder sale to get people to know about us. In November, we can count on gift buying to start and sales to edge up without any particular promotion. Then there is December, when booksellers do between 20 and 30 per cent of their total year's sales. Since it is our first year, we'll go for a median figure.

Now that we have planned our sales, we need to determine how much stock we must have. Since our goal for the year is four turns and we are working with a six-month period, our goal should, logically, be two turns. But industry figures indicate that some 60 per cent of retail book business is done in the last six months of the year. If we were to do only two turns, our average inventory at full retail price for the period would be half our projected sales of $58,000, or $29,000. But we want to do more than two turns. Therefore, we must operate on less than a $29,000 average inventory. Table 13.4 is the monthly inventory that we project.

These figures are our *planned stock*. Adding these figures together, we get a total of $175,000, which we divide by seven to obtain an average inventory of $25,000 for the six-month period. We then divide our sales for the period ($58,000) by our average inventory ($25,000) to obtain our turnover, which is 2.32.

If our turnover remained constant during the following six-month period, we would have an annual turnover for the fiscal year of 4.64. But we have set our goal at four. When we start to make our plans for the coming season, we must decide whether we wish to stick with four turns, in which case our goal for the second six months would be 1.58 turns, or go for 4.64. The deciding factor must be whether the rate of turnover will allow us to work with an adequate, representative stock.

From our planned-sales and planned-stock figures for the period, we can determine how much we should plan to spend for each month.

We begin July with $15,000 at retail price and want to end the month with the same amount. So during July we can only buy as much

TABLE 13.4
PLANNED STOCK

July 1	$15,000
July 31	15,000
August 31	25,000
September 30	25,000
October 31	30,000
November 30	40,000
December 31	25,000

as we sell, which we have already planned at $3,000. During August, however, we plan to increase our inventory to $25,000, for this is the month of back-to-school sales, and we want to build our inventory up for the return of the vacationers in September. So we can buy the amount we sell during August plus the amount by which we expect to increase our inventory. Expected sales of $4,000 and increasing our inventory from $15,000 to $25,000 give us a purchase budget for August of $14,000 (keep in mind that we are talking about retail price).

We plan to maintain our inventory at the $25,000 level during September. Once again, we may only buy as much as we sell, or $7,000. During October, we plan to build our inventory from $25,000 to $30,-000, and we expect sales of $10,000. So our October purchase budget is $15,000.

In November, our stock will peak in anticipation of December sales. We want to increase it from $30,000 to $40,000. We look for sales of $9,000. Our November purchase budget is $19,000.

During December, it is really too late for orders to be placed with publishers and nearly all of us rely most heavily on our wholesalers, so our purchases will be lighter if we have bought properly in November. Of course, there is that last-minute sleeper, but most of our buying will have been done. December is for selling. Our planned sales are $25,-000. We also want to reduce our inventory from $40,000 to $25,000. Therefore, we must deduct the amount by which we plan to reduce our stock, $15,000, from the amount of our planned sales. This gives us a purchase budget for December of $10,000.

From this, we can write down clearly for ourselves to see and remember exactly how much money we will have available to spend each month (Table 13.5). These figures represent our *planned purchases* at retail value. Actually, of course, the money we spend for it will be that amount less the discount we receive plus incoming carriage charges.

TABLE 13.5

PLANNED PURCHASES*

July	$ 3,000
August	14,000
September	7,000
October	15,000
November	19,000
December	10,000
Total	$68,000

*All the figures given are at retail. Do not forget that if you record your purchases at cost you must convert them to retail when computing a purchase budget in this manner, for you are working with sales at retail. The method for doing this is set forth in Chapter 14.

Our total purchase budget for the fall season, then, is $68,000. We know when our stock will peak and by how much. We can plan when we need to see our friendly banker for a loan to meet our bills, and we can project how long we will need the money so that we can pay it back in the shortest possible time.

We have worked here with a six-month budget rather than a whole year. Actually, a beginning store, before it buys a book, should work out such a plan for the entire year. Thereafter, a six-month planning period is more reasonable, since it will be based on actual-sales figures of the previous year and prevailing economic conditions. Such plans should be made at least one month prior to the period involved and reviewed periodically during the season.

In order to update the budget, it is necessary to adjust it for actual sales and actual purchases. If sales have been lower and purchases higher than projected, future purchases must be adjusted downward by the dollar amount by which we are overbought at the moment. Should sales be higher and purchases lower than planned, purchases might possibly, after careful study, be adjusted upward.

The task of budget adjustment is called "figuring your *open-to-buy* (OTB)."

III

The system of budget adjustment that I am going to set forth here is not the only one, nor do all successful bookstores use a formal system of open-to-buy. Whatever system is used, the basic elements of keeping track of where you stand are the same. You need to know how much stock you had on hand at the beginning of a given period, how much you actually received between that time and the present, the amount of goods you have on order, how much you sold during the period, and your planned-stock goal at the end of the period.

These are our basic elements, all computed at retail prices:

Beginning inventory
Goods received
On order
Sales
Planned-stock goal

By adding goods received to beginning inventory and then subtracting sales, we arrive at an approximate ledger inventory. If we add on-order for a stated period to this, we can determine how much money we have left to spend (open-to-buy) during that period by comparing the resulting figure to our planned-stock goal. Let's walk through this using the budget we have just set up.

First, let's look at how *actual purchases* have compared to planned (Table 13.6). Assume that we have just finished our first quarter in business.

TABLE 13.6

ACTUAL PURCHASES

Month	Actual	Planned
July	$ 2,500	$ 3,000
August	15,000	14,000
September	7,000	7,000

Our July purchases fell $500 below plan. But in August we bought $1,000 more than our plan. We pulled in the reins on ourselves during September and kept within the monthly plan. Nevertheless, our purchases ran $24,500 for the quarter rather than the $24,000 we had budgeted.

Next, let's see what *actual sales* were compared to what we planned (Table 13.7).

TABLE 13.7

ACTUAL SALES

Month	Actual	Planned
July	$2,000	$3,000
August	3,500	4,000
September	7,100	7,000

The net effect of July and August was to pull our sales for the quarter 10 per cent below plan. We had hoped to do $14,000, but we actually did $12,600.

TABLE 13.8

ACTUAL AND PLANNED STOCK

Month	Actual on Order	Planned to Buy
October	$13,000	$15,000
November	13,000	19,000
December	2,000	10,000

Now we must decide whether to reduce our sales plan (and therefore the rest of our budget) through the end of the year by 10 per cent or consider that September sales are more truly reflective of the community reaction to us than July and August. Before we go further, however, we must look at how much we have already committed for the next quarter. Table 13.8 shows what we actually have on order for the next three months compared to our planned purchases.

Now we have all the figures necessary to compute our open-to-buy for each month in the coming quarter. First, let's bring our *plan* up-to-date by adjusting it to *actual*-purchase and *actual*-sales figures (Table 13.9*a*).

TABLE 13.9*a*
OPEN-TO-BUY

July 1 inventory	$15,000
Goods received to date	+24,500
Total stock handled	$39,500
Sales to date	−12,600
Planned inventory, 9/30	$25,000
Inventory on hand, 9/30	26,900
Open-to-buy, 9/30	($ 1,900)

Parentheses around numbers are always bad news for someone, for they indicate a negative balance. In this case, they tell us that we were $1,900 *overbought* at the end of September. Table 13.9*b* shows how that will affect us in October.

TABLE 13.9*b*
OPEN-TO-BUY

Inventory on hand (O.H.), 9/30	$26,900
On order (O.O.), Oct. delivery	+13,000
Total O.H. and O.O.	$39,900
Planned sales, Oct.	−10,000
Estimated inventory, 10/31	$29,900
Planned inventory, 10/31.	$30,000
Est. inventory, 10/31	−29,900
OTB, 10/31	$ 100

If we don't buy another penny's worth between the first of October and the end, we will come out $100 under our stock goal and thus reverse our overbought situation. But how can we go an entire month without spending more than our $100 on special orders, basic stock, and best-sellers? We can't.

OTB is a tool. A tool is an aid. We must not become slaves to our tools but rather let them help us.

OTB has alerted us to a bad situation. If we do not take steps to correct it, the situation will only worsen. But the corrective steps should not include cutting off the primary sources of our sales unless the situation is desperate. One doesn't apply a tourniquet to the neck of a man whose temple is bleeding.

It would be rough in a bookstore to cut off all purchases of basic stock, best-sellers, and special orders. Without them, the store would have nothing but slower-moving, less-appealing stock, and customers would quickly look elsewhere for their needs.

Certainly, during periods of excessive stock, we need to examine more carefully our purchases of basic stock and best-sellers, applying as much caution as possible. And we should look around for dead titles that we have not yet returned. But mostly we should proceed with extreme caution in our buying for the rest of the season, remembering that we must include a certain amount of uncommitted money in our on-order each month to cover recurring order situations, including special orders, as well as promotional items of a timely nature.

Actually, things aren't as bad in this case as they might be, for we are not too heavily committed for November and December. Let's see how we stand for the rest of the quarter (Table 13.9c).

TABLE 13.9c
OPEN-TO-BUY

Est. inventory, 10/31	$29,900
O.O. Nov.	+13,000
O.O. Dec.	+ 2,000
Total O.H. and O.O.	$44,900
Planned sales, Nov.	− 9,000
Planned sales, Dec.	−25,000
Est. inventory, 12/31	$10,900
Planned inventory, 12/31.	$25,000
Est. inventory, 12/31	−10,900
OTB, 10/31–12/31	$14,100

So we can see that if we continue to watch our purchases for the next three months we can come out all right. The really crucial month is October. We must not commit too much of the $14,000 that we have left to spend too early, for we must give the Christmas-sellers time to emerge. There are always two or three sleepers in every season, and we must save some money for them.

There we have the mysteries of open-to-buy made simple. I find that very few booksellers have any records indicating how much money they have committed for books that are not yet in the store. Indeed, some keep no records of orders at all. Instinct can only take you so far down the right road before it detours you to the bank for an unnecessary loan.

So how do we arrive at an on-order figure? By extending all orders. This once was a great chore, but now with electronic calculators selling at less than $100, it is a swift and simple task for the small store as well as the large.

It isn't necessary to keep a journal of outstanding orders. A simple total will do. Remember each week to deduct the amount of the invoices you receive and process and add the total of all orders placed.

Do not deduct merchandise received for which you have not been billed. And remember to convert invoice amounts to retail, for we don't want to mix cost and retail figures.

Once again, you may adapt all or part of this to the needs of your operation and the time available. I have given you the whole merchandise budgeting picture because you will not be able to choose what you want until you know all the elements. Ideally, you will want to use the whole system, but practically, you may have to settle for less.

Budgeting Terms Used by Booksellers

14

G. ROYSCE SMITH

Executive Director,
American Booksellers Association, Inc.

There are a number of budgeting terms which, as used by booksellers, have never been properly defined. Here are some that turned up in Chapter 13, "Financing the Bookstore by Merchandise Budgeting."

budget "A plan for the coordination of resources and expenditures," according to *Webster's New Collegiate* (eighth edition). Right on!

The kind of budget that we had before us in Chapter 13 is a merchandise budget. There are other things that must be budgeted in a bookstore, and they are expenses and time. They are discussed elsewhere in this book.

A work sheet is useful in preparing a budget. Figure 14.1 is a form that can be made up by hand. *LY* means "last year." *TY*, "this year."

FIGURE 14.1 — SEASONAL SALES PLAN

MONTH	SALES		STOCK		PURCHASES	
	TY	*LY*	*TY*	*LY*	*TY*	*LY*
July	____	____	____	____	____	____
Aug.	____	____	____	____	____	____
Sept.	____	____	____	____	____	____
Oct.	____	____	____	____	____	____
Nov.	____	____	____	____	____	____
Dec.	____	____	____	____	____	____

The first step in completing this form is to fill in last year's sales, stock, and purchases if you have records for the previous year. Then fill in the blanks for this year's planned sales, stock, and purchases using the methods described in Chapter 13.

converting from cost to retail Most of us are familiar with computing the cost price of an item. If it retails for $4 and our discount is 40 per cent, we multiply by the reciprocal of .40, which is .60, to get the cost figure of $2.40 (instead of taking 40 per cent of $4 and then subtracting it). Converting cost to retail is the reverse of this process: dividing $2.40 by .60, we find that the retail is $4.

Most of us may not be indulging in this kind of small-scale exercise, but I cite it here simply because you may be recording sales at retail and inventory at cost and need to convert one or the other figure in order to compute turnover. In either case, you will need to establish an average *cost-of-sales* percentage in order to arrive at meaningful results.

cost of sales In their 1968 report prepared for the ABA, "Success Factors in Book Retailing," Ernst & Ernst recommended a standard form for a cost schedule with which your accountant may or may not agree. If he does, you would do well to adopt this form, for the ABA is going to be using it to develop and publish up-to-date statistics on our profession.

According to Ernst & Ernst, the proper elements in determining cost of sales are:

> Beginning inventory, at cost
> Purchases
> Inbound shipping charges
> Inventory markdowns
> Shrinkage

These are added together and from them are deducted:

> Cash discounts on purchases
> Ending inventory, at cost

This figure should be converted to a percentage of sales for use in *converting from cost to retail,* and vice versa, as described above.

expenses Ernst & Ernst, while allocating markdowns, incoming transportation, and shrinkage to *cost of sales,* lists the following basic expense categories:

W–2 gross salaries and wages
Rent
Depreciation and amortization
Advertising and promotion
Delivery charges on returns to publishers
Delivery charges on merchandise to customers
Supplies
Postage other than delivery and advertising

Taxes: payroll, state and local income and
property, and employee insurance
Bad debts
Professional fees
Telephone and telegraph
Miscellaneous (e.g., interest)

fiscal year An accounting period of twelve months. To hell with January 1. Start anytime you want, or that your accountant advises.

inventory The value, either at cost or retail, of stock for sale on hand. A *physical* inventory should be taken at least once a year. This means a hand count of each item in the store, either at actual cost, or at retail. It may be kept up-to-date on a monthly basis by adding:

Purchases
Customer returns

and deducting:

Sales
Returns to publishers
Markdowns

This updated inventory is called, variously, *ledger* inventory or *book* inventory. "Book" in the latter designation refers to "bookkeeping" and should not be confused by those of us who deal in a product of the same name.

sales per capita Sales divided by the number of heads in the shopping area.

At one time it was thought that every citizen would account for $1.50 to $2 in sales of books in a community per annum. I wouldn't venture a guess as to what that figure would be today, but it's worth investigating. If I were opening a new bookstore, I would stick with the figures above, possibly even the lower of the two, but I'm conservative. And some capitas are more bookish than other capitas.

sales per square foot Sales in dollars divided by the number of square feet of *selling* area in a store. Don't count stockrooms or shipping and receiving areas.

The 1968 Ernst & Ernst survey for ABA indicated that the average sales per square foot of all stores reporting was $85. I hope that figure is not correct. It is much too low. A healthy store should aim for sales of between $100 and $200 per square foot. Less than $75 indicates mortal illness. More than $200 indicates that it's time to consider expansion. $150 should make everyone happy, at least temporarily.

turnover The number of times the average inventory for a given period is sold.

Turnover is computed by dividing the gross sales for a given period by the average inventory at retail for the same period. Turnover may be computed for any desired period of time. Normally, it is computed for periods of one year or any fraction of a year. Computing turnover for longer periods of time would not seem to have much practical value.

To compute the turnover for any specific quarter of a year we total sales for the period (Table 14.1).

TABLE 14.1

TOTAL SALES

(First Quarter)

January	$3,000
February	2,500
March	3,000
	$8,500

We then compute the average inventory for the period by, first, adding the beginning inventory on January 1 to the ending inventories on January 31, February 28, and March 31 (Table 14.2).

TABLE 14.2

TOTAL INVENTORY

(First Quarter)

January 1	$12,000
January 31	10,000
February 28	12,000
March 30	12,000
	$46,000

We divide the sum of these figures by four to obtain the average inventory for the period. (Although the period covered is three months, we are entering four figures into our sum. Thus, we must divide by four.)

$$\$46,000 \div 4 = \$11,500 \text{ } average \text{ } inventory$$

Now we divide gross sales by average inventory.

$$\$8,500 \div \$11,500 = .74 \text{ } turns$$

If we maintain the same ratio between sales and stock throughout the year, we may project that the annual turnover rate will be four times .74, or 2.96. In other words, we multiply the turnover rate for the period by the number of times the period occurs in the year.

Always remember that in computing anything other than discounts, we must use only figures of the same kind. If we work with sales figures at retail, inventory figures must also be at retail. If either figure is at cost, the other figure must be at cost.

How To Make a Profit in Bookselling*   **15**

JOHN P. DESSAUER
President, John P. Dessauer, Inc.;
Official Statistician, Association of American Publishers,
Inc., and National Association of College Stores

The story goes that in 1957 R. I. Jones, a member of the public account-ing firm Arthur Anderson and Company, was told by a department store client that the store was planning to discontinue selling cigarettes because there was not enough profit margin in them. Jones remon-strated that the turnover on cigarettes was extremely high, that the costs involved were low and that therefore the store must surely be showing a profit on them. Not so, he was told: Over-all performance percentages showed that items below a certain gross margin could simply not be carried profitably by the store.

The myopia of that department store client was fortunate for all of us because it sent Jones to his drawing board to develop what he called "merchandise management accounting," a method of measuring profit-ability in retail operations. His work has had a profound impact on financial planning in the department store and other retail fields.

Merchandise Management Accounting

In this article I propose to adapt some of the principles of merchan-dise management accounting to bookselling.

"The basic aim of merchandise management accounting," state Charles F. Phillips and Delbert J. Duncan in *Retailing: Principles and Methods* (7th ed., Homewood, Ill.: Richard D. Irwin, Inc., 1967), "is to improve *dollar* profit (rather than *percentage* profit) through better determination and interpretation of costs by individual items." The factors affecting the profitability of specific items are basically: *list price, gross margin, turnover,* and *operating cost.*

---

*Adapted with permission from portions of a similarly titled series of articles (*Publishers Weekly*, April 2, 9, and 16, 1973).

It is the relationship of these factors in any given transaction that determines whether it will create a gain or loss for the bookseller. How does this relationship work? Consider a bookseller whose daily operating expense is $100. To retire that cost he could sell 100 books listing at $2 with a gross margin (publisher's discount less transportation cost) of 50 per cent; or 50 books listing at $8 with a gross margin of 25 per cent; or 75 books listing at $10 with a gross margin of 13.5 per cent; or 50 books listing at $5 with a gross margin of 40 per cent; and so on.

What would matter, in other words, would not be list price alone, or margin alone, or volume alone, but the *combination* of all three factors; to break even they would have to produce $100. Less than that would create a loss; more than that, a profit.

Assuming, for the moment, a constant gross margin of 40 per cent, and taking the last of our random examples as a starting point, we recall that to retire his cost the bookseller would have to sell 50 books listing at $5. Should he be unable to create such volume, the list price would have to rise, for example, to:

$8—requiring the sale of only 32 copies;
$10—requiring the sale of only 25 copies;
$15—requiring the sale of 17 copies, etc.

Similarly, an increase in volume, or turnover, would reduce the list price requirement:

75 copies—requiring a list price of $3.50;
100 copies—requiring a list price of $2.50;
150 copies—requiring a list price of $1.75, etc.

Were we to assume a constant in copies sold—50, for example—we would find that our margin requirements would move in relation to list price. At $10 we would require only 20 per cent, at $20 we would require only 10 per cent, but at $4 we would require 50 per cent, and at $2.50, we would require 80 per cent.

Did we, further, want to hold the list price at $5, the relationship of turnover and gross margin would show similar proportions: 10 copies at 20 per cent; 40 copies at 50 per cent; 34 copies at 60 per cent.

In all of the above examples, we were dealing with a constant cost —$100. When we vary that cost, we must deal with proportionate variations in the remaining factors of list price, gross margin, and turnover. If, for example, our costs were to be only $80 per day, we could retire them with sales of only:

40 copies at $5 with a margin of 40 per cent; or
50 copies at $4 with a margin of 40 per cent; or
50 copies at $5 with a margin of 32 per cent; etc.

To summarize the relationship of list price, margin, turnover, and operating cost in a formula, we could say that a break-even point is reached when

$$List\ Price \times Gross\ Margin\ = \frac{Operating\ Cost}{Turnover}$$

with turnover represented by number of copies sold.

Like all formulas and theoretical postulates, while the above can help us understand the basic dynamics, what really happens is infinitely more complex. In practice we must deal not with one list price, one margin, and one turnover rate or even one invariable daily cost, but with hundreds, perhaps thousands, of these in combination and sequence. Yet the success of retailing depends on our ability to make sound decisions with regard to them all; the more effective these decisions, the higher will be our profit.

Nothing is really simple in our business. Consider the following example.

A bookseller in a Midwestern city decided to join the paperback revolution. He remodeled. His dusty, small display window was replaced by a see-through glass wall. Featured in the front of the store were the trade (and a few mass-market) paperbacks. Farther back were new shelves displaying a good percentage of hard-cover stock, face out. The rest of the shop maintained a good hardbound selection with spine-out displays. Relics weeded out of his old inventory were marked down drastically and provided the main attraction in a sale that celebrated the renovation.

The results were dramatic. Traffic and sales volume increased, and the bookseller began to show a respectable profit. Now, he reasoned, if just partly converting the store to paperbacks had brought him such good fortune, would not expanding the new paperback section increase that fortune further? Didn't paperbacks sell much faster than the hard-cover books? And earn a better discount? And wouldn't it make sense to convert some of the wall racks displaying technical manuals, classics, and other slower-moving back stock to paperback fixtures also?

It was done—and profits declined drastically. What had gone wrong? The traffic in the shop was now greater than ever, paperback sales per title were higher than before; by all rights the bookseller should have been swimming in profits.

What had happened was that the remodeling had generated sales not only because of the paperbacks but also because of the more attractive display and trimmer stock selection in the rest of the store. When he expanded the paperback section at the expense of some of the hard-cover back-list titles, however, the bookseller was in effect substituting sales at lower list prices for sales at considerably higher list prices. The larger discount and more rapid turnover of the paperbacks were simply not sufficient to offset that disadvantage. What happened, in other words, is shown in Table 15.1.

TABLE 15.1

TALE OF A PAPERBACK EXPANSION

	BEFORE PAPERBACK EXPANSION		AFTER PAPERBACK EXPANSION	
	Sales	% of Sales	Sales	% of Sales
Hardback Sales . . .	$70,000	77.7 (7,000 units)	$48,000	59.3 (5,300 units)
Paperback Sales . . .	20,000	22.3 (9,000 units)	33,000	40.7 (15,000 units)
Total Sales	90,000	100.0 (16,000 units)	81,000	100.0 (20,300 units)
Cost of Sales				
Hardback	44,800	49.7	30,700	37.9
Paperback	12,000	13.3	19,800	24.4
Total	56,800	63.1	50,500	62.3
Gross Margin	33,200	36.9	30,500	37.6
Operating Expense. .	29,400	32.7	30,000	37.0
Net Profit.	$ 3,800	4.2	$ 500	.6

Note that the total number of units sold in the first instance was 16,000, while after the paperback expansion it was 20,300. The list-price average of hard-cover book sales before the change was $10, while after, it was $9—an indication that some of the most significant casualties were books at higher list prices.

Failure of the Bookman as Businessman

So the seemingly simple question of price and turnover leads to some very basic reflections about our business. Who are our customers? What kind of books will they buy? Are they "average" consumers or some very special breed? The full answer depends on many things: the character of the store, its location, the population of the community, and so on. Answers will differ for a paperback store located in a high-traffic downtown area, a personal bookshop located in a suburban shopping center, a college store either institutionally or privately owned, a leased section in a small-city department store, a venerable institution on New York's Fifth Avenue, or a shop in the heart of Greenwich Village.

But chances are there will be a common denominator in all the answers—diversity. The American consumer is not homogeneous. Rather, he represents a whole raft of minorities of tastes, interests, and reasons for purchasing books. He is radical, conservative, reactionary, middle-of-the-road, pacifist, hawk, skeptic, believer, lover, and hater—but whatever his views, moods or dispositions, he has at least one habit that endears him to our hearts: He buys books on his favorite subjects.

It is our job to serve him, and to do it well, so that he is satisfied and we can earn a decent living at it. We must learn to anticipate his various wishes, to have available for him at least those books he is likely to put in greatest demand. That means stocking best-sellers, but also enough of the many subjects that fascinate him and draw him to read—paperbacks, technical books, classics, poetry, hobby books, art books, mysteries—whatever suits *him* or *her,* for without their approval and support we shall go out of business.

In quiet moments I have asked myself why booksellers are so often charged with being remiss in fulfilling the dual role of representing their customers' tastes and running a competent business? I submit that there are three principal reasons, the first of which, I fear, is plain ignorance.

How many booksellers know what they need to know about the dynamics of retailing? How many have read one basic book on the subject, such as Phillips and Duncan's *Retailing: Principles and Methods?* How many are aware of the fundamental financial principles involved in retail profitability, such as we have attempted to outline here?

I confess that I grew up in such ignorance. Like most booksellers, I was nurtured on the notion that the only factor in profitability was the discount I got from the publisher.

Shortly after I entered the business in the 1940's, the first Kinsey report (*Sexual Behavior in the Human Male*) made its appearance and became an immediate best-seller. The store for which I worked had an ironclad policy not to stock books at less than full trade discount, and since the publisher was offering only a text discount on Alfred Kinsey's book, we simply did not stock it.

It did not take long before the dirty looks our customers gave us when we informed them of our policy persuaded us that here we'd better make an exception. The point is, however, that we did not have a single good economic reason not to stock the Kinsey book, and for a while we lost a good deal of money by not carrying it. The book sold for something like $7 in the days when a typical nonfiction best-seller sold for $3.50. The discount margin was therefore the same in dollars for both—$1.40. Given the lively turnover it displayed, we could not help showing a profit on this book, text discount or no. Not carrying it was simply a piece of ignorant obstinacy. It was not until years later that I learned from John Barnes, then president of Barnes & Noble, a man wise in the ways of specialized bookselling, that what matters in profit is basically the dollar yield of a transaction.

The second reason why booksellers are often poor business people is that by chemistry and background they are often romantic, slightly other-worldly people whose love for books and ideas, and for the other people who love books and ideas, attracts them to the business. When they contemplate sinking their life's savings into a bookstore, they do not always realize what a detailed, hard, and demanding business it can be. They are uncomfortable with business concepts and find it difficult to apply their considerable intelligence to such boring trivia as turnover rates, discounts, and profit.

The trouble is that in bookselling—as in any cultural industry, for that matter—the demands placed on the entrepreneur are both cultural and commercial in character. Only if the bookseller is efficient can he hope to perform even the cultural function to which he aspires.

The third reason for the paucity of business acumen in the bookselling community may be described as the "gold-rush syndrome"—an overemphatic preoccupation with best-sellers. This is the attitude that leads to: "It really doesn't matter what I do with my stock and my store; what matters is merchandising best-sellers—that will bail me out."

The trouble with this concept of course is that the book-buying public buys, or wants to buy, a lot more than the best-sellers—and the person who buys best-sellers may not necessarily be a consistent book buyer. To place all your eggs in the best-seller basket is to alienate the very people who are likely to be your most faithful customers.

Fidelity to Detail

Like all business, bookselling demands fidelity to small detail, the kind of enlightened decision-making that will appeal neither to the other-worldly nor to the compulsive gambler. On the contrary, it calls for people with a good deal of prudence, wisdom, and professional stature.

How such wisdom may be lacking even with the best of intentions, was recently illustrated to me when I decided to place a special order with a bookseller friend for a new title on computer applications in business. To my surprise he showed a great reluctance to accept it. "Why?" I wanted to know.

Because, he explained, it was a short-discount item, and his operating statement clearly showed that he could not profitably market books at short discount. "My costs are 33 per cent of sales, and though my discounts average just under 40 per cent, shrinkage, transportation, and markdowns bring my gross margin down to 35 per cent. That leaves me a measly 2 per cent profit before taxes—and you want me to order you a book on which I would get only a 20 or 25 per cent discount?"

"But those are *averages*," I said, "they represent composites of many transactions. They must include list-price sales anywhere from 50¢ to $50, and turnover figures anywhere from zero to several hundred. They involve books that had to be returned, hardback sales, bestsellers, back-list items—the works. How can you tell anything from that except your *over-all* performance?"

If the truth be told, his mistake is very common. Every day countless business people who keep excellent general financial records are misled by the composite experience they represent, and as a result, make unwise decisions.

In his pioneer work, "Merchandise Management Accounting in Practice," a booklet issued by the New York accounting firm Arthur Anderson and Company, R. I. Jones pointed out that the important level of decision-making for retailers must be the individual item, that reliance on averages tends to obscure the variation of profit on such items, and that without proper cost data the true profit or loss on an individual item cannot be determined. In their book *Retail Merchandise Accounting* (New York: Ronald Press), H. F. Bell and L. C. Moscarello devote an entire chapter to what they call "limitations in the use of percentages," explaining that "individual items sold within the same department do not necessarily incur all the normal layers of cost," and urging closer attention to such costs. [Discussion of the various items making up the cost of doing business will be found in Chapter 10, "Bookkeeping Basics," and Chapter 13, "Financing the Store by Merchandise Budgeting." Mr. Dessauer also treats the matter in great detail in the original *Publishers Weekly* articles from which this excerpt is taken.—ED.]

In order to increase the profitability of a particular title, series, or section, one must compute the applicable income (sales less shrinkage) and deduct cost of sales (list price of goods sold less publisher's discount and transportation cost) to arrive at a gross margin. From this margin the applicable operating expenses must be subtracted.

In some cases such expense can be measured directly. For example, if a particular department, such as the juvenile section, is large enough to have a salesperson assigned to it exclusively, the salary (including fringe benefits) of such a person could be charged entirely to that section. However, if no particular clerk had charge of the children's book corner and nearly everyone in the store occasionally took a hand in helping out with children's books, no such direct charge would be possible.

In the case of most smaller stores, the staff's responsibilities are usually too divided to allow direct measurement of salary costs. The same would be true of most other store expenses, which are too general in nature to apply directly to a particular section, series, or titles. An *allocation,* or proportionate attribution, of the expense is therefore devised to assign a fair share of the cost to the item being measured. For salaries and most other items of expense, the logical basis for making such allocations is in relation to net sales: The costs involved are related to the dollar sales of the particular item, measured in the same proportion as total costs in that category are related to total dollar sales for the store.

Occupancy cost (consisting of rent or real estate expense, amortization of fixtures, repair and maintenance, utilities—except telephone—and property insurance) can and should be measured directly by determining the floor space occupied by the item and assigning the proper portion of total occupancy cost to it. In so doing, one must consider the *period of time* occupied as well as the space, so occupancy expense can be assigned in accordance with a formula that divides total occupancy expense by the proportion of space occupied and then divides the result by the proportion of time (months, weeks, days) as well.

The cost per square foot of selling and stock areas must be weighted to absorb the cost of the non-stocked areas. This can be done simply by counting *only* the selling and stock areas in calculating total square footage, but then charging the *entire* occupancy expense to that net total. Example:

Total area occupied = 2,000 square feet. Books stocked in 1,000 square feet.
Total occupancy cost = $16,500.
Weighted cost per square foot = $16.50.

Furthermore, there is the realization that occupancy must be measured by *floor* space utilized and that therefore the manner in which books are displayed or stored has a bearing on the cost assignment. Multiple-tier shelves, for example, reduce that cost per book compared with flat display on a plain table.

Finally, in assigning costs, allowances must be made for the expense incurred by books that have not sold and have been returned. Personnel, occupancy, and general expenses attributable to such books should not be unfairly assigned to successful titles; otherwise the successes will be punished for the failures and the true costs of the failures will be hidden.

Income and expense analyses on specific titles can demonstrate that even books at short discount can be highly profitable. Consider, for example, technical and business books. These books generally have high list prices, and therefore, with a reasonable turnover and despite a discount of, say, only 30 per cent, they should be able to produce a profit for any store situated in an area where there is a solid demand.

There are fewer returns on such books, they can be displayed spine out, and once the professional and industrial community discovers at least a decent representation of the most important titles, they will begin to regard the store that carries them as a source. Every time a store pleases or attracts a customer, it has a chance to sell him something in addition to what he originally came for. An engineer, technician, or accountant regularly patronizing the store may begin to buy leisure reading, dictionaries, or gifts as well. And if some of the industries in the area can be persuaded to buy the specialized books they need for their executives and libraries from the bookseller, he may also be able to convince them that they should give books as gifts next Christmas.

The book-buying habit, like any other habit, easily becomes addictive. Making friends with the professional people in one's community may develop a whole new market for books.

Earlier we mentioned the tendency of booksellers, and publishers, too, to place excessive emphasis on "big" books that more often than not turn out not to be big at all but to lead instead to heavy, and costly, returns.

The smart bookseller's answer is to buy fewer books and buy them more wisely. It is well to ask the publisher's salesman who says he has a sure-fire best-seller bound to receive front-page reviews everywhere to send an advance copy for examination before ordering, or to place the order subject to confirmation after one is convinced that the title really is going to be a best-seller.

A bookseller should trust his own judgment. The seasonal announcement issues of *Publishers Weekly,* publishers' catalogs, and exhibits at the ABA Convention give an idea of what is forthcoming for the next season, what is supposedly going to be big on the new lists.

Homework is important. Many booksellers make up their own lists of books that they think are worth investigating and then read them.

No one is in a better position than the bookseller himself to choose the right books for his customers, and to supply the judgment, good taste, and business acumen needed to make a profit in bookselling.

Insurance and Protection   **16**

ELWIN B. SCHOEN
Partner, Herbert L. Jamieson & Co.

Although not every bookstore will need, or be able to afford, all of the types of insurance described in this article, it has been developed as a general guide to point out those areas of loss that can confront booksellers and the forms of insurance coverage available to cover them. As a guide it may be well to bear in mind that the 1968 Ernst & Ernst survey of bookstore operating costs shows a mean of .6 per cent of sales for all insurance costs other than employee benefits. Thus a store doing $100,-000 a year will have $600 to spend on business insurance of all kinds.

I. Package Policy

There are certain types of potential loss from which every bookseller will want protection. Fire, Water Damage to stock fixtures, and General Liability are the most important. It is probably to the bookseller's advantage to incorporate into one contract, with a potential saving in premium, the basic Fire and Extended Coverage on buildings, inventory, office furniture, and fixtures and General Liability insurance, together with Crime insurance and Valuable Papers if these latter types of protection are desired.

Having a single policy covering most of the insurable risks offers convenience as well as the possibility of broader over-all protection. Premium rates, of course, vary greatly depending on the location, the type of building, and other variable factors. Workmen's Compensation, and possibly Automobile Liability coverage, will still have to be written separately where required by law.

124

The coverages that may be included in the package policy are:

A. *Fire, Extended Coverage, Vandalism, Sprinkler Leakage, Water Damage*

1. *Insurable Value.*—Insurance valuations may be estimated by using one of three methods:

  a) The bookseller's own property records of building, equipment, and improvements.
  b) An appraisal by the company insuring the property. This is sometimes made without charge by the insurance companies.
  c) A professional appraisal. Done for a fee, this covers all real and personal property except inventories.

It is important that values be recalculated at least annually.

Inventory values are handled differently because of the constant movement of stock in and out and may be determined from the bookseller's own records. It is necessary to decide in advance whether to insure for selling price or cost and so specify in the policy.

The Standard Fire policy insures for the actual cash value of the property at the time of the loss, that is, the cost to repair or replace *less depreciation.* In most cases, however, for a higher premium the policy may be endorsed to insure buildings and improvements on a "repair and replacement" basis, eliminating any deduction for depreciation. The amount of insurance that must be carried is based on the replacement value of the property, subject to the coinsurance percentage.

2. *Coinsurance.*—Fire and other property insurance policies usually contain a coinsurance clause, which states that the amount of insurance carried must be equal to a specified percentage of the full value of the property. When this is done, the full amount of any covered loss will be paid up to the face value of the policy. If, on the other hand, the amount of insurance carried is less than the specified percentage, payment is made for only that portion of the loss determined by the ratio between the amount of insurance carried and the amount that should have been carried. It is, therefore, very important to check the amount of insurance periodically.

To illustrate this, assume that the full value of insured property is $100,000 and a 90 per cent coinsurance clause applies. This means that $90,000 insurance is required; if the policy is indeed written for $90,000, any covered loss up to and including $90,000 will be paid in full. If a total loss occurs, then $90,000—the face amount of the policy—is the maximum amount collectible.

If, on the other hand, only $70,000 insurance is carried, this is only seven-ninths of the required amount and therefore only seven-ninths of any loss will be paid up to $70,000, the face amount of the policy.

3. *Waiver of Subrogation.*—Most policies include a subrogation clause, which says, simply, that if the insurance company pays a loss, the policyholder will assign to the insurance company all his rights to make claim against any other party who may be responsible for the occurrence of the loss.

In certain instances, insurance companies will waive their right to make these subrogation claims; this can be done by naming all concerned parties in the policy or by issuance of a "waiver of subrogation" endorsement by the insurance company.

Since most booksellers occupy leased or rented premises and lessees or renters can be held responsible for fire damage to the building in which their stores are located if the fire originated within their areas, it is most important for the bookseller to limit his liability by requesting the owner to include the bookseller's interest in the owner's policy or obtain a waiver of subrogation from the owner's insurance company.

B. *Loss of Earnings and Extra Expense*

Loss of Earnings coverage is intended to pay for the loss of net profits and continuing overhead resulting from specified kinds of loss, such as Fire, Extended Coverage, Riot, Civil Commotion, Vandalism, or Sprinkler Leakage perils. Individual booksellers, according to their circumstances, will decide whether this type of protection, which is reassuring to have, is within their means.

Extra Expense coverage is sometimes needed where Loss of Earnings is not needed. For example, a store may be able to operate in another location without loss of income but at greater cost. This added cost is insurable under an Extra Expense coverage that usually stipulates a maximum limit of recovery per month on a gradually reducing basis. This, again, would be a matter of individual choice.

C. *Valuable Papers and Records*

Records involving accounting, personnel, taxes, contracts, and numerous other papers, if damaged or destroyed by fire, water, malicious damage, or other perils, may require substantial expense to reproduce. It may even be that reproduction is impossible.

Most Fire policies cover the cost of blank material and the labor required to transcribe damaged records but do not cover the expense of research and preliminary work, which is often the greatest cost. This cost may be covered by an all-risks Valuable Papers and Records policy, if the bookseller feels it is necessary. Smaller stores will probably not require it.

D. *Property in Transit*

The risks of loss or damage to property in transit may be covered by special floater policies to whatever extent is necessary. This subject has to be considered in the light of the bookseller's own method of handling incoming shipments from suppliers (which are the responsibility of the supplier until received) and outgoing (if any) to customers. Many booksellers find that not purchasing insurance from the post office or paying for a floater policy is cheaper in the long run. Some only insure shipments over a predetermined dollar value (say, $15).

II. Liability Insurance

A. *General Liability*

1. *Coverage.*—The basic Comprehensive General Public Liability policy covers the legal liability to members of the public for bodily injury and property damage caused by occurrences arising out of operations, ownership, or use of premises, a type of protection that is absolutely essential.

Although the policy is called "comprehensive," there are certain exposures that are not covered by the basic policy unless specifically added by endorsement. The need varies for these coverages, some of which require nominal additional premium. They include:

a) Personal Injury. The basic policy covers bodily injuries. In addition, however, the firm could be held liable for Personal Injury claims resulting from false arrest, detention or imprisonment, malicious prosecution, libel, slander or defamation of character, invasion of privacy, wrongful eviction, or wrongful entry. For example, an employee falsely accused of dishonesty might institute suit for personal injury. Personal Injury coverage does not include claims resulting from material appearing in advertisements or publications. These must be insured by separate policies.

b) Elevator Collision. If the bookseller is responsible for elevator operation, damage to elevator cars and property in the elevator resulting from a fall down the shaft, or material-handling trucks colliding with the elevators, may be insured for a slight premium.

2. *Limits of Liability.*—In recent years the trend has consistently been toward higher verdicts in cases arising from bodily injury. Recommended minimum Bodily Injury limit is $1 million per occurrence.

Property Damage limits depend a great deal on the locality of the property occupied and any operations performed away from the premises. The occupant of premises can be held legally liable for damage to property of others resulting from the negligent starting of a fire in his premises. The same is true regarding fires in office buildings, where the suggested minimum Property Damage limit would be $100,000.

3. *Contractor's Operations.*—The Comprehensive General Liability policy covers the bookseller's liability arising from operations performed for him by painters, window cleaners, builders, or other independent contractors. Such claims should, however, be the responsibility of the contractor; if he has adequate insurance to cover them, they will not enter the bookseller's experience or affect his premium. It is therefore important to obtain "certificates of insurance" from all contractors, covering not only their General Liability but also Workmen's Compensation and Automobile Liability.

B. *Automobile Insurance*
1. *Coverage.*—All automobile hazards relating to bodily injuries, property damage, and medical payments may be covered under a single automobile policy. However, it is preferable to add these to the Comprehensive General Public Liability policy. The principle exception is in the state of Massachusetts, where a separate statutory automobile policy is required.

It is important that all automotive equipment hazards be insured whether resulting from the maintenance, use, or operation of owned vehicles or the use of non-owned vehicles (that is, vehicles leased, hired, borrowed, or owned by employees and used in company business).

Voluntary Medical Payments coverage of $1,000 is recommended with respect to private passenger automobiles. This makes it unnecessary for guests or customers riding as passengers in a company vehicle to prove negligence in order to recover medical expenses.

2. *Limits of Liability.*—The limits of liability for bodily injuries should be as high as the General Liability limit. It is suggested that a minimum of $500,000/$1,000,000 be the general rule. With respect to property damage, a suggested minimum is $250,000 because of the extensive damage that can be done, particularly by vehicles running into buildings or damaging utility services that affect large numbers of people or operations.

3. *Physical Damage.*—All automobiles and trucks may be insured for material damage (i.e., fire, theft, glass breakage, vandalism, etc.).

C. *Workmen's Compensation*
Workmen's Compensation is legally required by some states. The Standard Workmen's Compensation policy is divided into two sections:

Coverage A offers statutory weekly indemnity, medical reimbursement, and other benefits according to the Workmen's Compensation and Occupational Disease Laws of the various states. These benefits are payable if the employee becomes involved in an accident arising out of and in the course of his employment, whether such accidents occur in or out of the employer's premises.

Coverage B offers coverage of employer's legal liability for work-connected injuries that are not compensable under the various state laws, such as a permanent injury that does not prevent the employee from pursuing his normal work. It also covers suits against the employer by third parties who may have been held responsible for injuries to an employee, contending that the employer was negligent. Coverage B normally has a limit of $100,000, except in certain states where the insurance companies are not permitted to limit this to a fixed amount. Wherever it is so limited, it is suggested that the basic $100,000 be increased to $500,000 for an additional premium.

D. *Umbrella Liability*

Rather than increase limits under primary policies, it may be desirable to investigate the use of a so-called umbrella policy, written by most major casualty insurance companies.

Umbrella policies are designed to provide $1 million or more per loss as excess over all underlying liability policies. Moreover, they cover nearly all exposures to loss that are not included in the underlying policies, but this feature is subject to a deductible or self-insured retention of $1,000 or more.

III. CRIME INSURANCE

This type of insurance may prove impractical to all but the larger operations, but it is included here as a part of the whole insurance picture. Some firms insure losses from infidelity of employees as well as risks of forgery, burglary or robbery of money and securities, and burglary or theft of office equipment. Your insurance agent can supply you with the necessary details.

IV. MISCELLANEOUS COVERAGES

Numerous other forms of insurance are available to cover risks that a bookseller may encounter. Space does not permit detailed explanations of all these coverages; a partial list of them may help point out a possible need.

A. *Accounts Receivable Records*

Loss of income resulting from inability to collect outstanding accounts because of damage or destruction of the records of accounts receivable from almost any cause may be covered under a special policy.

B. *Fine Arts*

Some stores have rare books or valuable paintings and other art objects that would be insured partially under business Fire insurance policies. Frequently, such objects have enhanced value beyond the actual cost of reproduction (in case of fire loss) and may also be subject to other perils, such as breakage and water damage, that are not covered by the basic Fire insurance contract.

C. *Plate Glass*

Ordinarily, the breakage of glass doors, windows, desk tops, partitions, etc., does not represent a serious financial loss and therefore may safely be assumed as a business risk. The premium cost to insure large numbers of such items would more than pay for an occasional breakage. On the other hand, if any of the glass contains valuable or expensive lettering, is of a decorative nature, or is exceptionally large, then an all-risks Plate Glass policy covering these specific items may be indicated.

V. Employee Benefits

The usual forms of employee benefits that a firm may provide include:

A. *Group Life Insurance*

This is usually annual renewable "term" insurance, issued at group rates to all eligible employees without regard to physical condition.

Accidental Death and Dismemberment insurance is often written as a companion coverage to Group Life insurance and provides specified lump-sum benefits for the loss of life, limbs, or sight arising out of occupational or non-occupational accident anywhere in the world.

B. *Accident and Sickness Insurance*

The states of New York, New Jersey, California, and Rhode Island have statutory non-occupational Disability Benefits Laws that require the employers in those states to provide basic benefits for loss of time due to accident or sickness.

Firms that are not in one of four states mentioned above may want Voluntary Group Accident and Sickness policies providing a similar scope of benefits, or self-insure the risk by continuing a disabled employee's salary under a formal or informal salary-continuation plan, usually for a short period of time.

C. *Long-Term Disability*

Many firms have not done anything to protect their employees against "economic death" caused by long-term disability. Extended disability of an employee forces management to make a spot decision on his compensation.

By adopting a Long-Term Disability Plan, management can insure the protection in advance and at the same time not tie up capital or upset existing benefit programs. Any benefits should be carefully integrated with the benefits payable under Social Security or Workmen's Compensation to avoid excessive benefits and keep costs at a minimum.

Such coverage is usually not individually available to small employers but may be secured through participation in the plans offered through the ABA.

D. *Medical Expense Benefits*

There are several approaches to this form of employee benefit, but the two most usual types of plan are:

1. *Basic Hospital-Surgical Benefits* plus supplementary Major Medical coverage. The basic benefits are usually the standard Blue Cross/Blue Shield plan for the area. The Group Major Medical policy fills in the gaps of the Blue Cross/Blue Shield or other base-plan coverage and provides the necessary catastrophe coverage for the serious disabilities. A group plan covering the above benefits is available through the ABA.

2. *Comprehensive Medical Coverage* offers reimbursement for hospital, surgical, doctor, nurse, and other medical expenses for the employee and his family, with a deductible of $100 and a maximum benefit of $250,000 for the lifetime of the person insured. The deductible screens out the small, easily budgetable expenses, and the coinsurance feature, in which benefits over the first $2,000 of hospitalization are paid at the rate of 80 per cent, keeps the cost in line and still provides coverage against the financial drain of serious disabilities.

E. *Business Life Insurance*

A Business Life policy should be considered if the untimely death of a key executive or sole stockholder would represent a serious financial loss to the firm. The proceeds can be used to help bolster the firm's credit, retire the stock interest of the deceased executive, and finance the selection and training of an adequate replacement.

VI. PENSIONS AND PROFIT SHARING

A. *Pensions*

A funded pension plan assures the employee that when he reaches the end of his productive years he will have an adequate retirement benefit that will permit him to live out his retirement in dignity and with financial security. A pension plan is very important from the standpoint of employee relations, both in attracting and holding good personnel. The benefit formula is definite in nature and the employee always knows where he stands regarding his retirement benefits. The retirement benefit, including Social Security, might equal 50–75 per cent of final average pay, although most plans are still on career-average pay.

Of the several recognized methods of providing the funds needed to meet the obligation to pay the retirement benefits, two main ones are:

1. *Pay-As-You-Go.*—This of course is not a funding method at all; you simply charge the cost of pensions against the year in which they are paid to the retired employees. While there would be little or no immediate cost of such a program, in future years it will be an ever-increasing burden on the firm's current profits as more employees reach retirement age. The pay-as-you-go approach represents poor business practice because, in effect, you are charging prior years' operating costs to the current year's profits. Payments into a pension fund are similar to charges for depreciation in equipment and you should charge the human depreciation to the year in which it occurs.

2. *Insured Pension Plans.*—Two forms of insured pension plans are Individual Policy Pension Trust and Deposit Administration.

In the early days of pension plans, the Pension Trust with individual retirement-income policies was the only form of pension funding available for the smaller firms; therefore, they were and still are the most numerous type of plan.

The Deposit Administration plan only guarantees the principal of the fund and the rate at which annuities may be purchased at retirement, but does not guarantee the adequacy of the fund to purchase the annuities when due. This permits greater flexibility in interest assumptions, which reduces the current cost of the plan. Most insurance companies now provide a "separate account" facility. This permits the employer to stipulate how much of his pension money may be invested in a common stock fund managed by the carrier. Usually a firm needs at least eight to ten employees for this option.

Stocking
and Ordering

How To Order   17

ROBERT DIKE BLAIR

The Vermont Book Shops (Middlebury, Waitsfield, and Burlington), and Vermont Books: Publishers.

Before we get into the basic mechanics of ordering books, let me offer a short personal sermon. After some fifteen years of publishing under the imprint Vermont Books and selling almost entirely to other Vermont stores, we published *Vermont Sampler* by poet-humorist Walter Hard, and *Life* ran a six-page article on him. And then *New England Laughs*—a paperback by E. D. Asselin—caught on and became a staple with northeastern bookstores.

As a result, we began to receive orders from many stores around the country. I was amazed and discouraged to discover how many of these orders were illegible, unclear, or simply not business-like. Some were long, chatty letters—to order perhaps one paperback. Quite a few were scrawled on blank paper without even a rubber-stamped name. Where we had both a paper- and hardbound edition, all too many orders did not specify which to send.

These are two fundamental rules for ordering: The order *must* be clear, and the process *not* wasteful of time.

Both will be served if you use a well-designed order form. Unless you have some particular reason not to, I strongly urge that you use the ABA Combination Order-Invoice Form, which you can get from the ABA, or have your local printer make up a similar form with extra space for information you might want. Publishers are accustomed to this form. They know where to look for special instructions without reading through a lot of fine print. It's an old friend to them. Please use it.

If printed forms seem too expensive, at least have a rubber stamp made of the store name and address and the words: "Please send at best trade discount."

Ordering Procedures

Organizing your orders. Set up whatever logical procedure seems best for you and follow it always until it becomes second nature. You will have stock control slips or cards of some kind, and notes on books you've seen reviewed in *PW,* locally, or requested by customers. These all should be uniform in size. (We use 3" X 5" cards for stock control and memo slips the same size. The notched cards placed inside paperbacks for control by some publishers and jobbers are also this size.) All go temporarily into three open files ("mass paper," "trade paper," and "cloth") with dividers listing major publishers and smaller publishers alphabetically, with the slips to be ordered first up-ended so they stand out like sore thumbs.

Another method: Write titles in a loose-leaf notebook, Atheneum and Arco on page A, Bobbs and Beacon on page B, etc. Clip special orders to appropriate page. Cross out titles as ordered. [*See also* Chapter 11, "Inventory Control."]

Where to order. You almost certainly will order from wholesalers and also direct from publishers. With each individual title you order, the question is: Wholesaler or publisher? In general, wholesalers get the books to you *more quickly,* and you have only one order form and invoice to process rather than many. Disadvantages: Wholesalers by necessity have a limited stock and may well be out of many of the titles you order, and their discount very often is less than that of the publisher. Contact (or, preferably, visit) wholesalers in your area listed in the *ABA Book Buyer's Handbook* to learn their service and terms.

- If you need a current or standard stock book quickly, and you're willing to accept the wholesale discount, order from the wholesaler.
- If the book is from a publisher who gives prompt service, and you have other titles to order to bring the discount to 40 per cent, or if it is not a title you'd expect the jobber to have, order from the publisher.

The primary reason for buying from jobbers is fast service, but if the jobber is out of the book, you've lost a week's time. When you must go direct to the publisher, try to have accumulated titles to order that you do not need at once in order to qualify for full discount.

How to order. Be certain your order can be understood by the order-fillers (many booksellers think these people often can barely read and write). A minute's research at this point can save much time later: Does the book come in both paper *and* cloth? Does it carry a text (rather than trade) discount? Or both? You must specify which you want. With technical or textbook titles, citing author and International

Standard Book Number (ISBN) helps, and with large publishers this is a good idea in any case.

Paperbacks: In series, give the title's series number (e.g., Anchor: A208). Some jobbers insist on book numbers for all mass-market paperbacks. If ordering both cloth *and* paper books from one publisher, put them on separate sheets (you still will get incorrect shipments).

If your title information is incomplete, add notes: "Ship only if under $10 retail," or "If hardbound is o.s. [out of stock], paperback is acceptable." Be sure the note is not ambiguous.

How soon will you receive the books? Your distance from the source obviously determines the shipping time, and you should figure two days for your order to reach the publisher in the first place. In 1964, ninety-seven bookstores kept careful records for one month of fulfillment times for all shipments. Based on these statistics, the New York accounting firm of J. K. Lasser & Co., in their summary titled "Order Fulfillment Study," reported thirteen days as the median time elapsed between order and delivery. Of this, the publishers' processing took four working days (not counting weekends). SCOP orders took slightly less time, and large orders (twenty or more titles) took two more days to process. The service is no faster today.

Rush orders. The Lasser report showed that writing "Rush!" on an order had little or no effect. When special-handling shipment was specified, the publishers' processing time was reduced by about a day (apparently they try harder on such orders), and time in transit should be reduced too.

Telephone orders. Say, at once, "This is a bookstore calling long distance. I want to place an order." Ask whether books are in stock, when they can be shipped, and note the order-taker's name in case of error.

Mass-market paperbacks often seem a lot of effort for a small dollar gross, but do show a good profit margin when ordered direct (40 per cent discount, with the books "laid in"—no transportation charge). Minimum order direct usually is twenty-five books (with sometimes a minimum of three or five per title). You may find a local magazine jobber who'll give fast service, though at a lower discount. Some of the larger wholesalers give 40 per cent for fifty books.

Wherever you order, please be sure your orders are clear and can be understood. It's so important!

Wholesale Bookselling   **18**

HARRY T. HOFFMAN
Ingram Book Co.,
Nashville, Tennessee

An effective trade wholesaler can be extremely helpful in making your sales and profit objectives. In fact, if you can find an effective wholesaler, he should become your major source of supply. The question of how best to use your wholesaler is a difficult one to answer. Many stores use a wholesaler to "fill in" on current and back-list titles when their inventory becomes low and they need books rapidly. Other stores are more wholesaler-oriented and order more of their total needs from the wholesaler because they believe that in the long run the single source concept—one order for books of many publishers, one shipment, one invoice, and one check—offsets any additional discounts they may earn by buying direct from a publisher.

It is perhaps most important to know what you can expect from an effective trade wholesaler and in turn what he will expect from you.

What To Expect from an Effective Wholesaler

There is no overabundance of effective wholesalers who specialize in serving the retail trade. All told, there are not more than six or seven that have the resources to carry the inventory quantities necessary to fill retailers' needs. Fortunately, the six or seven are distributed so that virtually every section of the country is fairly well covered. These wholesalers who specialize in serving retailers generally have in stock the current and back-list titles that account for the greatest percentage of total book sales. The theory of 20 per cent of the titles doing 80 per cent of the volume is especially true in the publishing industry and the chances are that the major trade wholesalers will have the 20 per cent in stock. So the first thing that you should expect from your trade wholesaler is an in-depth inventory of those titles that will comprise up to 80 per cent of your total volume.

Rapid shipment is the second thing that you should expect of your wholesaler. Most major wholesalers will ship your order within twenty-four hours after the order is received. Retailers should relate the capability of wholesalers to ship quickly to their own over-all need to turn their inventory rapidly. Consideration should be given as to what additional inventory turns mean to a retailer in terms of the cost of tying up money in inventory. In today's economy, 15 per cent is a conservative figure when it comes to analyzing how much inventory costs. Most profitable stores attempt to turn their investment in inventory at least 4.3 times a year. An effective wholesaler can offer a very positive contribution to attaining this objective.

The third thing to expect from your wholesaler is really intangible, yet extremely important. This is personal service. You should be able to "reach" your wholesaler in terms of solving problems that may occur. Although there are many publishers with excellent customer service departments, wholesalers, with a smaller base of customers, will in general give you more attention. Service is one of the main reasons for the wholesaler's existence, and problems that occur are generally handled promptly and courteously.

To summarize, a retailer should expect three things from his wholesaler:

1. An in-depth inventory of titles that will comprise a large percentage of the retailer's total sales.
2. Rapid delivery of these titles.
3. Excellent personal service in handling individual problems as they occur.

What a Wholesaler Expects from a Retailer

Retailers should realize that a trade wholesaler operates on an extremely small profit margin. The old cliché—"I don't make much money but I sell an awful lot of books"—is more fact than fiction when discussing wholesaling. It is probably the major reason why there are not more effective trade wholesalers in the country today. In view of this, and because it is important for wholesalers to remain financially healthy, it is important that retailers look to the wholesaler as "partners in distribution." By understanding the need for a wholesaler to be as efficient as possible in order to remain viable, the retailer can help his partner in several ways. There are three very basic considerations: ordering, returns, and payment.

When ordering from a wholesaler, it is important to place your order as he designates. Each wholesaler probably has a "best way" to receive an order based on his particular internal order-processing system. If you will discover this best way and place your orders accordingly, not only will you receive better service, but you will be helping your wholesaler keep his order-processing costs down.

Returns are always a problem for retailers, publishers, and wholesalers. The wholesaler, however, is probably most affected by retailer returns because he must handle the returned book at least five times. He must handle it when it is originally received from the publisher, when it is placed on his shelves, when it is shipped to the retailer, when it is received as a return from the retailer, and when it is put back on his shelf or returned to the publisher. All of this handling of a book, plus the paper work involved, immediately makes the transaction unprofitable. To try to offset the cost of this unprofitable transaction, most wholesalers will penalize retailers for returns by charging a handling charge. While wholesalers understand the need to make some returns, they feel that returns should be very minimal. The ability of wholesalers to get books to retailers rapidly should offset the need for excessive volume buying. In a way, this may appear to be contradictory, for wholesalers do want large orders. However, if a retailer uses his wholesaler effectively, he will not order a six-month supply of a title at one time. He will order enough to cover his immediate needs, taking into consideration consumer demand (sometimes difficult) and length of time it takes to receive another order (not so difficult when dealing with a wholesaler).

The final major consideration a wholesaler expects from a retailer is that the retailer meet his payment requirements. Wholesalers believe that it is only fair for retailers to pay on time in view of the service a wholesaler offers. Because of the rapid delivery provided by wholesalers, a retailer should be able to increase his return on investment and should be literally willing to pay for the service he is being rendered by paying bills promptly. In view of today's cost of borrowing money, along with the low margins with which a wholesaler must work, it is absolutely essential that his money not be tied up in accounts receivable.

Also, because of the wholesalers' need for a good cash flow, dating programs are usually out of the question. Throughout the peak seasons, when dating is frequently most desirable, an effective wholesaler should be in a good enough inventory position to supply books in demand without requiring retailers to stock excessive quantities; therefore requests for dating by retailers of wholesalers are generally not considered.

To summarize, a wholesaler expects three things from a retailer:

1. Retailers should be aware of how the wholesaler with whom he works wants to receive orders. By following the ordering re-

quirements of the wholesaler, the retailer can be assured of better service and a healthy wholesaler.

2. Returns, while generally accepted by wholesalers, should be kept at a minimum. The handling and rehandling of each order, plus the paper work involved, can lead to hard times for the wholesaler.

3. Payment should be made to wholesalers within their stated terms. Delayed payment can play havoc with a wholesaler's cash position and can be the chief factor in his demise. Pay on time and don't ask for dating.

Improving book distribution. Most major trade wholesalers feel very strongly about their responsibilities in improving distribution. Most of them are convinced that the economies effected by publishers and retailers working more with wholesalers can make publishing, retailing, and wholesaling more profitable. Most major trade wholesalers believe that the key to effective book distribution is the wholesaler, and they are taking positive steps to improve the distribution process. These steps include adding data-processing equipment to make order-handling more efficient, adding titles to their inventory in order to offer a greater selection to retailers, adding mass paperbacks to their inventory to give additional sources of supply to retailers, building warehouses in strategic locations to be closer to retailers, and making more information available through catalogs, brochures, and microfiche to assist retailers in planning their orders. In general, wholesalers are directing their efforts toward improving the distribution process. They can succeed if retailers and publishers will consider them partners.

The Publisher's Rep   **19**

RICHARD H. NOYES
Chinook Bookshop,
Colorado Springs, Colorado

Buying a new season's titles well in advance of publication can be one of the most fascinating aspects of retail bookselling. It is an art form of sorts, with many subtleties. It is one of the things that the owner or manager of a smaller store often wishes to handle himself. There are some booksellers who prefer to order "cold" from catalogs, ads, and reviews without the personal advice, counsel, and support of the publisher's field representative. I cannot imagine why.

The capable publisher's salesman is a valuable ally because he is frequently the retail bookseller's chief source of contact with the publisher. We are sorry for those booksellers whose stores are too small or too remote to have the privilege of visits from a full contingent of reps on a regular basis. Their professional competence and integrity are of first importance.

One could sketch the ideal trade publisher's rep as follows:

He is at least reasonably well educated; a reader, of course, and at home in a number of subject areas. He is sincerely empathetic with retail bookselling, and knowledgeable about it. Convinced of the importance and quality of his product, he believes in the basic integrity of the house, or houses, he represents.

The good salesman will have read the books he sells and will have formed his own opinion of their quality and sales potential in his territory. He will have attempted to determine just who is going to buy each title and for what reasons. Of course he respects the bookseller's judgment and the individuality of each account, yet he will feel obligated to question the bookseller's order if it is considerably over or under what he thinks it should be.

The good salesman will be completely informed of the sales aids available to the bookseller and the promotional literature his company is offering. He is eager to help the bookseller sell books, by suggesting statement stuffers, cooperative advertising, and other material available from his publisher.

The conscientious rep maintains contact with his accounts between visits, informing them of special discounts, dating on stock offers, last-moment publicity efforts, sleeper titles, and so forth. The publisher or publishers he represents respect his judgment and he can be effective in helping to solve their shipping, billing, and returns problems with the stores. He recognizes the errors of overselling and overbuying and the problem of returns, and looks forward to a profitable long-term association with his accounts.

Finally, the rep serves as a valuable source of information and scuttlebutt about bookselling and booksellers in his territory, and about interesting developments in the trade in general.

Some Questions About Reps

If these are accepted standards for the ideal publisher's representative, you might use them as a yardstick to evaluate the men and women who call on you. You might ask yourself some of these questions when a rep next visits you:

Can he relate his new season's list (and his back list) specifically to your store and to the peculiarities of your town and area?

All too often a rep will come into your store as though he's wearing blinders. Statements like: "I don't know if you can handle expensive art books," or "If you do anything with quality fiction," may indicate that he hasn't even bothered to look around.

A wise rep makes the effort to study the records of your past purchases, to familiarize himself with your inventory and layout, and even to find out something about your community. A few hardbound copies of Nikki Giovanni's and Diane Wakoski's poetry on your shelves can suggest that his publisher's newest volume of avant-garde poetry is worth mentioning. Perhaps books on aircraft and aviation in general are particularly saleable because a flying school happens to be in your town. Maybe the rep's new gardening book and baking cookbook will only end up in your returns, simply because they were written for a different climate and elevation.

Has the representative related his new list to the season's offerings of other publishers?

It's not too much to expect of him; he can study *PW*'s seasonal announcement numbers. It is important to know, for example, that his publisher's new pictorial history of handball is the only new title on the subject. Though the six new novels on his list are receiving "major promotion from coast to coast," are they truly that saleable in competition with the numerous fiction offerings of many other publishers?

Can the rep place a new nonfiction title in the perspective of the other titles currently available in that subject area?

The fact that his new manual of falconry is the only one ever devoted to the techniques used in North America is important information in areas where that hobby may be popular.

Is the rep aware that his new fondue cookbook has twice as many recipes and is $2 less expensive than any other available book on the subject?

Has he simply memorized the prepackaged, and perhaps overoptimistic, sales information spoon-fed by his editors during the periodic sales conferences, or has he actually questioned the editors, his sales manager, and his favorite booksellers, and perhaps even checked with the *Subject Guide to Books in Print?*

Trade book publishers are all competing for the space on your shelves. The representative who is not able to relate a new title to other books in the field is asking you to order on blind faith. It's like a rep who says, "I don't know anything about children's books, but this one looks cute." Why does he bother to visit you if he can offer no more than the hackneyed prose of his publisher's catalog, using exactly the same adjectives and superlatives?

Is the representative professionally honest enough to present his offerings candidly and avoid the sins of overselling?

Excessive returns do not reflect well on his record, and they are expensive mistakes for the bookseller as well. Most reps remain in their territory for some time; a buyer's memory can challenge an elephant's if he feels he's been the victim of a misrepresentation.

One experienced buyer has suggested that "each book you order should be forever." Certainly you will want to be bolder than usual sometimes and order a single copy of an off-beat title, but you should never order any amount of any title with the reasoning that "it can always be returned later."

The competent rep will realize that the size of the initial order is less important than a judicious sampling of a wide range of titles. More significant is the ability of a store's stock-control system to respond quickly when a title suddenly catches on. The availability of a good jobber in the region also lessens the need for heavy initial orders. The publisher who grants additional discount for the total quantity of your whole season's order, rather than for the quantity of a single title, best serves the interests of the small and medium-sized bookstores.

Is your representative enough of a professional to review your seasonal stock orders with you in detail, or does he just check in for his routine "pitch" a few times a year.

If you have an unusual question about a new title, which he himself cannot answer, he should be willing to query his home office and call you or send you a card with the information you need.

It is certainly not out of order for you to request galley proofs of a title that is of special interest to you and your area, but in fairness to the publisher you should realize that advance galleys are very expensive and not make such requests unless a favorable reading will be worth while in terms of sales.

If you ask your rep to go out on the floor and check your stock for his titles, he should do so thoroughly, weeding out deadwood and following through to see that you receive the credit to which you are entitled. In short, you should expect full personalized professional service from your publisher's rep, such as your customers expect from you and your staff every day.

When you hear such pat phrases as "major advertising and promotion," "coast-to-coast appearances," and "one-free-for-ten," sit back, put down your ordering pencil, and ask a few questions.

Exactly where will the author appear and when? Is it definite that he will be on Johnny Carson's "Tonight Show" or is this just wishful thinking on the part of the publisher? Where and in what media will all that advertising money be spent? If the ad budget is $10,000, for example, $1,000 or more must be used just to advertise to the trade. What is left is not a large amount in view of today's advertising rates, and in any event, will two or three ads in the *New York Times* really help the sale of the book that much out your way?

An additional copy free when you order ten copies sounds like a nice extra, but remember that the cost of that copy to the publisher is allocated to the title's ad budget, which decreases it even further. If you're going to order ten copies anyway, then be certain to claim your extra free one, but if five or fewer are what you intended to order, you are almost always wrong to increase the quantity.

There are a number of phrases you'll learn to hear with skepticism: "Our editor says this guy is the next Vonnegut." "You remember his last book was a best-seller." "This won the Prix Goncourt in France last year." "This is the year for it; you can't have too many." "This is another *Jonathan Livingston Seagull.*" "Our advance is ——." "Order five and see what happens." "We're really gonna get behind this one." And then, the ultimate putdowns: "If you can't sell this . . ." and "Your competitor down the street bought two hundred copies."

If you're the owner of a store just getting started, the pressures on your time and energies are particularly great. Pause on occasion and consider how to make the hours you spend with the publishers' reps more productive.

A bookseller in California asks her representatives to "talk through" the catalog all the way before she decides what title and what quantities she will order. She feels that on the second time through the catalog she is better able to bring the various titles (and the representative) into perspective.

Another experienced bookseller-buyer prefers to order with the rep as he turns the pages of the publisher's catalog. He writes down a variety of data in the margins, and this specially annotated copy of the catalog is circulated among his sales staff, after which it is filed in an accessible spot for quick reference. He finds he can control the pace of the sales interview by turning the pages himself and can also better judge the salesman's presentation; he is unimpressed if the rep consistently uses the same words and descriptions that are in the catalog.

However, the bookseller should remember that the publisher's rep has his pressures and problems, too. He is in the middle, and often that's a delicate role. He must live with his own home office and its internal problems, as well as with you and yours. It is his publisher who pays his expenses, salary, and bonuses, and surely his house has a right to expect that more of its books will be sold because of the representative's visit. Yet possibly he has been assigned sales quotas that are too high or geographically unrealistic, or has been misled about a title's real importance. Perhaps he has interceded for you in a special billing situation, and his credit department's typically negative and inflexible policies have not helped his cause or yours.

The "with it" publisher will invest a lot of faith in his salespeople and give them much responsibility. Representatives should be authorized to approve returns on the spot, for example, and the home-office machinery should respond to their requests for help in straightening out a store's paper-work problems.

The "with it" bookseller will recognize that he has an obligation, also, to assure an open and creative line of communication between himself and the rep. It all boils down to a matter of common courtesy. If you've made an advance appointment with him, be there on time with an open mind and be candid. Remember, he works on a tight travel schedule. Give him your order then and there if you can, or confirm it promptly. Don't waste his time—it's valuable, too. Show some interest in him personally. Just as you are turned off by a pompous, hard-sell approach, so can your manner help or hinder positive communication. In the words of one of our favorite reps, "I've got a delicate ego, too. If a bookstore plays it square and shows a little friendliness, I'll stand on my head to help."

How To Get Through Christmas in a Small Bookshop

20

GODDARD LIGHT
Lighthouse Bookstore,
Rye, New York

In discussing our preparations for the Christmas season, when we do better than one-third of our year's business, it should be noted that ours is a very small suburban shop, employing during the regular part of the year just one other full-time person in addition to myself.

I am very certain that the single most important thing at Christmas (or at any time) is staff: with a good staff the battle is half won. In the fall we begin adding to our staff so that by the end of November we have three additional salespeople on the floor at all times, and for the last week before Christmas at least two, sometimes as many as four, other part-time helpers. These latter are college students home for the holidays.

Over the years our staff has included a former secretary of Andrew Mellon, as well as the wives of a lawyer, a professor, a banker, an ad man, a cartographer, and an editor, among others.

Money is a factor, certainly, but I would feel that most of our people like the idea of working in a bookstore and I am sure that some of them would not have worked at all anywhere else. They frequently have come in and asked if we could use them. More often we suggest to a customer whom we frequently see or to a neighbor that we could use an extra hand at Christmas time. Those working for us or who have worked for us make suggestions. Only once have we had to run an ad for sales help. What with college and high school students available, we've had quite a variety. I am sure that every store has had its selection of interesting and knowledgeable people.

It hasn't always been this way—four or five of us on the floor at Christmas. This began as a one-man shop with a part-timer at Christmas. Then we grew, not in size but in volume, and the staff had to grow as well.

Years ago, the mayor of our town was in the store one day before Christmas and I was bragging—or carrying on, at least—about how hard I worked: " . . . at the store until 2:00 and 3:00 A.M. . . . checking stock, writing orders, posting charges . . . and up again at 7:00 A.M. . . . to the store . . . phoning . . . " I was younger then. It must have been pretty boring.

The mayor said, "It doesn't sound as if you manage things very well."

I was deflated and mad—but he was right. I still bring work home, but I'm now out of the store at closing time or shortly thereafter. Not that I don't work Sundays; I do, and I take no time off during the week, at least at Christmas time. But the 3:00 A.M. bit is long since over and it is good that it is. The hard fact, however, is that I still *like* doing things myself, which is a bad habit for a businessman to get into. This is one of the main reasons, I would suspect, that I have remained and prefer to remain small.

With some difficulty I have learned to turn some things over to someone else, and surprisingly, they get done. Twice when I have been out sick—once I was out from early November right up to Christmas week—they got done very well, indeed. This too was a shock to my ego. The whole thing should have fallen apart.

Christmas planning must start January 1. After Christmas I try if possible to keep most of my Christmas staff on, staggering the work so that there are sometimes as many as five part-timers making up one week's work, plus a day off for me. I try to use one or the other of them more during vacations or at periods when we need an extra hand around, particularly at billing times. Presuming that all my help are willing to play it this way, we can go into the following Christmas with a thoroughly trained staff. Sometimes it doesn't work!

For years I had flattered myself with the thought that this was a small shop and that if worse came to worse (which, of course, it did) I could run the whole damn thing myself. Well, I now know that this can no longer be a one-man shop, *ever,* and that planning for Christmas help must start somewhere around January 1, which it does.

I would put first, then, in preparing for Christmas, the assembling of a good staff, sufficiently large to get through the toughest day one can expect.

Ordering Non-Book Items

As for planning stock, I'll begin with some non-book items (so if your shop carries books only, skip this). Non-book items are easier than books are to plan for in advance. It is easier to know what to buy. They are more predictable. Who really knows what practically unheralded book (and every year there are several) is going to take off, leaving you, the jobber, the publisher, everybody, without stock two weeks before Christmas? But cards, stationery, and related items can and should be ordered in the spring or early summer.

We keep a detailed control book for all counter Christmas cards and insist that our suppliers send only those quantities that our past performance indicates as being warranted. We've had some pretty severe battles trying to convince them that we mean just what we say. The hope is that they are now convinced.

What we want is last year's sales in cards, plus 20 per cent, less the carry-over. Hallmark, like some other card companies, makes a very good control book in which this information can be kept. The trouble is that some salesmen seem to be very poor in arithmetic; so we now do the figuring ourselves. Since we order Christmas counter cards from sixteen different companies, we can end up with quite a lot of merchandise we don't want if we're not careful. We also carry a complete assortment of gift wrappings.

In recent years we have done a very nice business in imported Advent calendars. These should be in the hands of the recipients before December 1, so we have them on display early in October, and fortunately, the space devoted to them becomes available again before the peak Christmas rush. We order these from Mainzer and Wilkinson. (For addresses of these and other suppliers, see *ABA Sidelines Directory*.) Engagement calendars are another important item.

Personal greeting (PG) books we put out as they arrive, and most of them are in by late August. We have a back room which for most of the year is used as an office but which during Christmas we call our "PG room" and where we also put our everyday card racks during this and other holiday seasons.

We offer no discount for early ordering, though our biggest competitor, a gift shop across the street, does, but we were surprised and delighted to take a thousand-card order once in July. When they started giving discounts, we were sorely tempted to follow suit, for it seemed to us likely that their policy of giving 10 per cent off on card orders placed before November 1 might hurt us. We didn't, and it didn't. Dollar volume went up 4 per cent.

For some years, Charles Anderson in neighboring Larchmont has been preparing a list of PG card companies with which he deals, and the way they perform. The current list can be had by writing the American Booksellers Association. It is extremely helpful in building a department.

It cannot be said, however, that PG customers just walk in, particularly if there is, as with us, serious competition nearby. We spend more money for PG advertising in the fall than for anything else. We assume, perhaps mistakenly, that people know we sell books. We also want them to know that they can get locally, here, as fine a selection of Christmas cards as they will find in neighboring White Plains or in any of the big New York department stores. We now have such a selection, but in some instances it was a struggle to get it. Many top companies are reluctant to sell the small bookstore. And it has taken a great deal of letter-writing to get the good selection we have.

In August we start addressing a mailing to anybody who has ever ordered cards from us in the past, urging them to "come in and do it early—do it beautifully—do it *now!*" We'll send these out the first week in October. Most of the major card companies make such a mailing piece, and many of our customers thank us for reminding them and respond by coming in and getting this part of Christmas out of the way early. As anybody knows who has ever handled PG's, this can be a big help in reducing the number of last-minute orders.

The question of how long to leave PG books out is a matter of geography—how close you are to your source of supply and how dependable your mails are. (The slow companies we remove at Thanksgiving.) When we can phone in the order to a company in the vicinity and get United Parcel delivery, we display the company's PG book until practically the last day. We have even taken one order the day after Christmas for a customer who sent cards out at New Year's.

We keep a record book from year to year on all of these sales indicating name, address, phone, quantity, card company, and price. If we haven't seen a regular customer by the middle of November, we get on the telephone to him.

How We Begin Ordering Books

The foregoing might lead one to believe that maybe we don't sell any books at all. Actually, Christmas PG's account for only about 8 per cent of our annual volume, but since there is no investment in stock, it is a nice bonanza at a 50 per cent discount. However, fundamentally we are a bookstore. Books provide the satisfaction of feeling that we are actually contributing something to the community. We like them, and the fact that a living can be made selling them is so much icing on the cake. Despite problems, it is a good life, except at Christmas, when it can be grueling.

I recently met a woman who had been in the trade. Hearing that I had a bookstore, she said, "Bookselling isn't a business. It's a way of life." Well, maybe it is, but it better have a bit of business in it, too. The guy she used to work for had to close his doors; he couldn't pay the rent.

It is difficult to begin ordering books for Christmas. I don't think there can be a rule of thumb for them as there is for cards. For quite a few years now, I've been going to the ABA Convention in June. Although I do very little buying at the time, it does help greatly to see how the fall season is going to shape up.

No later than August it is good to look at the *ABA Hardbound Basic Book List.* Basic stock has a way of going out of stock and not being replaced. In October you just won't get to it. The fall juveniles begin to appear in August, and we order them as they are published. The big adult titles generally come along later.

We spend a whole night with the *PW* "Fall Announcement Number" as soon as it comes out. Then the complete fall picture will have to begin taking shape: What to do about the window, newspaper advertising, getting out mailings, and most important of all, what to order— what to order just to have and what to order in quantity and get behind and push.

Since we deal almost exclusively with a jobber and see very few salesmen, there are titles we miss and quantities that we underestimate, which we pick up as reviews begin to appear. The Sunday and daily editions of the *New York Times* are our biggest help in this.

By this time of the year it is almost a full-time job to keep up with publishers' catalogs as they come in. These, too, play a major part in our thinking when we order. As with everyone else, we order with the intention of selling, *not returning.* Returns, which we make twice a year—January and July—amount to only about 2 per cent of our annual purchases. Since net profits have been taking a beating for some time, what we can save on penalties for returns is so much money in the bank.

Toward the end of September, we begin to think about how we are going to accommodate all the merchandise we already have and are shortly to be receiving. We have no basement, so slow-moving items go on higher shelves or in the back of bins. Reserve supplies go home to the garage. Whatever painting and refurbishing we are going to do for the year will have to have been done. It is a question now of making the maximum use of limited space—pointing toward the big three weeks before Christmas.

The whole year really depends on this—a time when you do more in one day than you do in most weeks during the rest of the year, and reorder much more in a week than in a normal month. It can be a bad year and Christmas will pull it out. Or a good beginning can go down the drain, as it almost did with us one year, when the main street was torn up in September in order to put an electrical conduit underground, and then through the first week in December had to be repaved from one end of the business section to the other.

Getting the Show on the Road

For several years we held a book fair at a local private school, usually after Thanksgiving, which grossed upward of $3,000. We gave 20 per cent to the school mothers who handled it for their school fund.

This is, of course, not an ideal time to do a book fair, but the school wanted it then so we did it. We have, in the past, had as many as three fall book fairs. It was murder and we have had to give them up.

Our Christmas window goes in the first week in December at the time the general Christmas festivities of the business community begin. We have a Christmas-window "artistic director," a neighbor who once a year puts her creative talents to work in our behalf. Once a customer bought the entire set of decorative material she had made—bought it *after* Christmas—and had us pack up the whole shebang and send it to her daughter in England. This window also won first prize in the local Chamber of Commerce competition.

The important thing about a Christmas window—or any window at any time—is that it be eye-catching enough to make the passer-by look, stop, and, most important of all, take note of the goodies that are there for just about everybody on the Christmas list. Our window is loaded, artistically of course, with books—really quite jammed.

We feel that a book attractively gift-wrapped is a good advertisement for our store. Without going overboard on this, we do try to have an eye-catching Christmas gift-wrapping, which we have in the store in summer waiting to be used. The fact that we will gift-wrap *and mail* does help business; and a lot of this business comes by telephone. It is always a source of wonder to me how much telephone business there is, and how often the judgment on what book to send is left up to us. We charge for the postage.

We make quite a thing out of publishers' prepublication and pre-Christmas offers, giving over a major part of our nonfiction flat display space as well as part of every November and December window to them. We make our own slit cards:

SPECIAL

BEFORE XMAS $14.95

LATER $17.50

Generally we variously display around thirty titles in this way. It would help if all publishers would let these special prices run until Christmas and then go to the regular price. When there is a variety of cut-off dates—from late November until April of the following year—and when the publisher changes his mind in midstream, as he frequently does, it makes for confusion and continuous checking every time stock comes in. If a publisher puts the special price and the cut-off date on a clippable corner of the jacket, as many of them do, with the regular price underneath, this is a very big help indeed.

Another great help is the "Pre-Publication and Pre-Christmas Special Price Offers" list prepared every fall by the ABA and sent to all members. This list is a survey of all publishers and includes publication date, title, pre-pub or pre-Christmas price, regular price, and cut-off date of the special price, and is arranged alphabetically by title. Every year there are over a hundred such offers. Distribution of the list is generally made early in November, late enough to reflect publishers' changes and early enough to be of service when it is really needed.

We do not sneer at the so-called coffee table books. Some of our best-selling Christmas books are among the high-priced gift items, and not only the ones with pre-pub prices. If it is a good book on a subject somebody wants, the price (at Christmas time) is not a deterrent. Sometimes it is a help, as for example when a customer *wants* to spend $15 on Uncle Frank. Many of these books are beautifully produced. The fact that they sell means something. People are buying them—art books, boating books, the Sierra Club Books. It takes an awful lot of paperbacks to make up the price of one $25 item, and sometimes a lot more work and salesmanship. I'm not faulting the paperback, but at Christmas we set our sights higher and that is where our customers seem to want our sights to be.

Wholesalers at Christmas

If our jobber has it, we have it; if he doesn't . . . ? The fact that our store is served by a local jobber with frequent truck service is a boon I would wish for every small bookseller in the country. As long as our jobber has stock, we have it. And unless there is reason to order in big quantities to take advantage of pre-pubs or for purposes of display, there is no need to have any title pile up. A few day's supply is all we want or need.

When to stop taking special orders is a nagging question, the answer to which will depend largely on one's local circumstances and even then cannot be answered with certainty. Taking orders on books we do not have in stock represents around 25 per cent of our annual volume. Even the largest store cannot have every book currently in print, and it is my understanding that the large store also depends heavily on special orders. Having a well-stocked jobber who delivers daily is a great help. We can say to any customer right up to the day before Christmas, "If our jobber has it, we will have a copy for you tomorrow afternoon." Surprisingly, this covers us on about 50 per cent of the books we are asked for but do not have.

But, what about the other 50 per cent? Until almost two weeks before Christmas, we promise pre-Christmas delivery—either overnight from our jobber or, barring calamity, from the publisher if he ships from the New York–New England area. One year we hit calamity mainly because of the horrible mail service. Our customers' patience and understanding in that year of disaster was a thing to wonder at.

From about three weeks before Christmas, we mark every special order we take either "At Once" or "Wants." "At Once" means that the customer will only accept delivery if our jobber has the book and we can have it in the store the next day. "Wants" means that the customer will accept delivery even if the book arrives after Christmas. About half of our customers tell us to do the best we can and they will take their chances. Frequently we give them an ABA gift certificate to cover them in the event that the book does not arrive in time.

We mark on all orders to publishers at this time: "Rush—for Xmas —Thanks!" And this seems to mean something. We frequently get better action out of publishers' shipping departments at this very hectic time of the year than we do at any other time. Right here might be a good point at which to say, "Thanks, fellows!"

The last day and after. The last shopping day before Christmas can be one of the best. For us and other booksellers we know, it has frequently been by far the biggest day of the year. We plan for it accordingly. We have one extra person on the floor and we do the best we can to have a complete stock. By the end of the day, our shelves are all but empty. Big ticket items, some of which we have just been watching sit there all fall, are gone—most of them. This is generally a great day for small stocking stuffers, and for cartoon and humor books— "something nutty for Dad." On a really good day before Christmas, just about everything but the shelves can go and, of course, everybody wants everything gift-wrapped, separately. It's pretty wild! But we have already set up an extra set of wrapping facilities where the PG books had been and we get through the day.

How to get through Christmas *easily* is, I guess, something nobody knows. When it's over, I always feel a trifle sad, almost reluctant to leave —like after a good vacation—locking the front door Christmas Eve. Sometimes I go next door and have a drink with the barber before going home. It's all over. For ten months it will be just the everyday running of a store. There won't be the same excitement, but there won't be all that work and that worry about deliveries. The question really is, how do any of us ever get through it? It's a testament to human fortitude that we do.

The January Cleanup*   **21**

AMERICAN BOOKSELLERS ASSOCIATION STAFF

The dust should not have been allowed to settle on the cash register Christmas Eve without your having thought about how you're going to clean up your inventory during the weeks that follow. This doesn't mean simply by making returns, although that is one aspect of freshening an inventory which no one should overlook.

Returns, markdowns, and sales are the three paramount devices for cleaning up an inventory, but first you must know what you have to get rid of. It will be clear enough that you have eleven copies of a $15 cookbook left over. But what about the three copies of the $8.95 book on sailing that have been sitting around since late last spring? Are you aware of them and of the book on bird-watching that always sold so well in the past but has been superseded by another, newer book? And what about the most recent crop of fiction that is sitting untouched where you put it the day it came into the shop last October? Are you only really concerned about the expensive gift books that tie up so much of your cash?

January is one of the two times of the year when you must—if you never do at any other time—take a moment to think about every book in your stock. If you are going to sell it, when do you think you will? This month, next month, next summer, next Christmas?

If your answer is next summer, look at it. How long have you had it already? Not too long? How long is that? Do you mean that you don't really know how long you've had it, but it's a good book and someone is going to come in someday and buy it? Do you have a lot of books around on your shelves like that? Do you, perhaps, find that you have so many like that around that it has become necessary for you to start

---

*Reprinted from "Educational Section No. 2," *ABA Bulletin* (New York), January, 1972.

putting them away in the basement? And the attic at home? And the garage? They're all good books, and someone is going to buy them someday?

Maybe so, at 5¢ on the dollar.

So look, really look, at every book on your shelves, tell yourself exactly how long you've had it, and be honest with yourself about your chances of selling it before it has been in your shop for twelve months.

How can you tell exactly how long it's been in the shop? By aging it when it is received. There are many different ways of marking stock to indicate age. One of the simplest and oldest is to pencil in a letter beside the price. Some stores use a letter for each six-month period, while others use a different letter for each month.

A quicker, neater aging mark may be made by purchasing rubber tips which fit over the top of a pencil and which may be used to apply the code in charcoal, which can be rubbed off with tissue paper without leaving a trace. The stamps can be purchased from stock or made to order by any rubber-stamp-maker. An uninked stamp pad and a supply of granulated charcoal from your office-supply house are all you need to complete your coding equipment.

Another, more modern aging system is to use small colored dots such as those manufactured by Dennison Manufacturing Co., Framingham, Massachusetts. Dennison makes them in a variety of sizes under the name "Pres-a-ply Marking Labels." They are self-adhesive and removable, in most cases, without leaving a trace. Instead of changing letters with each time period, you change colors. Applied to the lower corner of the spine of a book, these colored dots are virtually invisible to customers, but make it easy for the bookstore employee to spot at a glance how long books on a shelf have been around. The age of the book may readily be determined without handling each book to look inside for a season letter.

As you conclude that some decision must be made about how much longer you can afford to keep each book in stock, you will have to decide whether you can sell it at the price it is marked, sell it at a reduced price, or return it to the publisher or wholesaler from whom you bought it.

When you bought the book in the first place you must have had someone in mind to whom you could sell it. Did you make the effort to sell it or did you simply leave it on the shelf and hope the customer would stumble on it? If you still have faith in your original decision, you owe it to your customer, the book, and yourself to make the effort to sell it or to tell your staff how to sell it.

There are three reasons for marking a book down:

1. The book is eligible for return but is too shopworn to be acceptable to the publisher.

2. The book was once considered basic stock but sales have dropped off, and it is no longer eligible for return.
3. The book is eligible for return and is in pristine condition, but it is cheaper to mark it down than return it.

When is it cheaper to mark a book down rather than return it? When you can sell it for 5 per cent less than the credit you would receive from the publisher. The key word in this sentence is "sell." If you must look up invoice numbers or else suffer a flat 46 per cent on the return, it is certainly cheaper (and more fun) to sell the book at half price, especially if you must write for permission to return in addition to the expense of packing and shipping.

Listing books for return can be an expensive and tedious job. It is best done in a loose-leaf notebook with alphabetical dividers. Of course, if you are using the Dennison dot system of aging, you can send out any employee to yank all the books with dots other than green ones off the shelves. Even so, the buyer must make the final decision about what happens to each book. And in doing this, he must remember that *every day a book stays on his shelves it has cost him just a little bit more.* The post-Christmas season offers the best opportunity to clear the decks for the upcoming year. A little extra effort at this point may mean the difference between profit and loss a year from then.

Departments 1: Books

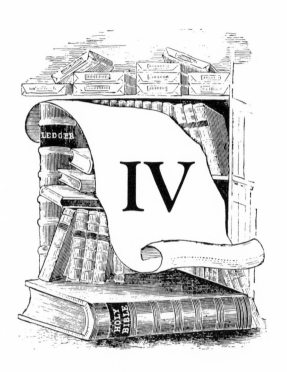

A Note on Stock Selection 22

G. ROYSCE SMITH
Executive Director,
American Booksellers Association, Inc.

If you are a new bookseller, you may wish for someone to hand you a list of books to stock. If you are an experienced bookseller, you will know why this is not possible. Even if every town and every location in every town were demographically identical, it would still not be possible. Finally, you and the customers you attract will determine the nature of your stock. Nor will it be static; it will change, for your customers will change, and more importantly, you will change.

Change is evident everywhere around us each day, and the speed of change has accelerated drastically in the last thirty years. As a bookseller, your antennae must constantly be out, alert to trends before they happen. But before you can adapt to change, you must begin.

Developing an idea about the kind of store yours will be is basic to site selection and store design. Valuable information on determining purpose and developing image is contained in Part I of the *Manual* in the chapters on sites and design and in the first chapters of Part VI, "Promotion and Advertising." This kind of planning will have a profound effect on your initial stock selection, but the most important factor influencing your decisions will be experience. If you don't have any, we urge, implore, and exhort you to go out and work in at least one bookstore for as long as you can. You will save yourself a lot of money, headaches, and mistakes, including the basic mistake of being temperamentally allergic to working in bookstores.

Actually working with books, with the buyer who chooses the books the store will sell, with the salespeople who sell them, and with the customers who ultimately buy them is invaluable. No written words can substitute for experience. You will quickly learn that there are books of which you have never heard that are extremely popular; that the store's buyer is less apt to buy new fiction, for example, on the basis of plot than on the basis of the reputation of author and publisher and the size of print orders and ad budgets; that the salespeople in a bookstore develop special talents for determining and remembering each regular customer's preferences; and that the customer expresses his pleasure or displeasure at the way you select books, call them to his attention, and service his special requests by becoming a regular customer or staying away forever.

So there is no magic list. However, here are some additional pointers that will supplement experience in helping you to compile a successful list for your store:

- Wholesalers' and publishers' representatives are very helpful in choosing initial selection and in reviewing basic stock periodically. But do not simply say to a publisher's rep, "Send me $2,000 worth of your best books." Work with him.
- Look at what other booksellers are doing as often as possible. Visit bookstores every chance you get. While visiting stores most like your own may prove most helpful, visit every kind of bookstore you can. Some of your best ideas may come from the least likely places. Keep your eyes and mind open.
- Meet with other booksellers as often as possible. Booksellers are a giving lot and freely share their ideas, enthusiasms, and frustrations.
- Read your trade publications. *Publishers Weekly* and *ABA Newswire* are musts. Keep on top of the ads in *PW* as well as the news of books and bookstores. The *ABA Newswire* will keep you alert ahead of time to the authors who are really going to be pushed in the media. It should be the first piece of mail you open on Monday morning.
- Use lists, but use them cautiously. ABA publishes basic book lists for cloth and paper *(Hardbound Basic Book List* and *Paperbound Basic Book List)*, yet I can say with confidence that there is not a single title—not even dictionaries and Bibles—on these lists (or any other) that is carried by every store in the country. Be selective.
- If someone says, "I just can't get enough Voyager Books," do not take them literally and order huge quantities of each title as one bookseller I know did. Try them. Find out how many is enough for your store. Proceed with care.
- Keep lists of titles which are called for but which you don't carry. Review them and your special orders with an eye to improving your basic stock.
- Please listen to your customers. They tell you more than any other source or combination of sources. There is a knack to listening.
- Know when a title or a subject is dead. Get rid of it. Replace it with what matters; what people want.

What follows is a discussion of specific sections of the bookstore and specialized subject areas where it is possible to discuss actual titles. Again, approach these titles with care.

Setting Up a Children's Book Department

23

JUDITH M. NOYES
Chinook Bookshop,
Colorado Springs, Colorado

So you want to be a children's bookseller? That's great. You have ahead of you one of the most personally rewarding and most enjoyable experiences of bookselling. All that talk about the future of the world depending on the minds and hearts of the young (preferably minds that can stretch and hearts that can understand) is true! And you, the bookseller, with a little time and energy and a great deal of imagination and wit, can play a significant part in preparing the young for a life of enlightened participation and responsible leadership. Get the right book to the right child at the right time (your absolute, ultimate goal) and you kindle sparks and open up vistas.

Let's assume—correctly, we believe—that a *good* children's book department is essential to the *good* general bookstore you are planning to open or have opened. And let's assume that you have managed somehow to assign a portion of your retail space to this department. How much space depends, of course, on how much emphasis you are planning to give the section, but with children's books, keep in mind that quality, not quantity, is the key. If possible, choose an area of the store that is slightly out of the traffic pattern; there should be a leisurely feeling that will encourage thoughtful browsing. Do something to establish the children's book department as a physical entity, even if it's as simple a technique as painting the shelves and fixtures a bright color, different from the rest of the store, or decorating with murals and mobiles. Here's where your artistic gifts—or those of an artistic friend who would probably paint a mural in exchange for some art books—can find an outlet. Use your imagination to make this area appealing to both children and their adult companions.

Many stores have small reading tables and child-sized chairs. Make sure if you do this you set aside some books especially for them to look at, the ones you've removed from stock for this purpose. It would be the height of recklessness to sit them down with their eager, grubby little fingers before a pile of gorgeous $5.95 picture books that you're hoping to sell.

In our own children's book department, which occupies approximately 400 square feet out of a total of 5,000, we have a two-story, 4'X6' playhouse inhabited by a Steiff Plush Animals monkey family, where youngsters can play while the parents shop. My husband built it for about $60, and although several salesmen have told us we were wasting valuable selling space, we've found it is one of our most effective (and least expensive) bits of advertising and public relations. "Take me to the shop with the monkey house," say the three-year-olds. We know that soon the command changes quite naturally to: "Take me to the *book* shop." Some shops with superior children's book departments have benefited from such additions as hobby horses, outdoor swings, and giant cutouts of well-known children's book personalities. Some give away small tokens appropriate to the shop, such as bookmarks and bookplates. (But avoid lollipops and balloons—you're a bookstore, not a gas station.) The moral of the story: Try to make your children's book department something unique, something every small customer as well as his parents will remember with pleasure.

Organization

So, you have your department, and you've done your best to make it inviting. You've ordered the books (we'll get to that later), they're beginning to arrive, and now where do you put them? You will find, to some people's dismay and others' delight, that children's books vary tremendously in size and shape, especially those for the preschoolers. We happen to find the variety of shapes and sizes far more interesting in terms of aesthetics and display. Pegboard, you will find, is often the answer to the space-shy bookseller's dilemma. Cover part of the section with this adaptable stuff, paint it a warm background color, and, using those handy-dandy wire fixtures, cover it with those outsized and glorious-looking picture books that cannot fit your shelves. You not only solve a space problem but create a showcase for the wondrously handsome productions that all your customers will enjoy.

Organization? First, by age. Picture books, ABC's, Mother Goose (keep a variety on hand—from traditional to wildly contemporary, if you have both kinds of customers), and the sturdy books (printed on stiff stock) and the books printed on cloth should be together. Beginning-readers series can easily be shelved spine out in this section. Give face-out display to the most beautiful books, new or old, and let the others stand spine by spine. We would suggest three basic age groups (for those who are not sure about age levels, most publishers code the book on the dust jacket): babies through third grade, third through fifth, and fifth up. Anything for over twelve belongs in the adult section. If you or your personnel are in the dark as to matching age to grade, just start with age six for first grade and proceed accordingly.

Another organizational factor to be considered in addition to age is subject; some subject arrangement seems practical and effective. You might group your science books together, for example, and it will help speed up things greatly if you put poetry collections together, and set aside an area for horse stories, dog stories, and books about sports. Music and dance books, fairy stories, and books about crafts are other subject areas that can be organized in this way.

A word here about paperbacks, an important and constantly growing area of children's book publishing. Smart publishers are adding more paperback juvenile titles to their lists every year, and bright booksellers know that if you stock them, the youngsters will beat a path from home and classroom to your shop to buy reading matter that they can afford to buy with their own allowances. We look for increased activity from the publishers in this field, especially for the youngest readers.

Ordering Stock

Now, to backtrack a bit. Surely the most difficult problem facing the beginning bookseller is what to order. Your own "remembrance of times past" will help you in selecting the very important back stock of classics, but what of the hundreds of new books appearing each season? The publisher's representative can be very helpful here. If he's a good one (and most of them in our experience have been competent and likeable chaps), he will weed out for you the obvious library titles on his list, and point out the books that his publisher believes to have a potentially strong trade market. He should be able to tell you something about the author and illustrator, the plot (if it's fiction), and how it compares with other books on the subject (if it's nonfiction). If it's a book for a preschooler, he should have with him either finished copies or enough samples of text and art work so that you can have a good idea of the end product. As a rule, we wouldn't buy picture books for the preschool or early elementary years without seeing a good portion of the book. Take the time to read it before you order—it only takes a few minutes, and the wise salesman would rather have you do so, realizing that you will sell many more copies of a book you know and that you'll go to bat for one you've fallen for. Also helpful in choosing new books are the excellent forecasts of children's books in *Publishers Weekly;* follow them faithfully.

To set up a strong back stock, there are many aids for the new bookseller. The *ABA Hardbound Basic Book List,* prepared by seasoned and reasoned booksellers across the country, is a good starting place. Bowker's *Best Books for Children* contains over 4,000 titles arranged by both grade and subject.

The Children's Book Council, Inc., 175 Fifth Avenue, New York, N.Y. 10010, can send you information, book lists, and all kinds of promotional materials for a very nominal fee. Their pamphlet, "Selling Children's Books," is perhaps the most useful and concise guide available for training you and your staff in the children's department. [The text of a major portion of this pamphlet is given in Chapter 24.—ED.] They also have bookmarks that list all the winners of both the Caldecott Medal and the John Newbery Medal; you may want to set up a shelf of at least some of these prize-winning children's books, since many parents, teachers, and librarians will ask for them.

And here are some books that will help you in choosing your stock and in learning more about the field of children's literature:

ARBUTHNOT, MAY HILL. *Children and Books.* New York: Lothrop, Lee & Shepard Co.

EGOFF, SHEILA, *et al. Only Connect: Readings on Children's Literature.* New York: Oxford University Press.

KLEMIN, DIANA. *The Art of Art for Children's Books.* New York: Clarkson N. Potter.

LANES, SELMA G. *Down the Rabbit Hole: Adventures and Misadventures in the Realm of Children's Literature.* New York: Atheneum Publishers.

LARRICK, NANCY. *A Parent's Guide to Children's Reading.* New York: Pocket Books.

National Council of Teachers of English. *Adventuring with Books.* New York: Scholastic Book Services.

SMITH, JAMES STEEL. *A Critical Approach to Children's Literature.* New York: McGraw-Hill Book Co.

You will, of course, want to add books of special importance to your region and community and books by local authors. A Western bookstore will no doubt set up a full shelf of books about cowboys and Indians; a Boston shop will feature stories relevant to Revere and the Revolution. And the ladies-with-three-names who write for children and speak on the local church-circle–women's-club circuit will be selling their books over the creamed chicken, so be sure you stock them—and maybe get the authors in to sign them. Use your head, too, about subject matter. If your shop is in the Great Plains, don't go overboard on oceanography; if you're in a coastal community, you'd better have a whole shelf of books on fish and ships.

A few suggestions. Both in choosing and selling the books, there are several things to keep in mind. Ask yourself if the author has written this with a *child* in mind, or is it one of those cutesy bits of wade-throughable whimsy that, as one of the most respected children's book editors has remarked, "are bought by repulsive adults to give to other even more repulsive adults"? Is there substance to the text; will it stand up to the test of being read many times over without becoming tiresome? Is the format appropriate to the age of the child? (Older children feel that oversized books look babyish.) Is the type size good and, again, appropriate to the age? (Look for clear, big type for the beginning readers—that is, up to grade four.) Do the illustrations enhance the text and are they significant in themselves rather than just being pictures of the action? Of course, the best test of all is how the children themselves respond. If you're a parent or grandparent, with youngsters around the premises, or if you have small neighbors or friends, round them up once in a while and have a reading-aloud session. Their reactions will tell you worlds about the worth of a book, and they are always honest.

Be sure that you and whoever else is working with the children's books know the stock inside and out. When we train a new staff member, we wind up the lectures by "playing games": What have you got about horses for a nine-year old? What is a good first book of poetry? What's the difference between these three editions of *Little Women?* What do you suggest for a twelve-year-old whose reading level is fourth grade? How about a "terribly bright" child who is eight years old and loved *War and Peace*? (You, the bookseller, are counselor and psychologist, as well!)

You'll probably find that people (men *or* women—my husband is one of the most enthusiastic salesmen of children's books I know) who have had considerable experience with children, their own or other people's, are more comfortable in this department, but there's really no reason why any intelligent, friendly person shouldn't be able to do a good job with a little bit of homework.

Once you get this carefully chosen, attractively arranged children's book department set up, don't just sit back and wait for the customers to find you. Get out and tell the community what you have to offer. Let PTA program chairmen know you're available to talk to them about children's reading (and take some books along); church and civic groups are also interested in this kind of talk, especially during National Library Week. Invite school teachers to bring a class at a time to the shop during a relatively slow period, and talk to them about books and publishing. Many stores have created immeasurable good will (and handsome sales) by sponsoring regular story hours in their shops. Have a permanent children's window if you can; otherwise be sure to devote an occasional window display to that department—and not just at

Christmas. Investigate book fairs and autograph parties; they're not everybody's cup of punch, but many stores have found them extremely profitable. You'll notice that none of the above ventures (with the exception of the parties) will cost you a penny—just time.

So, children's bookseller, scan the column of "Births" in your local paper and rejoice. Every one of those button-eyed bundles is a potential book reader and book buyer. *You* can play a part in introducing them to Bambi and Babar, Tom Sawyer and Mary Poppins, to science and fantasy, humor and the arts. What a responsibility! What a challenge! What fun!

Selling Children's Books*   24

CHILDREN'S BOOK COUNCIL STAFF

The most effective way to sell children's books is to read children's books and then tell customers about the books you have read, and speak with enthusiasm. But time is not available to you, or to anyone, to read the 2,000 or so new children's books published each year.

In the meantime, you may find it helpful to study a few rudimentary facts about children's books and how others have sold them.

Your best help will come from bookseller friends who have sold children's books successfully over a long period of time. Your local children's librarian is often of help on a variety of matters having to do with children's literature. When it comes to children's books, everyone concerned has the same aim: Get the right book into a child's hands at the right time.

Keep in mind a few points experienced booksellers consider important:

- In all of selling there is probably no single area as personal as children's books. The salesperson can determine what the customer will buy, for the customer comes to you for help in a way he does not come to any other person selling things.
- You will know more about children's books than most customers after a few weeks of hard work on the selling floor. This knowledge should give you confidence and make it possible for you to be positive when talking about children's books with customers. Most customers need and want your help.
- Your general attitude, sense of concern, and hospitality will mean more to your store in repeat sales in the children's book section

---

*Adapted from a pamphlet of the same name prepared by the staff of the Children's Book Council, Inc., New York.

than almost any other factor. If a customer, whether a child or a grandmother, believes that a sympathetic friend has been found, that customer will return.

- Remember that it has required some extra effort for a customer to come to a bookstore. The usual present for a child is money, a game, a toy, clothes, and so on. If a customer comes for a book, he wants something special. He deserves special help.

Finding What's Requested

The most important thing for a salesperson to do when first selling children's books is to learn the stock and find out how the store's management has arranged the books. Many booksellers have prepared lists of books known to sell well. Those books should be the first on your familiarity list, both as to location in the store and content. Read them at the first possible opportunity.

The easiest moment in your day when selling children's books is no doubt when a customer comes to you to ask for a specific book, you know where the book is, and you ring up the sale in the cash register in a matter of minutes. More often than not a customer will know the title of a children's book more readily than the author's name, but sometimes people may ask for a book by author. How can the book be identified? *Children's Books in Print,* though useful, is not up-to-the-minute. In addition, it does not include every children's book. If you conclude in talking about the wanted book that it is a recently published one, a good place to find out more information about its exact title and author would be the semi-annual special children's numbers of *Publishers Weekly,* which have good roundups of new books. *Subject Guide to Children's Books in Print* is good when a customer asks for a book by subject. Of course, when you know your stock you can point out all the books you have available on any subject.

In the adult section of a bookstore, potential customers know more or less what they want, either for themselves or as presents. In the children's section, with the exception of the customer who wants a particular book, confusion and embarrassment are more the rule than the exception. People don't know what they want. Whether you feel it or not, be positive, make the customer feel he is welcome and not a dope for not knowing exactly what book to buy for a child. There is a book for every child, whatever his age or interests, with prices for every pocketbook.

First, ask how old the child is, and whether it's a boy or a girl. Then steer the customer to the section of the department where the right book is most likely to be. Put one book in the customer's hands, just to let him know that this is the general area in which a book may be found.

While the customer is looking through the book you have picked, you will have time to think about phase two of your approach. However, before getting into phase two, what is the right section to lead a customer to after he tells the age of the child?

The Right Section

Where you take the customer depends on how your stock has been arranged. Some stores arrange children's books according to two important factors: the age of the child and children's interests. And sometimes books are grouped together according to a child's reading ability, in four major groups:

1. *Books for Babies.*—There are two kinds of "books" available for infants. The first is probably not really a book at all, but an object designed to develop perception skills. These objects sometimes make noises; they may be made of cloth; they usually provide the baby some sort of manipulative experience. The second is a regular book for infants, sometimes called "sturdy book," on stiff boards. Such books usually show pictures of simple, familiar objects. To please a baby the most, the pictures should be in bright colors.

2. *For Preschoolers.*—Some children, even before they are two, are ready for Mother Goose. A Mother Goose book is always an appropriate gift for a new baby, as is any book to be enjoyed in the future. When a child has reached two, and until he is in school and learning to read, this is a time for people to buy picture books for him. The first picture books he sees should depict familiar, cozy objects, such as animals and children, and should have very simple stories. Color is important in such books, which may be number books or alphabet books, designed, as are all books at this level, to be read many times.

If the child is already a good listener, and seems ready for a more complex story than the simplest books on your shelves, show the customer picture books with more pages and a lot more text. Especially if the customer buying the book for the preschooler is the child's parent, tell him that he shouldn't hesitate to buy books a few years beyond the child's level, now or later. A book intended for a somewhat older child can be read to the child now, and by the child later. If you encourage the customer to share books with his family, a child may come to the realization early in his life that books can be great fun.

By the time the child is ready to go to school, he is probably ready to hear ridiculous stories, and he may be partial to nonsense. If the child has not had poetry books by the time he is five, suggest a book of nonsense verse.

3. *Early School Years (First, Second, and Third Grades, Ages* 5–8). —This is an age group in which children are likely to have widely

varying capacities when it comes to reading. Some children are reading almost independently by the end of their first full year in school; others are not independent readers until the third grade. As a salesperson, you don't want to make the mistake of asking if the child for whom the book is being bought is a "slow reader." That would never do! If the customer says the child is a seven-year-old second-grader, get the information you need by saying, "Then I don't suppose he's ready to read without your help, is he?" If the answer is "No," say, "It's so much fun to read together, isn't it?" Then show the picture books with strong story lines, in which plot and character figure prominently. If the child is reading independently, however, show the books that are designed specifically for him. Publishers frequently will designate a book as part of a series for newly independent readers, but there are many books with easy vocabularies and good stories that beginning readers like.

A parent buying books for children in this age group should be reminded not to neglect books on subjects the child is known to have interests in, even though the books may be beyond the child's reading range. As mentioned, the child can read them himself later on.

4. *Fourth Grade (Ages 9–10) and Beyond.*—If it's going to happen naturally, it's probably going to happen by the fourth grade. This is when a child will start reading all kinds of books independently, so the child's personality and preferences become the most important factor from now on. Stores usually recognize this fact in arranging stock for this age group and beyond more by interests than by age groups. They may include an arrangement for readers nine to twelve, but close study usually shows that books about a particular subject will be together. This is also true of books intended for the over-twelve reader.

The Appropriate Book

Assuming that the customer has been directed to the right section for selecting a book, what is the next crucial question, phase two in your search for the right book? Ask if the child is an avid reader already. Parents and others close to a child may assure you that the child is brilliant, and they may be perfectly right. On the other hand, they may be wrong, and it would be unfortunate to select a book appropriate for a brilliant ten-year-old as a gift for a non-reader of the same age. There is an appropriate book for very child.

One way to test a positive answer to your question is to ask which book the young reader has recently read and enjoyed. If you get a concrete answer, your book-selection problem will be solved and not necessarily by suggesting a book in an identical area. If, for example, an eleven-year-old girl has been reading a lot of books about ballet dancing and famous ballerinas, suggest a book in a related area, on costumes, say. Most customers will appreciate your thoughtful suggestion.

If you conclude that the child is an average reader, ask the customer to tell you of the child's interests and hobbies. If the customer knows them, select a book in an appropriate area. When you make your selection, don't overlook fiction titles in the area of the child's interests. In any event, don't sell a customer a nonfiction book if he doesn't know the child very well.

If, as frequently happens, the customer doesn't know much about the child, select a puzzle or riddle book for a beginning reader; a humorous book or a story about a family situation dealt with in a light-hearted way for a slightly older reader; a collection of poetry for a girl over nine; a short-story collection for older boys; a mystery or a book about horses or dogs for either a boy or girl of almost any age.

The most important thing in book selection at this point is not to let your own literary taste or missionary spirit get the best of you. Don't select a book that may turn a child away from books entirely.

Classics. Some books, as a result of their acceptance by children in successive generations, become classics, standard titles familiar to everyone working with children and books. Such titles will undoubtedly be on your store's best-seller list, and you will want to read them right away if you don't know them already.

Some stores have special sections where classics, particularly those published in an earlier generation, are shelved. Customers will gravitate to books whose titles they recognize. Of course, sell as many classics as you can if your customers ask for them. If on the other hand, your customer has more or less drifted to your classics section out of fear of buying newer books, you, as a salesperson, should know that there are pitfalls in relying on established titles. Many don't stand up when re-read, especially by a child who does not appreciate their interest as literary history or even curiosity. Reliable stories familiar to grandmothers may be filled with funny language, are frequently about people who are meaningless to today's young readers, and as frequently reflect values that contemporary life has made archaic. When you have the chance to influence a decision between a contemporary book and a classic of an earlier generation, choose today's.

- When you are showing books to a customer, don't show more than three or four books at a time. It will confuse the customer to have to select from a large assortment.
- Don't panic if you find yourself waiting on several customers at the same time. The important thing is to be sure that each is left with something to look at while you are attending to another's needs.

If a customer comments that a children's book is too expensive, it may be proper to agree with him, but whatever you do, don't stop there. It cannot be *too* expensive, given the value received. Remember, also, to point out to the customer the vast number of high-quality, low-priced books that are available. In the case of picture books, each color added to an illustration to make a page more attractive adds greatly to the final cost of the book. The artists selected to illustrate children's books are the most talented available. And don't forget to tell the customer that a children's book will be read over and over again, and passed on to younger brothers and sisters, quite unlike most adult books.

If the customer isn't an adult, but a child, don't worry. A child will tell you what he wants. If it's his own allowance money he's spending, or perhaps money given to him for his birthday to buy books, he will make his selections judiciously. Your help is valuable to a child when you direct him to the areas of his interests. Whatever you say, don't tell a child what he *should* read. He gets that sort of advice from everyone. If a child wants your advice, tell him to buy the book *he* wants to read, not the book someone has told him he should read.

Prize-winning Books

There are many prizes for children's books. Take the time to read not only the winners, but the runners-up for the important awards. If there is a local (city, state, or regional) children's book prize, be sure to know the names of current and recent winners. (It's also a good idea to know where books by local authors are shelved. Always tell anyone asking about such a book that people in the store like it very much. Don't ever say it sells a lot of copies unless you know for certain that it does. More often than not, you are talking to the author, or his wife.)

Some of the U.S. and foreign awards of particular interest to booksellers are:

- John Newbery Medal. Given annually by the Children's Services Division of the American Library Association (ALA) to the author of the most distinguished contribution to literature for children published each year.
- Randolph Caldecott Medal. Given annually by the Children's Services Division of the ALA for the most distinguished picture book for children published each year.
- National Book Award: Children's Book Category. Administered by the National Book Committee, the award is presented annually to a children's book that a panel of judges considers the most distinguished by an American citizen published in the United States in the preceding year.
- Notable Books. A selection, usually around fifty, of books published each year. The selection is made by the Book Evaluation Committee of the Children's Services Division of the ALA.

- Child Study Association of America Children's Book Award. An annual award for the best book of the previous year that deals realistically with some problem in the world of the contemporary child or young person.
- *New York Times* Choice of Best-Illustrated Books of the Year. A selection, usually around ten or twelve books, by a panel of at least three judges.
- *Boston Globe*–Horn Book Annual Children's Book Awards. Two awards, one for a book with an outstanding text and one for a book with outstanding illustrations.
- Mildred L. Batchelder Award. Annual award to the publisher of the most outstanding translation of a children's book first published abroad in a foreign language. Administered by the Children's Services Division, ALA.
- Jane Addams Children's Book Award. Annual award by the Women's International League for Peace and Freedom and the Jane Addams Peace Association for a children's book that best combines literary merit and themes of brotherhood.
- Hans Christian Andersen Prizes. Biennial awards by the International Board on Books for Young People to an author and an illustrator for their entire works.
- Carnegie Medal. Annual award by the British Library Association to a writer of a children's book of outstanding merit.
- Kate Greenaway Medal. Annual award by the British Library Association for the most distinguished work in the illustration of children's books.

Books cost a lot of money, but so does a quart of ice cream, which disappears a lot faster than books. The kind of nourishment any reader gets from a book can last a long time, however, if the reader is reading a book he responds to. That is the whole thing when it comes to finding the right book for any reader, particularly children. Give a child a book he can respond to, and he'll seek out more books, perhaps in his library or school, and perhaps in your bookstore. If a child believes books have nothing for him, everyone has failed that child.

Technical Books in the General Bookstore

25

SAM WELLER
*Sam Weller's Zion Book Store, Inc.,
Salt Lake City, Utah*

We operate a general bookstore that maintains a good stock of the newest titles and a strong back list of books in every category. We feel that the technical section of a store is indispensable for customer attraction and service.

Technical books may be considered as falling into two basic categories: (1) the "how-to" books (how to build a whatever so it won't fall down), and (2) reference books such as handbooks, books of tables and formulas, and advanced studies in the sciences.

To purchase stock for a basic technical section, the owner of a small bookstore should be prepared to invest at least $1,000 to $2,000.

The cash registers in our store have separate keys for ringing sales in separate departments. Each day we can tell exactly what any given subject does when cash-register totals are combined with charge totals. In our operation, technical-book sales amount to 10 per cent of our gross sales.

We feel it is wise to keep the technical books near the wrapping counter to encourage impulse sales and discourage theft. Technical books are expensive and often are published in small format. Because of this, they are an easy and tempting mark for the shoplifter. We have found it best to install our technical section where personnel can keep an eye on the books.

Most of the books in a technical section should contain basic information for the beginner in each field, leaving advanced works to be special-ordered. The stock should be chosen from the *ABA Hardbound* (and *Paperbound) Basic Book List* with special reference to what is likely to sell well in your area.

There are several publishing houses whose technical books sell well and whose discounts are large enough to make stocking the books worth while. John Wiley & Sons, McGraw-Hill Book Company, Prentice-Hall, Inc., Hayden Book Company, Bobbs-Merrill Company, Goodheart-Willcox Company, Chilton Book Company, and Hearst Books are but a few of the houses whose discounts to the dealer vary from 20 to 40 per cent. [The profitability of short-discount books is discussed in Chapter 15, "How To Make a Profit in Bookselling."—ED.]

In my estimation, Wiley offers the finest books dealing with the earth sciences and also computers, mathematics, and architecture. McGraw-Hill has excellent architectural titles and business books as well as the finest technical handbooks. Their electrical, chemical, plumbing, and piping handbooks must not be overlooked. Prentice-Hall has fine books for the layman about real estate, insurance, and salesmanship. Hayden has an important line of books for the non-professional on radio, electronics, transistors, television, etc. A division of Howard W. Sams & Co., Audel Books, is important to the advanced technician and the novice. Audel's four-volume *Carpenters and Builders Library* is a fine set for anyone interested in a complete course in building techniques. Goodheart-Willcox also has fine books on carpentry, electricity, and automotive repair.

Basic stock is the backbone of the bookstore and to maintain it we have an inventory control system. An inventory slip is placed in each book. When the book is sold, the slip is removed from the book and returned to the inventory control desk. The category of the book is written on both a control card and the control slip. This determines where it is to be shelved and makes it easier to find for both old and new clerks. [*See also* Chapter 11, "Inventory Control."—ED.]

The above procedure enables us to tell the rate at which any particular book is selling. If a book does not sell one copy in a year, we usually drop that title from stock. Of course this annual limit does not apply to general trade books; technical books are different. More leeway is necessary because their specialization makes the rate of sale slower. In some cases, even though some particular titles may take longer than one year to sell, we keep one copy in stock simply because we want to be able to offer a book on that subject. Maybe it doesn't pay off, but I enjoy surprising a customer once in a while. On second thought, I think it does pay off, because the customer will remember the store where he was able to get what he wanted and will come back again.

In our locality, books (both simple and very technical) on geology and related earth sciences are important because such organizations as Kennecott Copper Corporation, the Anaconda Company, Exxon, and Phillips Oil Company as well as many small mining companies are located here. They maintain staffs of researchers who buy many categories of technical books in addition to geology, and their personnel also purchase books on selling, investments, computer data-processing, accounting, and so forth.

We feature technical books in our windows constantly. A small space is always reserved for new titles and new editions of standard texts. We take full advantage of the free catalogs publishers send us by passing them out to our customers and mailing them to local organizations. When we buy, we try to keep in mind the wants of our best customers.

We will special-order any technical titles we do not normally carry in stock. There are problems connected with some special orders. It is easy enough to order a book if it is listed in *Books in Print.* But every now and then a customer asks for a publication we are unable to find listed or one published by a company that does not often sell to retail booksellers. This may happen when a customer has been reading a trade magazine devoted to his special field of interest. We ask the customer to supply us with the title, author, publisher, and price. More often than not, he will do so and will ask us to order the book just to save himself the trouble of writing for it. If the book is supplied to us at no discount, we then raise the retail price or add a service charge to cover our costs.

We have found that it is quickest and easiest to order medical books from a good medical book wholesaler. Some medical publishers will not sell direct to bookstores anyway, but will refer orders to a wholesaler.

No part of a bookstore succeeds by merely being there. Advertising is extremely important. Technical-book publishers provide advertising aids, such as statement stuffers, posters, and window-display material. Use them—they're free.

Many technical books literally sell themselves. An engineer, contractor, or electrician usually knows exactly what he wants and asks for it, and the sale is completed. But the hobbyist or home-remodeler will appreciate your help in suggesting just the right book to provide the answer to his problem. It helps to have at least a limited variety of titles on the very basic do-it-yourself subjects. People like to choose.

A LIST OF OUR BETTER-SELLING TECHNICAL TITLES

Architecture

CALLENDER, J. H. *Time-Saver Standards: A Handbook of Architectural Design.* New York: McGraw-Hill Book Co.

GIEDION, SIGFRIED. *Space, Time & Architecture.* Cambridge, Mass.: Harvard University Press.

HALSE, ALBERT. *Architectural Rendering.* New York: McGraw-Hill Book Co.

RAMSEY, CHARLES G., and SLEEPER, HAROLD R. *Architectural Graphic Standards.* New York: John Wiley & Sons.

Astronomy

ASIMOV, ISAAC. *The Universe.* New York: Walker & Co.
MOORE, PATRICK. *Amateur Astronomy.* New York: W. W. Norton & Co.
REY, HANS A. *The Stars.* Boston: Houghton Mifflin.

Automotive

Chilton's Auto Repair Manual. Radnor, Pa.: Chilton Book Co.
Chilton's Foreign Car Repair Manual. 2 vols. Radnor, Pa.: Chilton Book Co.
JOHNSON, LARRY. *Fix Your Volkswagen.* So. Holland, Ill.: Goodheart-Willcox Co.
Motor's Auto Repair Manual. New York: Hearst Books.
Motor's Truck & Diesel Repair Manual. New York: Hearst Books.
MUIR, JOHN. *How To Keep Your VW Alive.* Santa Fe, N.M.: John Muir Publications.
PURVIS, JUD. *All About Small Gas Engines.* So. Holland, Ill.: Goodheart-Willcox Co.
TOBOLDT, BILL (ed.). *Fix Your Ford.* So. Holland, Ill.: Goodheart-Willcox Co.

Aviation

DOHM, JOHN. *Flying the Omnirange.* No. Hollywood, Calif.: Pan American Navigation Service.
HOYT, JOHN R. *As the Pro Flies.* New York: McGraw-Hill Book Co.
LANGEWIESCHE, WOLFGANG. *Stick & Rudder.* New York: McGraw-Hill Book Co.
SMITH, FRANK K. *Week-End Pilot.* New York: Random House.
TAYLOR, RICHARD L. *Instrument Flying.* New York: Macmillan Publishing Co.

Chemistry and Physics

LANGE, NORBERT A. *Handbook of Chemistry.* New York: McGraw-Hill Book Co.
The Way Things Work: An Encyclopedia of Modern Technology. 2 vols. New York: Simon and Schuster.
WEAST, ROBERT C. (ed.). *Handbook of Chemistry and Physics.* Cleveland: Chemical Rubber Co.

Electronics

American Radio Relay League, *Radio Amateur's Handbook.* Newington, Conn.: American Radio Relay League.

COOKE, NELSON M., and ADAMS, HERBERT F. *Basic Mathematics for Electronics.* New York: McGraw-Hill Book Co.

GERRISH, HOWARD. *Electricity and Electronics.* So. Holland, Ill.: Goodheart-Willcox Co.

HORNUNG, JULIUS L., and MCKENZIE, A. A. *Radio Operating Questions & Answers.* New York: McGraw-Hill Book Co.

KAUFMAN, MILTON. *Radio Operator's License Q[uestion] & A[nswer] Manual.* New York: Hayden Book Co.

MARCUS, A., and MARCUS, W. *Elements of Radio.* Englewood Cliffs, N.J.: Prentice-Hall.

VAN VALKENBURG, MAC E., *et al. Basic Electricity.* 5 vols. New York: Hayden Book Co.

————.*Basic Electronics.* 6 vols. New York: Hayden Book Co.

Geology

DANA, E. S. *Dana's Textbook of Mineralogy,* ed. W. C. Ford. New York: John Wiley & Sons.

FENTON, CARROLL L., and FENTON,, MILDRED A. *The Rock Book.* New York: Doubleday & Co.

HILLS, E. S. *Elements of Structural Geology.* New York: John Wiley & Sons.

HURLBUT, C. S. (ed.). *Dana's Manual of Mineralogy.* New York: John Wiley & Sons.

LAHEE, FREDERICK H. *Field Geology.* New York: McGraw-Hill Book Co.

LEWIS, ROBERT S., and CLARK, G. B. *Elements of Mining.* New York: John Wiley & Sons.

PEARL, RICHARD M. *Handbook for Prospectors.* New York: McGraw-Hill Book Co.

POUGH, FREDERICK H. *A Field Guide to Rocks & Minerals,* ed. Roger T. Peterson. Boston: Houghton Mifflin.

SHELTON, JOHN S. *Geology Illustrated.* San Francisco: W. H. Freeman & Co.

TAGGERT, ARTHUR F. *Handbook of Mineral Dressing.* New York: John Wiley & Sons.

VANDERS, IRIS, and KERR, PAUL F. *Mineral Recognition.* New York: John Wiley & Sons.

Handbooks and Manuals for Engineers and Builders

American Institute of Steel Construction. *A Manual of Steel Construction.* New York: American Institute of Steel Construction.

American Institute of Timber Construction. *Timber Construction Manual.* New York: John Wiley & Sons.

American Society of Tool and Manufacturing Engineers. *Tool Engineer's Handbook,* ed. F. W. Wilson. New York: McGraw-Hill Book Co.

BAUMEISTER, T., and MARKS, LIONEL (eds.). *Standard Handbook for Mechanical Engineers.* New York: McGraw-Hill Book Co.

ESHBACH, OVID W. *Handbook of Engineering Fundamentals.* New York: John Wiley & Sons.

FINK, DONALD G., and CARROLL, JOHN M. *Standard Handbook for Electrical Engineers.* New York: McGraw-Hill Book Co.

FRENCH, THOMAS E., and VIERCK, CHARLES J. *Engineering Drawing & Graphic Technology.* New York: McGraw-Hill Book Co.

HUDSON, RALPH G. *Engineers' Manual.* New York: John Wiley & Sons.

KENT, R. T. *Kent's Mechanical Engineers' Handbook.* 2 vols. Part I ed. C. Carmichael. Part II ed. J. Salisbury. New York: Industrial Press.

OBERG, ENK, and JONES, FRANKLIN D. *Machinery's Handbook.* New York: Industrial Press.

PEELE, R. (ed.) *Mining Engineers' Handbook.* New York: John Wiley & Sons.

PERRY, ROBERT A. *Engineering Manual.* New York: McGraw-Hill Book Co.

SEARLES, WILLIAM H., *et al. Field Engineering.* New York: John Wiley & Sons.

Walker Building Estimator's Handbook. Chicago: Frank R. Walker Co.

Home Repair

ALTHOUSE, ANDREW D. *Modern Refrigeration & Air Conditioning.* So. Holland, Ill.: Goodheart-Willcox Co.

ALTHOUSE, ANDREW D., *et al. Modern Welding.* So. Holland, Ill.: Goodheart-Willcox Co.

Better Homes & Gardens Handyman's Book. Des Moines, Iowa: Meredith Corp.

BRUSHWELL, WILLIAM (ed.). *Painting & Decorating Encyclopedia.* So. Holland, Ill.: Goodheart-Willcox Co.

DALZELL, RALPH, J. *Plan Reading for Home Builders,* ed. Frederick S. Merritt. New York: McGraw-Hill Book Co.

DALZELL, RALPH, J., *et al.* (eds.). *Masonry Simplified.* 2 vols. Chicago: American Technical Society.

DURBAHN, WALTER E., and SUNDBERG, ELMER W. *Fundamentals of Carpentry.* 2 vols. Chicago: American Technical Society.

GRAHAM, FRANK D. *Carpenter's & Builder's Library.* 4 vols. "Audel Books." Indianapolis: Howard W. Sams & Co.

Manual of Home Repairs, Remodeling and Maintenence. New York: Grosset & Dunlap.

ORAVETZ, JULES, SR. (ed.). *Plumbers & Pipe Fitters Library.* 3 vols. "Audel Books." Indianapolis: Howard W. Sams & Co.

WAGNER, W. H. *Modern Carpentry.* So. Holland, Ill.: Goodheart-Willcox Co.

———.*Modern Woodworking.* So. Holland, Ill.: Goodheart-Willcox Co.

Insurance

GORDIS, PHILLIP. *Property and Casualty Insurance.* Indianapolis: Rough Notes.

HUEBNER, SOLOMON S., and BLACK, KENNETH, JR. (eds.). *Life Insurance.* New York: Appleton-Century-Crofts.

Werbel's Health Insurance Primer. Smithtown, L.I., N.Y.: Werbel Publishing Co.

Werbel's Life Insurance Primer. Smithtown, L.I., N.Y.: Werbel Publishing Co.

Investment

ENGLE, LOUIS. *How To Buy Stocks.* Boston: Little, Brown and Co.

GRAHAM, BENJAMIN. *Intelligent Investor.* New York: Harper & Row.

LEFFLER, G. L., and FARWELL, L. C. *The Stock Market.* New York: Ronald Press.

LOEB, GERALD M. *Battle for Investment Survival.* New York: Simon and Schuster.

Legal

BLACK, HENRY CAMPBELL. *Black's Law Dictionary.* St. Paul., Minn.: West Publishing Co.

CATALDO, BERNARD F., *et al. Introduction to Law and the Legal Process.* New York: John Wiley & Sons.

DACEY, NORMAN F. *How to Avoid Probate!* New York: Crown Publishers.

Management

DRUCKER, PETER F. *Concept of the Corporation.* New York: John Day Co.

———. *The Effective Executive.* New York: Harper & Row.

———. *Managing for Results.* New York: Harper & Row.

LAIRD, DONALD A., and LAIRD, ELEANOR C. *Technique of Handling People.* New York: McGraw-Hill Book Co.

LASSER, JACOB K. *How To Run a Small Business,* ed. B. Griesman. New York: McGraw-Hill Book Co.

McGREGOR, DOUGLAS. *The Professional Manager.* New York: McGraw-Hill Book Co.

ODIORNE, G. *Management Decisions by Objectives.* Englewood Cliffs, N.J.: Prentice-Hall.

Mathematics

HOGBEN, LANCELOT. *Mathematics for the Millions.* New York: W. W. Norton & Co.

SELBY, SAMUEL M. *Handbook of Tables for Mathematics.* Cleveland: Chemical Rubber Co.

Smoley's Four Combined Tables. Chautauqua, N.Y.: C. K. Smoley & Sons.

Smoley's Logarithms and Squares. Chautauqua, N.Y.: C. K. Smoley & Sons.

Smoley's Slopes and Rises. Chautauqua, N.Y.: C. K. Smoley & Sons.

Smoley's Three Combined Tables. Chautauqua, N.Y.: C. K. Smoley & Sons.

Medical

Blakiston's New Gould Medical Dictionary. New York: McGraw-Hill Book Co.

DORLAND, WILLIAM A. *Dorland's Illustrated Medical Dictionary.* Philadelphia: W. B. Saunders Co.

GRAY, HENRY. *Gray's Anatomy of the Human Body,* ed. C. M. Goss. Philadelphia: Lea & Febiger.

HOERR, N. L., and OSOL, A. (eds). *Blakiston's Illustrated Pocket Medical Dictionary.* New York: McGraw-Hill Book Co.

HOLVERY, DAVID N. (ed.). *Merck Manual.* Rahway, N.J.: Merck & Co.

MILLER, BENJAMIN F. *Complete Medical Guide.* New York: Simon and Schuster.

TABER, CLARENCE W. *Cyclopedic Medical Dictionary.* Philadelphia: F. A. Davis Co.

Real Estate

KRATOVIL, ROBERT. *Real Estate Law.* Englewood Cliffs, N.J.: Prentice-Hall.

MCMICHAEL, STANLEY. *How to Make Money in Real Estate.* Englewood Cliffs, N.J.: Prentice-Hall.

MCMICHAEL, STANLEY L. (ed.). *McMichael's Appraising Manual.* Englewood Cliffs, N.J.: Prentice-Hall.

RING, ALFRED A. *Real Estate Principles & Practices.* Englewood Cliffs, N.J.: Prentice-Hall.

SEMENOW, R. *Questions & Answers on Real Estate.* Englewood Cliffs, N.J.: Prentice-Hall.

Salesmanship

BETTGER, FRANK. *How I Raised Myself from Failure to Success in Selling.* Englewood Cliffs, N.J.: Prentice-Hall.

WHITNEY, ROBERT A., *et al. New Psychology of Persuasion and Motivation in Selling.* Englewood Cliffs, N.J.: Prentice-Hall

Secretarial

DORIS, LILLIAN, and MILLER, BESSEMAY. *Complete Secretary's Handbook.* Englewood Cliffs, N.J.: Prentice-Hall.

GREGG, JOHN R., *et al. Gregg Shorthand: Diamond Jubilee Series.* New York: McGraw-Hill Book Co.

HUTCHINSON, LOIS. *Standard Handbook for Secretaries.* New York: McGraw-Hill Book Co.

MILLER, B. *Legal Secretary's Complete Handbook.* Englewood Cliffs, N.J.: Prentice-Hall.

MONROE, K. M., *et al. Secretary's Handbook.* New York: Macmillan Publishing Co.

Home Reference Books   **26**

ELSA LICHTENSTEIN
Barnes & Noble, Inc.,
New York City

All bookstores can and should stock reference books. Selling them is a challenging and rewarding part of the business. A good department adds prestige to your store and dollars to your sales. The following is intended for the beginner contemplating opening a bookstore, or planning a department.

It would not only be foolhardy to plunge right in with much inventory and no experience, it is absolutely essential to go very slowly feeling your way, while learning as much as you can. There are certain factors to be considered before you start. Do you have a school nearby? Are you in or near a business district? What is the average economic level of your community? Is there a library reasonably close? All this information can contribute to the success of your efforts.

Let us now consider the most basic stock with which you will operate. At least three or four of the best-known college dictionaries must be on your shelves; perhaps not more than two of each. The ones that move fastest you will restock. The ones which stay on your shelves too long you will drop. It's as simple as that.

A small selection of atlases must be available in a moderate price range under $10, and one or two between that and $35. Remember that dictionaries and atlases not only are necessities for some people but are excellent gift suggestions for graduations, birthdays, Christmas, and many other special occasions.

The next to consider is a one-volume encyclopedia along with the popular almanacs. One or two thesauruses, a volume or two of quotations, something on vocabulary-building, grammar, and style, and one or two books of etiquette and letter-writing ought to be in evidence. And last, a small selection of foreign-language dictionaries and phrase books in French, Spanish, German, and Italian will put you in business.

It certainly is not necessary to carry much inventory. Here is where selectivity counts. It is preferable to have one first-rate book to recommend confidently than an assortment of cheap inadequate books in your store.

Once you have assembled your selection don't make a secret of it. Publishers of dictionaries at holiday times often have a neat easel sign that you can put in your window to remind passers-by that dictionaries make tasteful gifts and that your store carries them. You can make an attractive display in the store either on shelves or on a table, but always as a unit. The displays ought to be in a prominent spot, conducive to browsing. Make certain that you keep aware of your customers' requests and preferences. Always be alert for those titles for which you might be getting calls as well as for those you have which develop consistent sales. The latter might be stocked a little more heavily to avoid the deadly sin of being out of stock.

As for selling reference books, the more you familiarize yourself with them the more authoritatively you can discuss them. Many people need guidance and most want to be "sold." If you develop honest convictions about the merit of a particular dictionary, thesaurus, or atlas, you can project a genuine enthusiasm that is contagious and a wonderful aid in selling. Each dictionary, for example, has certain selling features. Read the jacket copy. Note and point out to the customer the word count, if one is indicated. One dictionary may have especially good readable type. Another may have clear and concise definitions, while still another may offer more detailed definitions. Still another may be unusually handsome in format or possess features not found in any of the others. Try to determine what makes each one distinctive. Most bookstores sell twice as many of the thumb-indexed editions as the plain.

Train your clerks to ask questions to determine for whom the book is intended. What is the level required? Is it for the whole family? Is it for an individual, and if so, try to learn what his or her requirements might be. Don't let a clerk guess at the answers to specific questions. If he doesn't know, he should say so, and get the information from a competent source.

In helping a customer come to a decision, I have on occasion suggested that he choose a word or two and together we compared the definitions in the dictionaries under discussion. This can be effective since the customer is led into making his own choice. He will be delighted and certain that he has chosen well.

One reference book that might serve you well is R. R. Bowker's *Home Reference Books in Print.* It describes and evaluates English-language dictionaries, some world atlases, and other American reference works. There is an additional aid in the *ABA Hardbound Basic*

Book List. Among its categories is a list of reference books and dictionaries that are considered to be basic stock by its compilers, who represent a broad spectrum of booksellers from various parts of the country
and from a representative selection of stores. Make good use, also, of the
Subject Guide to Books in Print.

As time goes on and you gain in experience and slowly develop
your market, you can begin to expand to reference books in specific
subjects. These too can become staples. Watch for *Publishers Weekly*'s
annual reference-book number. This is invaluable to all of us. Remember, too, at holiday times to explore the assortment of display materials
from the publishers. Above all, keep in mind that reference books,
subject occasionally to new editions, can be sold year after year, year
in and year out. They are not subject to fads or topicality, and there are
always new and expanding markets.

The following is a short bibliography of the most basic books:

Dictionaries and Encyclopedias

American Heritage Dictionary of the English Language, The. Boston:
Houghton Mifflin Co.
Columbia-Viking Desk Encyclopedia, The. New York: Viking Press.
Random House Dictionary of the English Language. New York: Ran-
dom House.
Webster's Eighth New Collegiate Dictionary. Springfield, Mass.: G. &
C. Merriam Co.
Webster's New College Dictionary of the American Language. New
York: World Publishing Co.

Atlases and Almanacs

Hammond Ambassador World Atlas. Maplewood, N.J.: Hammond, Inc.
Hammond Citation World Atlas. Maplewood, N.J.: Hammond, Inc.
Information Please Almanac. New York: Simon and Schuster.
Rand McNally International Atlas, The. Chicago: Rand McNally & Co.
Rand McNally New Cosmopolitan World Atlas. Chicago: Rand
McNally & Co.
World Almanac & Book of Facts. New York: Doubleday & Co.

Thesauruses and Style

Roget's International Thesaurus. New York: Thomas Y. Crowell Co.
Roget's Thesaurus in Dictionary Form, The. New York: G. P. Putnam's
Sons.
STRUNK, WILLIAM S., JR., and WHITE, E. B. *Elements of Style.* New York:
Macmillan Publishing Co.

Foreign-Language Dictionaries

*The Cassell's New French (New German)(Italian)(Spanish)*and*(Latin) Dictionary* is available from Funk & Wagnalls Publishing Co. (New York). *The Berlitz French (German) (Italian)* and *(Spanish) for Travelers Phrase Books* are available from Grosset & Dunlap (New York).

Miscellaneous

Amy Vanderbilt's Etiquette: A Guide to Gracious Living. New York: Doubleday & Co.

BARTLETT, JOHN. *Familiar Quotations.* Boston: Little, Brown and Co.

DORIS, LILLIAN, and MILLER, BESSEMAY. *Complete Secretary's Handbook.* Englewood Cliffs, N.J.: Prentice-Hall.

Emily Post's Etiquette. New York: Funk & Wagnalls Publishing Co.

INGALLS, EDNA, and SHEFF, ALEXANDER L. *How To Write Letters for All Occasions.* New York: Doubleday & Co.

(For a larger store, the following are additional titles to be considered.)

BERNSTEIN, THEODORE M. *The Careful Writer: A Modern Guide to English Usage.* New York: Atheneum Publishers.

Columbia Encyclopedia, The. New York: Columbia University Press.

Funk and Wagnalls New Standard Dictionary of the English Language. New York: Funk & Wagnalls Publishing Co.

New York Times Atlas of the World. New York: Quadrangle Books.

Earth and Man, The. Chicago: Rand McNally & Co.

Robert's Rules of Order Newly Revised. Glenview, Ill.: Scott, Foresman and Co.

Webster's Third New International Dictionary. Springfield, Mass.: G. & C. Merriam Co.

Paperback Bookselling 27

GEORGE STEPHENS
Manager, Paperback Department,
Harvard Cooperative Society,
Cambridge, Massachusetts

The once humble paperback has taken an important place as a practical household and classroom necessity within the structure of our culture. Paperback bookstores and paperback departments in both general and college stores have become an integral part of the bookselling community. From relatively few titles in 1960, the number of paperback titles increased to more than 116,000 in 1974. It is estimated that the projected growth rate for mass-market paperbacks will continue at 12 per cent per annum until 1980. Consequently, everywhere in the United States large numbers of paperbacks are being "supermarketed" with the action aimed at all ages, levels, and classes.

There are even days for the paperback bookseller when, happily, the turn is so high that he has all he can do to shelve the books and take his daily stock checks. Of course, this healthy situation compounds the problem of providing sufficient space for even a fraction of that mind-boggling number of titles in print. The physical layout of a bookstore built as recently as the late 1950's or early 1960's and intended to support 8,000 to 10,000 titles now has to accommodate 15,000 to 20,000. There isn't a bookman in the country who doesn't cry out at least occasionally: "Where are we going to put it all?" Odd-sized catalogs, non-books, and "now" books complicate the problem. As the number of titles increases, so does the paperback inventory, and the demand.

This spiraling production followed by mass consumption has produced the exciting environment of the paperback supermarkets. In them, we see hundreds of young people seeking moderately priced books corresponding to their current "mind-blowing" interests, such as higher states of consciousness, meditation, yoga, drugs, the occult, new life styles, arts and crafts, ecology, the rights of women, science fiction, and fantasy. In a recent *Publishers Weekly* survey, booksellers report that their customers are getting younger. Within the present youth culture, there is a new breed of reader who has chosen, perhaps grudgingly, to give the paperback industry a prominent place. This restructuring of bookstore clientele profoundly affects book distribution. Youth, tuned in to ephemeral trends, passing fads, and flash interests, is nothing new in this world, but the number of new readers is a new challenge to publishers, distributors, and retailers to provide enough of the right reading material.

Publishers have discovered a big market potential in paperback reprints of children's books, which had in recent years been virtually priced out of the bookstore market. There is now a wide selection of excellent books for children in paperback and the number constantly increases.

Fastback Wholesaling

The link between paperback bookstores and the wholesalers is absolutely vital. Paperback outlets carrying more than 15,000 titles cannot function at top level without this important relationship. Within the past five years, competiton has created a new breed of paperback wholesalers striving to offer the quickest possible service at substantial discounts. One must distinguish between the magazine wholesaler and the specialized book wholesaler. The former usually deals primarily in the current mass-market titles only. A specialized book wholesaler will deliver a full representation not only of every mass-market publisher but almost all trade paperback publishers as well. In addition to new titles he will also be able to help his customers to maintain the back-list titles that constitute a basic stock. A well-stocked paperback wholesaler, some of whom carry more than 40,000 titles, may be able to supply as much as 80 to 90 percent of the entire required stock. Whether a store will use a wholesaler to that extent depends on whether the individual bookseller feels that it is more profitable to purchase direct from the publisher in those cases where the latter offers discounts on quantity purchases substantially higher than those offered by the wholesaler. (At this writing there are a few wholesalers who do offer a straight 40 per cent on both mass-market and trade paperbacks with no return privileges and with freight charges extra.)

In all events, in case of emergency or for a fast fill-in, the wholesaler is essential. When that red-hot best-seller has not yet arrived at the bookstore and sales are being lost every minute, he will do his utmost to supply it immediately. It is not at all unusual for the wholesaler to receive shipments from mass-market publishers before retail stores do, and in such cases he may call on the bookstores asking for orders.

Delivery to nearby dealers can take place within a few hours or perhaps by the next day.

Useful in-store services can also be provided by the wholesaler. His salesmen will often check the stock in the store weekly or monthly, then later, without extra charge, deliver and shelve what has been ordered as replacement stock. He can also provide—at no cost to the store— catalogs, weekly reports on fast-moving and new titles, specialized booklists and bibliographies of various sorts. Some wholesalers are even capable of providing assistance in store layout or the designing and building of fixtures.

Those smaller paperback bookstores that have limited buying budgets find that placing conservative orders at weekly intervals with a wholesaler is much safer than placing heavy orders at less-frequent intervals direct with the publisher, who may take as much as three to five weeks to make deliveries. Dealing with wholesalers in such cases may prevent a dangerously overbought condition.

The average wholesaler offers discounts of about 30 per cent on mass-market paperbacks and 36 to 38 per cent on trade paperbacks. A few now offer a straight 40 per cent on non-returnable purchases and charge the freight to the retailer. There is no question, however, that direct buying from the publisher, when possible, still provides the best discount: 40 per cent on mass-market, shipping prepaid. There are certain areas, however, where franchise arrangements with wholesalers prevent the publisher from selling direct to retailers.

Trade paperbacks carry nearly the same discounts as hardbound trade books: 40 per cent and up, depending on the quantity and the individual publisher's discount policy. Representatives of trade paperback publishing houses make periodic calls on most of their accounts, at which time stock checks are taken on the back list, and new titles are ordered. Frequently, orders for back-list and new releases may be combined to earn an improved discount—in some cases running as high as 50 per cent. If a representative fails to call on you, try to persuade him or his sales manager that it would be worth his while to do so. Failing this, request a stock checklist. The object is to get the highest discount whenever possible, unless other costs, such as increased paper work and shipping charges, make it uneconomical.

Paperback publishers frequently offer fixtures gratis, or as part of a package that includes a specific stock order. If a bookseller has custommade fixtures, it is possible that publishers will offer a subsidy of so much per pocket on the fixture.

Inventory Control

Whether you deal in paperbacks on a moderate or a supermarket level, an effective inventory control system is essential to prevent both overbuying and understocking. It may be a card system, a list system, or even several systems going at once, but you must have something to control the buying level. My own form of inventory is just plain visual or "eyeballing." An alert buyer can walk his aisles, seeing at a glance holes and missing titles. Holes in the new-book section are particularly easy to detect. This section always draws customers. The new titles, if the range is extensive, may be divided into separate categories: fiction and literature, psychology and education, history and economics, and so on. In some college stores, this section alone can occupy as much as three hundred linear feet of shelves. Constant vigilance is needed to keep the pockets full. Further visual stock checks may be taken of the oversized "now" books, non-books, and "with-it" books that because of their unshelvable dimensions are displayed flat on tables or on special racks.

But eyeballing alone is not sufficient because the large number of titles that must be carried requires a more formal method of control. Most booksellers concur that the card system is effective in maintaining the back list in all categories. For each section there is a file of 3"X5" cards on each of which is written all pertinent information, including a maximum-minimum level and the quantity in the stockroom or other storage area. Cards for titles that need reordering are pulled from the files and given to the buyer.

The Looreen card system of perpetual inventory is widely used. The store's name and address is printed on a card, often furnished by the publisher. This card bears the title, author, and publisher of the book it represents. Each book in stock carries one of these cards, which is to be removed by the cashier or clerk at the time of sale, and periodically at the end of the day or otherwise forwarded to the buyer or person in charge of inventory control. This simple system is cheap and easy to maintain. When a substantial number of cards have been accumulated, or a specific time has elapsed, the buyer uses the cards to prepare his orders to the wholesaler or publisher. [*See also* Chapter 11, "Inventory Control."—ED.]

To set up a basic stock, or to review the requirements for adequate staple stock, there is no better or more authoritative aid than the list published by the ABA, *Paperbound Basic Book List.* This list is revised every other year by experts, and is an excellent source of information for anyone wanting to clean out, reduce, or change his basic stock. It would also be an asset for the relatively inexperienced individual who is opening a paperback bookstore for the first time. All paperback buyers, no matter how knowledgeable, should keep this ABA list on their reference shelf as a guide.

There is nothing more important, perhaps, than keeping oneself continuously informed, in order to anticipate the public's wants and tastes. More important even than a daily reading of reviews, news releases, newswires, *Publishers Weekly,* and so forth is to keep an out-of-stock list at the service desk. Surprisingly, there are many bookstores that do not do this. All requests, no matter how trivial, should be recorded. A paperback buyer lives with this daily list, which indicates the direction his business is moving—and it can move alarmingly fast! The last seventeen copies of Dylan Thomas' *Collected Poems* might have been sold while you were at lunch. Many requests on this "out" list may be ignored, but it is a gauge of the wants and needs of the community you are serving, may serve as an indication of weaknesses within the inventory system, and, most important of all, shows where sales and money have been lost that day. In bookselling, "in stock" is the name of the game.

The out list also provides a means of supplying single copies of mass-market paperbacks without resorting to a special order. The ABA Single Copy Order Plan won't work with mass-market publishers, who understandably are reluctant to accept orders under $25 from bookstores. Nevertheless, conscientious booksellers will want at least to make the attempt to locate whatever a customer may need. Should the wholesaler be unable to supply the title, then it may be placed on the next salesman's order, even though this may involve a delay of several weeks. Whatever arrangement one makes to supply a single copy of a mass-market book, it should be a loose commitment. Unless he needs the book at once, the customer will be grateful for your interest and effort in finding the book for him, if you can.

On the other hand, there are no barriers when ordering trade paperbacks. When a local supplier cannot provide a higher-priced paperback, a buyer may use the Single Copy Order Plan, a system honored by most publishers.

Returns. The publisher wants to see his most saleable merchandise on bookstore shelves. When a title stops moving, the paperback publisher usually prefers to replace it with another title with greater sales potential. The issue here is simply one of the profitable use of space. The more money the store makes, the more the publisher makes. Almost all of them have set up a prescribed time span for returns—usually six months or twelve months from the date of invoice. Mass-market publishers seem to have a loose return policy. All that is usually needed is an official shipping label and a packing slip to make the return—at the store's expense. Several mass-market publishers request that the book be destroyed after ripping off the cover for return. When the covers are received, the account is credited. Easy return policies assist the paperback buyer, who must of necessity often extend himself on certain mass-market titles. This built-in figure of constant credit on his returns allows the bookseller to experiment with more new titles, to speculate in a new category, perhaps foreign-language paperbacks. A warning, however: Unless bills are paid, credit will be cut off and future shipments canceled.

Very heavy returns can be expensive. Expensive because the unsold books take up valuable space on the sales floor and in the stockroom, expensive in time consumed in preparing the charge-back and packing and in the cost of shipping. The liberal returns policy must be used intelligently.

I know a bookstore owner who never makes returns. This seems ridiculous, because to me the paperback business is built on the returns system. Returns are an important aspect of the general flow of business. When good judgment so dictates, there is a time to be conservative, but there is also a time for creative speculation. Test out new impulses, new ideas, and check your sales figures for the progress of your experimentation.

Selling Tips

With today's shrinking profits and inflation, it is necessary to find ways of picking up extra business. There are gimmicks that can pick up as much as $400 or $500 in a single day. Large paperback operations have had tremendous success with hurt-book sales. A "hurt" book is simply a returned book that a publisher has accepted from his accounts and resold to another account at a very large discount. Some publishers assign these hurt books to a shredder for pulping, while others resell them to their dealers—sometimes for prices as low as 19¢ each. There are many examples of success along this line. One large metropolitan dealer offered approximately 6,000 slightly hurt paperbacks at one-half of the list price, and did $3,000 extra business on one Saturday afternoon.

A paperback bookstore will do well to offer frequent special sales and bargain prices. If there is space to spare, keep a couple of tables heaped with tempting bargains, be they special purchases, slightly hurt, or just markdowns from the store's own stock. The important thing is that a bargain is as tempting to a paperback customer as to any other type of retail customer. Bargain offers can be promoted through radio and newspaper ads, or even a sign in the front window.

The use of paperbacks as gifts is constantly increasing. Boxed sets, assortments of mysteries, Westerns, or Gothic novels, or the customer's own selection of titles can provide a relatively high unit of sale. By offering free gift-wrapping, the bookseller can further encourage gift purchases.

One should not overlook the fact that the media often offer unexpected free advertising opportunities, such as author appearances on television or radio talk programs, and reviews and articles in newspapers and magazines. The *ABA Newswire* lists all scheduled TV and radio interviews with authors to be done in major cities within the next month.

The sound paperback bookstore depends partly on the quality of its stock and the arrangement of its titles, not just chosen from run-of-the-mill mass-market best-sellers but carefully selected to serve the broadest cross-section of the community. The arrangement of the titles may be by category, based on the twenty-six major headings listed in *Paperbound Books in Print,* or in the *ABA Paperbound Basic Book List.* Within each category, books may be shelved alphabetically by author's name.

It is equally important that the salespeople be well informed and helpful at all times. Clerks must also be made aware that a paperback is easily pilferable and that only they act as a deterrent against "ripoffs." Urge them to be alert, observing both the suspicious and the non-suspicious, without offending the latter. Particularly vulnerable are paperback operations located in or near colleges and schools where there's a certain element of the student body with an irresponsible attitude toward others' property.

In any store, turnover is important. Maintaining the recommended four-times-a-year turnover of stock may not be a simple matter for some paperback booksellers. Others report turnovers of five, six, and even seven times a year. Inflation has affected production costs, including paper, thus making paperbacks somewhat more expensive than they used to be.

There is thus more reason than ever to intensify promotion of the best-seller mass-market during slow seasons—promoting the hot books and using sales gimmicks to increase sales.

Should business fall off and the retail price of paperbacks continue to rise, then as buyers we must exercise restraint and use fewer copies to test titles. By buying fewer of a title, we keep our investment within limits.

Whatever the problems, paperbacks are here to stay and the paperback bookseller can look forward to making a respectable profit while serving his public.

Remainders and Reprints   **28**

ROBERT C. McGEE
*Walden Book Company,
Stamford, Connecticut*

With the upward price spiral in new-book publishing, remainders and reprints have a very healthy future in the retail bookstore. In many instances, remainders and reprints account for 20 to 30 per cent of a bookstore's volume.

Those of you who are new to the book world may ask what a remainder is. *Remainders* are books that (1) were printed in much larger quantities than sales warranted, (2) didn't sell due to limited interest or overpricing, (3) have later been issued in paperback editions, or (4) have simply run their course at full price.

It is important for you not to think of remainders as books that are not saleable. Many of these books were at one time national best-sellers. Most are books that were either overpriced or had a limited audience at their original price. Remainders are indeed saleable. In addition, they also (1) create traffic, (2) stimulate and enhance the image of the store, and (3) produce *profitable* sales volume.

One of the fastest-growing remainder categories is that of *reprints.* These are books, usually with many color illustrations, that have proven their marketability by selling unusually well as remainders. They are reprinted in very large quantities and marketed through remainder houses at about half the original published price. There is *real* value in reprints. The value is so apparent to the customer that many dealers have had excellent results blending reprints with regular stock. This is especially true in such categories as antiques, cookbooks, and art. Reprints have become the basic stock books that were once hard to find in remainder houses, assuring that proven sellers continue to be available once the original stock is exhausted.

When a publisher decides that he must reduce his inventory of slower-moving titles, he has two choices. First, he may offer them directly to booksellers either at a lower net price, leaving the selling price to the bookseller's option, or at a lower retail price less a standard discount. Let the bookseller be cautioned that "self-remaindering," as this process is called, is usually done on a non-returnable basis. Once you've bought it, it's no longer the publisher's mistake if it doesn't sell —it's yours, as are all further losses if you can't sell it at the price for which you bought it. There are no advertising allowances granted.

The publisher's second choice is to offer lots of books to the highest bidder among the several wholesalers specializing in remainders. By far, most remainders travel this route. There are half a dozen remainder houses in the New York area. The current remainder specialists are listed in the supplementary section of the *ABA Book Buyer's Handbook.* They are also the primary source for reprints. Among the services they offer (which most publishers who self-remainder do not) are advertising allowances, special mailing pieces, ad copy, glossies, and return privileges.

Remainder houses also offer a third category of promotional book —the special import—which complements the remainder and the reprint. *Special imports* are books printed abroad which have no U.S. list price and are therefore offered without a comparative price. They are generally profusely illustrated books that represent a real value for the money, but frequently stores take care to offer them separately as "special values" rather than "sale books." This, in addition to being a more honest designation, avoids the problem of answering the embarrassing question, "How much was this originally?"

Selling Techniques

Now that we have defined them and discussed where they come from, how do we merchandise them? Some people keep permanent remainder tables, others use remainders only for promotions, and there are others who combine both these approaches.

The permanent remainder table. Many booksellers prefer to keep displays of remainders at all times, continually freshening the stock with small quantities of new titles as they become available. Slower-moving titles are not replaced as they are sold, while fast-moving titles may have an effective life of several months. This method is especially effective for the smaller bookstore that operates on a limited advertising budget. The trick here is to display your books in a key traffic area and to sign your tables properly with value slogans. Soon you'll have a steady stream of regular customers checking for your latest bargains.

If you should want to advertise the titles on the table or the table itself, you may be permitted to accumulate an advertising allowance on all purchases during the year to be used for a future newspaper ad.

Usually this amount is 10 per cent of the net purchases and must be spent during the same year that the books were received. Advertising is rebated on proof of tearsheet and is reimbursed on a 75/25 cooperative basis (75 per cent of your supplier's money to 25 per cent of your money).

The promotional approach. A second approach to remainders is to buy a specific sale assortment from the remainder house, running a newspaper ad and returning the unsold portion usually within one month. Advertising policies are uniform here. You are entitled to 10 per cent of net purchases (that is, less returns) for newspaper advertising. Radio and TV advertising must usually be approved in advance because of the large variance in rates. All advertising is based on the cheapest local line rate on a 75/25 cooperative basis.

There are three methods of buying a remainder promotion:

1. *The Package Promotion.*—Notify the remainder house that you are planning a sale. State the date you plan the event, the number of titles you require, and total dollars you want to invest. Your supplier will make your selections for you and send you the necessary promotional materials. These arrangements should be made six weeks to two months in advance of the planned date. The success of the package promotion depends entirely on your supplier's ability to select books that will sell in your area. Try to help him to make a good selection for your store by indicating to him the type of books you sell best.

2. *The Hand-picked Promotion.*—While some remainder houses have salesmen on the road with jackets representing their latest acquisitions, hand-picking usually involves the buyer's coming to New York, where the remainder houses are located, and selecting his own books from the sample showrooms. Sometimes it is possible to select your own titles from available catalogs. However, it is important to realize that most remainder catalogs are outdated within several weeks after publication. The market moves too quickly to allow reliance on the catalog method. In either case it is important that you select about 20 per cent more titles than you plan to receive. Some titles go out of stock within a matter of days. The "overbuy" method prevents your supplier sending you substitutes that you do not want if you give him, as you should, a dollar figure which you want the order to approximate.

3. *A Third Method.*—Select the best available stock from a variety of sources. This often provides a better and stronger category assortment, and you can pick up sales on a hot remainder that is available for a short period of time. It also gives you greater

protection against duplication of titles by competing remainder wholesalers.

Advertising the remainder promotion properly is tremendously important. Timing is of the essence and will vary by trade area. Traditionally the two strongest periods are January/February and September/October. However, watch your competition and schedule around them if possible—or simply make your sale better than theirs.

Advertising

Select the local paper with the largest circulation, if you can afford it. Generally, Sunday ads are best because of the book interest created by book reviews and other feature sections. The average family spends more time with its Sunday paper than with the dailies. Do not advertise a remainder sale on the book page. This limits your market. Aim for the higher-readership general news sections of the paper. You've undoubtedly selected a variety of books that will appeal to the non-book-buyer or the occasional book customer as well as the serious reader. Don't take a chance on missing this diverse market by advertising in a special-readership section.

However, special sections can also be effectively utilized by running small feature-page ads—sports books on the sports page, cookbooks on the women's page, business books on the financial page, and so on. Small remainder ads in feature sections can add a real plus to your sales volume. Here, you are after a special audience and the special sections are ideal.

Allow enough advertising copy to sell your books. Generally, higher-priced books require more descriptive copy while books under $5 can sometimes sell in large quantities from just a few descriptive lines. The advertising copy supplied by your remainder source can frequently be edited without losing its effectiveness.

Always include a mail-order coupon in your ad. Make sure it is large enough to be easily filled out. Mail orders average from 20 to 30 per cent of total promotional sales with most dealers. Don't let the fact that you have never actively solicited mail order deter you. You'll be pleasantly surprised with the results. Do not permit C.O.D.'s, however. Too many are refused, and the cost is on you.

Use the smallest readable newspaper type available. Book readers and bargain hunters are used to reading small type. Indeed, it seems to attract them. Adequate sales copy is essential to selling your books. Don't waste your space with large type and white border space no matter what the advertising textbooks say. Use several illustrations or photographs to dress up your ad. The remainder houses supply free glossies. Try to arrange your books in broad category groupings with a heading for each one. Many times this will attract the customer who doesn't take the time to read your entire ad.

Make sure you know the lead time required by your local paper in reserving ad space. This will vary greatly from one area to another. You should also know the schedule on which you will receive and must return proofs. It is also good to know the latest time at which you may cancel the ad if the proofs are totally unsatisfactory.

Always use the comparative prices supplied by the remainder house. The greater the comparative savings, the better the sales. But be honest. False comparatives create mistrust—and rightfully so.

Pick a name for your book sale and feature it with a **bold** heading across the top of your ad. Immediately below, list the savings spread in percentages (e.g., 20%–50%) and the dollar price range ($.98–$9.98). Some examples of possible sale headings are:

> Winter [Spring, Summer, Fall] Sale
> George Washington's Birthday Book Sale
> Semi-Annual Clearance Sale
> Mother's [Father's] Day Book Sales
> Pre-Holiday Gift Book Sale
> Pre-Inventory Sale
> [Your Own Store's] Birthday Book Sale
> Valentine Book Sale
> Graduation Gift Book Sale

You can also use local historic dates. Watch your city's department store advertising. They'll use every conceivable heading for their special events. You might find a few that you can use. Think up some of your own.

Use art work to emphasize the name of your sale if possible. If you haven't a resident artist in the family, use the books of ready-made art that your newspaper can supply free. You'll find pages of cupids, graduates, Washington-chopping-down-cherry-trees, spring sunbursts, and people-breaking-down-doors. Of course, it's better if you can come up with something original; but if you are short of funds or ideas, canned art is better than no art.

The remainder houses will supply you with samples of ads that have actually been successful in other stores. One final word of caution about ads: Be certain that you have *in the store* all the books you are advertising before you O.K. the final proof.

Display and Signing

Now that the title selection has been made and your newspaper ad is placed, the final preparation for the sale-day event involves display and signing. This sounds like a simple ingredient of a successful sale—and it is. However, it is also the most often overlooked. Here are a few hints that you'll find helpful:

- Feature your sale in a high-traffic area. Don't hide it in a hard-to-find corner of your shop. If you've got a bargain to offer, make it easy to find.
- Stack up your books for impact. Avoid that flat look. Pyramid your stock to give the impression you have more than you actually do.
- Proper signing is essential. Utilize window signing to highlight a sample selection. Demonstrate the values of the books in your window with cards showing the original and new prices mounted directly onto the dust jackets of the books with double-faced masking tape. Use large signing at your store entrances and smaller signing on each of your table displays. Sign each and every table. Don't make the customer guess.
- Mount a copy of your newspaper ad on signboard and feature it at your store entrance. This will help call attention to the event for those who missed your ad. It will also help to identify the style of your ad in the minds of your customers, so that they'll recognize it when you run one again.

Remainders are exciting and profitable. Join the hundreds of book-sellers already enjoying tremendous extra sales through remainder promotions. Your customers will love them.

Foreign Books for the American Bookseller

29

ANTHONY I. LEE
Schoenhof's Foreign Books, Inc.,
Cambridge, Massachusetts

Foreign-book selling is an activity that most American booksellers have viewed with great caution. They have seen it as a dark and mysterious territory where the unwary are likely to catch their feet in hidden and tangled undergrowth, taking the inevitable headlong fall. This attitude is understandable. It is demanding enough for the bookseller to keep up with the ever-burgeoning output of the increasing number of American publishers without compounding his problems by entering into a field that will require familiarizing himself with even more authors, titles, and publishers—the whole, to make it worse, obscured behind murky veils of a few foreign languages with which he might not be wholly familiar.

However, there is a definite market for foreign books, and many booksellers would like to know how they can cater to, stimulate, and profit from this market. Fortunately, it is possible to provide guidelines and pointers to help the bookseller who wishes to venture into this field.

The Market

When he considers dealing in a particular type of book, the first thing a bookseller will ask himself is whether he has a market for that type of book. Where foreign books are concerned there are three potential markets for the bookseller to evaluate. His decision must take into account the existence of these markets, or a combination of them, in the area in which he is doing business.

The first market might be termed the "ethnic-group market." A bookseller might be situated in an area where there is an appreciable gathering of first- or second-generation immigrant Americans who still speak the language of their country of origin or nationality at home and in their community. As a market for foreign-language books, this group must be very carefully evaluated. The question that must be asked is whether the members of this community want to read books in their native language. In most cases the answer will probably be that they do not. The older members of the community will often only read newspapers and magazines bought at a local store. The younger members frequently have only a speaking knowledge of their parents' native language and their reading matter is all in English. One by-product of the proximity of such an ethnic group is the customer who wants to buy a book as a present for a grandmother, grandfather, aunt, uncle, etc., who does not read English. This request is complicated by the customer not being sufficiently familiar with the relative's language to have an author or title in mind. However, it is not too difficult to stock a few suitable books to offer should this kind of request be made with any regularity.

Before an attempt is made to define the second and what is probably the largest market for foreign-language books, it would be worth while to consider the general level of interest in foreign languages in the United States today. Briefly, interest is very high. Many colleges, it is true, have dropped their language requirements, but nevertheless public interest in foreign languages is quite substantial. There seems to be a tremendous fascination in knowing another language, in adding a new dimension to one's ability to communicate. This is reflected in the increasing number of private language schools and large enrollments in language classes at adult education centers and university extension schools. The interest in foreign languages is further stimulated by the increasing accessibility to all, and especially to the young, of foreign travel. The bookseller who already stocks trade language-learning books, foreign-language dictionaries, and phrase books has probably seen evidence of this. If so, there are very good reasons to consider developing the potential market that the bookseller tapped when he sold his customer a teach-yourself language book and a paperback dictionary.

Thus, the largest market for foreign-language books, leaving aside required school and college textbooks as outside the scope of this article, is, perhaps, paradoxically, made up of customers whose first language is not the language in which the book they are buying was written.

The majority of foreign-language books bought in this country, outside of textbooks, are probably bought by English-speaking people who learned the foreign language in question as part of an academic discipline, their knowledge of the language possibly improved by study or travel abroad. In many cases their interest in the language will have no professional or academic motivation. They simply will have maintained their interest in foreign languages and literature. In the vicinity of colleges and universities especially there will be many people, language specialists or otherwise, who wish to read foreign books, perhaps just to go beyond the books listed for their courses, yet who are unable to find a selection of foreign books at their college bookstores. The bookseller contemplating selling foreign books would of course be well advised to research other sources of supply, such as college bookstores, with which he might find himself in competition. An amorphous market, difficult to profile, but there nevertheless.

The final group of potential foreign-book buyers, a little easier to profile than the language-conscious American group, is a cosmopolitan group, composed of people from abroad who are in the United States either on business or for educational purposes. While this group has much in common with the ethnic groups mentioned first, it differs in that it is formed of people who have recently arrived to stay in this country, who might only be here for a limited period, and who are thus more closely in touch with the cultural life of their home countries. Also, because of their reasons for being in the United States and the socio-economic background suggested by their international mobility, they are more liable to be book buyers. At any one time in any of the large population centers in the country, there are likely to be a large number of people who fall into this category. The members of the group might be constantly changing but the group itself is always there.

Kinds and Sources of Stock

Once the bookseller who is interested in selling foreign books has decided that there is a market, or a combination of markets, for books in French, German, Spanish, Italian, Russian, or whatever language, in his area, his next two considerations will be sources of supply and what to stock. These two considerations are closely connected and the decision on the first will go a long way toward resolving the dilemma of the second.

Where the supply of foreign books is concerned, the bookseller has a choice of two sources. He can order direct from publishers abroad or he can work with an importer based in the United States. The bookseller for whom foreign books will only be a small part of total business, who does not intend making a large-scale specialty of selling foreign books, will find little advantage in dealing directly with foreign publishers. The principal drawbacks would be the additional cost of dealing with a variety of suppliers (who would also be located in a variety of countries and working in a variety of currencies); long waiting periods for shipments (most books ordered from abroad take from five weeks to three months to arrive); and the impossibility of returning unsold books, since most foreign publishers do not offer returns privileges, except in certain limited circumstances, and even then, shipping costs both ways make mistakes or poor judgment in ordering very expensive. The possibility of buying books a little cheaper by ordering direct rather than dealing with a domestic wholesaler does not make up for the extra work, risk, and expense involved. As will be shown below, it is possible to sell with a reasonable margin, comparable with that on American books, when buying from a wholesaler of foreign books. Finally, ordering from abroad does not provide the bookseller with the close working relationship that he can have with a wholesaler based in the United States, a relationship that could be especially helpful to the bookseller who is unfamiliar with the field and is just getting started.

There are several importer-wholesalers in the United States. Some specialize in books in one or two languages, some stock books in a wide variety of languages. A list of such wholesalers, with their specialties, can be found in the *ABA Book Buyer's Handbook.*

When ordering through a wholesaler, the bookseller can expect delivery of the books that the wholesaler carries as regular stock items within two to three weeks. On most books, the wholesaler will give him between 20 and 40 per cent discount. It must be realized, of course, that the wholesaler himself will only receive between 30 and 40 per cent discount from the foreign publisher, so to give a discount himself he must raise prices accordingly. Different wholesalers will have different policies on the discount they give and the amount by which they increase the price of the book. The bookseller should bear in mind that there is no real list price for an imported book and he should price his books in a way he feels is fair and reasonable in terms of the price he paid and the market he has for them. He is not necessarily doing the best for himself by buying from the wholesaler who gives the biggest percentage discount; net price and service should be the main criteria.

When dealing with a wholesaler, the bookseller can expect to enjoy a returns privilege much in accordance with the returns policies of most American publishers. The bookseller should take the trouble to find out what the wholesaler's policies in this matter are when first examining sources of supply. Usually the returns privilege does not apply to books that have been specially imported and that the wholesaler does not usually carry in stock. For this reason the bookseller is advised to limit his orders to books the wholesaler does stock on a regular basis. This naturally leads to the question of what the bookseller should consider stocking in his foreign-book department, and what he should avoid.

It will probably surprise most booksellers to know that the books that will form the best stock for his foreign department are probably on his shelves already—in English translations. The steadiest-selling foreign books in the United States are the works of important modern and classic authors with whom the bookseller will probably already be familiar. One might mention as examples Camus, Sartre, Gide, Molière,

Balzac, Flaubert, Cervantes, Lorca, García Márquez, Goethe, Mann, Grass, Böll, Moravia, and Pavese. These are names known to most American booksellers and indicate the type of books he should consider for his foreign department. One important point is that literary works are the most reliable sellers; another is that the most important literary works written in French, Spanish, German, and Italian are available in attractive and inexpensive paperback editions. Despite the rising cost of foreign books and of importing, prices compare favorably with the prices of American paperbacks.

In general it is best to avoid carrying new novels that have not yet been published in an inexpensive paperback series. They are very expensive and a large investment is required to carry a wide enough selection to build volume. An exception is the book that is enjoying great popularity in English translation. This often creates good sales in the foreign-language original, but of course, by the time the English-language translation has been published the original may well be available in an inexpensive edition. It is also wise to avoid art books and other pictorial books and gift editions, since the high prices of these books make them appear poor buys next to the ubiquitous bargain-priced American remainders.

The request for a foreign-language book to give as a special gift, mentioned earlier, is often best answered by suggesting a bound edition of a well-known classic. These are available in various series that are not exorbitantly priced and a wholesaler should be able to quote something suitable from his stock.

One final word of warning on what not to stock—foreign translations of works written in English. Most people who buy foreign books want to read a work in its original. The market for German translations of Hemingway might be big in Germany but it is very small over here.

Last words. Mention has already been made of the rising price of foreign books. Inflation abroad, combined with the weakness of the dollar, has caused dollar prices of imported books to increase greatly. Thus the bookseller should not be surprised if books he reorders come in at a higher price than a few weeks before. This is one of the great disadvantages of importing books. One cannot tell what the price will be on the next shipment, except that it is unlikely to be lower.

Many booksellers might wonder how important it is to have a knowledge of any foreign languages to be able to run a successful foreign-book department. It would certainly be helpful to have some knowledge, and obviously a bookseller's knowledge and interest will be important in his decision whether or not to sell foreign books. His major customers for foreign-language books can be of great assistance. However, interest and confidence are more important than a thorough knowledge of the language of the books being sold. It is important to be able to keep track of the foreign titles; familiarity with the books themselves is often provided by the bookseller's familiarity with the English translations.

Finally, and with the previous paragraph in mind, here is a suggestion for the bookseller who is interested in having a foreign-book section but is unsure of how he will fare at handling books in foreign languages or of what sort of market he will have for them. If he wants to experiment, without going in too far, he might set up a section containing some of the bilingual readers and anthologies available from various American paperback publishers. These, together with the books for learning foreign languages mentioned earlier, should give him a good opportunity to test both himself and his market for the selling of foreign books.

Rare and Out-of-Print Books

30

SOL M. MALKIN

Founder of Antiquarian Bookman *and*
Field Editor of AB Bookman's Weekly

Imagine a separate book world within the world of books where dealers set up their businesses where they please (store or office, home or barn); where the minimum markup is 100 per cent: where they can call upon over 5,000 fellow dealers throughout the world and a stock of over 200 million volumes, practically from the beginning of the printed word; where books are safely packed and mailed with no extra charge for postage; where there is no competition from publishers and discount houses; where colleagues help one another in time of need to provide fellow dealers with a unique service that makes happy customers all the time—an ideal imaginary book world that never was nor ever will be? Perhaps . . . but the above is at least 99 per cent true in the antiquarian book trade.

Many new-book dealers think of the antiquarian bookseller as a secondhand junkman or as a weird character who obtains books by sorcery, prices them by cabalistic necromancy, and sells them by black magic. To be sure there are still a few dealers who might fit that description, but in general, the antiquarian bookseller is a highly competent, trained bookman who is in this field to take advantage of his knowledge and love of books for both pleasure and profit.

Many new-book dealers still equate "antiquarian" with "secondhand." Would you call an original Hepplewhite chair "secondhand furniture"? In fact, the antiquarian takes in the old and the new, the used and the out-of-print, the rare and the specialized work. Thus, a book can be new, perhaps a review copy, a remainder (entire or partial), or an out-of-print title that the antiquarian dealer is glad to obtain and save for stock, certain that the title will be in demand in the future.

An o.p. (out-of-print) book is not necessarily a used or an old book. A new book can go o.p. very quickly and not be reprinted. Even if later the title is available in a paperback edition, the customer will often want the original cloth-bound work, especially if the reprint is abridged, has poor paper, inferior press work, or foggy halftone illustrations.

It is impossible in this limited space to discuss all the complexities that go into the making of antiquarian bookselling. But there are three major and profitable parts of this field that can be conducted by every new-book dealer searching for out-of-print and unusual books: buying and selling out-of-print books, rare books, and fine bindings—or (1) the complete book service, (2) the complete sales service, and (3) the complete bookshop.

1. *The Complete Book Service*

Any bookseller can offer a complete book service and take advantage of the 200-million-plus stock of his fellow dealers. No bookseller should turn away any customer who asks for any out-of-the-way or o.p. book.

Every major country has a major trade magazine that acts as a medium for obtaining books no longer available from publishers. In the United States that is the function of *AB Bookman's Weekly: The Specialist Book Trade Weekly,* or *AB* (which stands for *Antiquarian Bookman*), as it is usually abbreviated in the book world. Dealers simply send cards to *AB* (Box 1100, Newark, N.J. 07101) listing o.p. or special titles their customers want. *AB* prints these want lists of thousands of dealers throughout the country in its weekly issues, at regular rates.

Thousands of fellow dealers throughout the country—and in over fifty foreign countries—check these lists against their stock and advise the advertisers if they can supply the desired titles, giving edition, condition, and price postpaid. Within a week to ten days, each advertiser may receive anywhere from a single to a few dozen such quotations, depending on scarcity and demand for the required book. The price requested may be anywhere from 25¢ to $5, with $2.50 as average, depending on edition and condition. The dealer advises his customer he can get a reading (poor) copy for $1.50, a first edition for $5, or a fine first for $10, marking up the price at least 100 per cent in making the quotation. It's pleasantly surprising to find how often the customer wants the better, more expensive edition in fine condition.

Once the customer makes up his mind, the advertiser advises the quoter to send the book and, if the amount is small, encloses check with order to save bookkeeping on both sides. (Usual terms to known dealers are thirty days net.) Note that the advertiser has not had to invest in any stock to make this transaction—which invariably results in a happy and pleased customer who will return and, in addition, tell his friends about the complete book service he gets from his local dealer.

The cost of advertising in *AB* to the subscribing dealer is 30¢ a line; 50¢ a line to non-subscribers. Most book wants (abbreviations O.K.) will fit on one line. Many antiquarian booksellers include this cost in their charge to customers—some ask an extra charge of 50¢ to $1 for this service, especially to transient or unknown customers. This is a small cost for a unique, world-wide search service that any bookseller can offer to his customers. No matter if the customer does not know exact title, name of author, or edition, fellow dealers will call upon their extensive knowledge of books in their specialties and advise you of the correct information. This is another plus value in the antiquarian book world. New-book dealers are welcomed into the international community of booksellers, and the knowledge and friendships gained are priceless.

The fact that there is such an international search service available makes the bookshop offering an antiquarian book service unique in any community. Do not think of o.p., used, or rare books as sidelines (they are more profitable than greeting cards and other sidelines), and they are an integral part of a complete book service.

2. *The Complete Sales Service*

Although the life of a new book (fiction or nonfiction) could be anywhere from three months to a year or so, an o.p. book never dies. New-book dealers often have opportunities to purchase good private libraries in their communities, but only too often they turn them down because they are not in the antiquarian business. Many bookstores have found it profitable, however, to display out-of-print books (as well as remainders) with new titles in special classifications. Despite the multitude of new subject books in most fields, there are still many back-list and o.p. titles that will be preferred by customers.

Despite careful buying and returns privileges, a new-book dealer will often be stuck with books that cannot be sold in his community. Here again, *AB Bookman's Weekly* plays an important part. There is a special "Books for Sale" section in the back part in which dealers can advertise items for sale at the same 30¢-a-line rate to subscribers. It is intriguing to find that certain titles will be in great demand in some sections of the country while unsaleable in others.

Then, after some experience with advertising and receiving quotation cards, you, too, may be bitten by the quoting urge. In those slack hours in every bookstore, scanning and quoting the lists of "Books Wanted" in *AB* will turn out to be enjoyable as well as profitable. Here is an excellent opportunity for new-book dealers to take advantage of their experience and booklore and reduce their stock of slow-moving titles.

3. *The Complete Bookshop*

A shop that carries only new books is like an iceberg—visible is not just a sixth but a millionth of the total number of titles that have been printed since the Gutenberg Bible (1450–55). No matter how valuable space may be in the most expensive sales area, a separate section of used, o.p., fine-binding, and rare books will pay extra dividends and plus sales. In the beginning, a new-book dealer would do well to add a small general stock of antiquarian books, and then, with experience, specialize in one subject, perhaps a hobby of his own personal choice.

Under no circumstance should a new-book dealer attempt to set up a separate antiquarian bookshop without extensive experience and training in the field. This is a world in itself and requires the most expert help (in scarce supply).

A concise summary of the o.p. field is contained in "The O.P. Market" in the annual issues of *AB Bookman's Yearbook: The Specialist Book Trade Annual.* Complete and practical suggestions will also be found in *ABC of the Book Trade,* reprints of which are available from *AB*, Box 1100, Newark, N.J. 07101.

Setting Up an Out-of-Print Department 31

SAM WELLER
*Sam Weller's Zion Book Store, Inc.,
Salt Lake City, Utah*

Antiquarian bookselling is an integral part of the book business. It complements all phases of bookselling, including new books, paperbacks, and remainders. A book's going out of print does not always mean that it goes out of demand. In a few instances, books with special illustrations or other features may become more valuable than when they were in print. They are more rarely found but far more exciting to discover.

There are many collectors in the book field, specializing in almost every area. Some people collect certain authors' works and may or may not insist on first editions. Some collect everything written about certain subjects and these range from toys or trains to medicine, philosophy, or religion. Old comics or science fiction are in vogue right now. As mentioned in Sol Malkin's article (Chapter 30), specializing in used books on a hobby of your own would be a quick way to get into selling used books with some knowledge of what you need to stock.

In setting up an out-of-print department, you must first consider how to buy the stock. An advertisement in the yellow pages of the telephone book and also one in the classified ads of your local newspaper may bring in individuals who wish to sell their books. Reading *AB Bookman's Weekly* is not only helpful to learning the used-book market, it provides possible sources for special items. Advertising in *AB Bookman's Weekly* will follow when you have built up a want list for your customers.

Books should be purchased and prices determined by anticipating possible future sales. Dealers' catalogs are usually good pricing guides. In buying books, buy at a quarter to a half of your selling price if you already have customers in mind, less if not; run-of-the-mill stuff at 10¢ to 50¢ each; rare books, a third to a half of what you think you can get. Current books bought used are priced at about a half of current list price dependent upon condition, so they must be bought at a quarter of list. Reflect that you may have to give shelf space to a book for several years before it is sold, so initial investment must be low.

Each locality engenders its own specialties and these should be built into collections. First editions of better-known writers are always good. Sets of authors' works or periodicals bound into sets are always worth more when complete. Regional books are important in many areas.

Very important in antiquarian bookselling is compiling and maintaining a customer list. Sometimes finding a specific title takes months or a few years. Names of customers with collections or particular areas of interest should be kept on file so they can be notified when items of interest to them come in.

The older editions of the *Cumulative Book Index* (H. W. Wilson Co.) can help you locate exact author's names and titles. It helps to know what other bookdealers specialize in and where to inquire for a specific title. If you don't know where to ask for a title, you may be able to find a copy by advertising in the *AB*. Should the ad be unsuccessful the first time, more ads are run later at no charge to the customer.

Quotations are received from various dealers throughout the country and the advertiser is notified that the book is available and of the price and condition. If he approves the purchase, a check for the amount is airmailed to the quoting dealer, citing his quotation. If no quotation is received for a given book after two or three ads, the advertiser is notified and at his option *AB* continues to keep his want on file in case one shows up.

The out-of-print file should be worked systematically throughout the year for remaindered or reprinted titles. If you have the time and have a good stock, compile a catalog and include other dealers in your mailing.

A complete service in finding books makes good customer relationships. The person who is told that there are ways to find a copy of a book that is out of print is a more satisfied customer.

Portrait of a Lending Library   **32**

CHARLES B. ANDERSON
Anderson's Book Shop,
Larchmont, New York

The rental library is the most profitable department in our store. It gives us a higher return than personalized Christmas cards or any sideline we have yet discovered. The yearly gross profit has never been less than 65 per cent of receipts and in most years of its history, beginning in 1947, has been closer to 70 per cent. To arrive at our gross profit figure, we determine the cost of all books added to the library and of all direct expenses, such as the cost of plastic bookcovers, library cards, and printing, and subtract it from gross rental receipts. In our new store, the library occupies about 6 per cent of the total selling and display area and accounts for between 5 per cent and 6 per cent of our gross business. There is no other department in our store, or in any other bookstore that I know about, that pays off so well in gross profit, net profit, or profit per square footage of space—any way you want to take it.

Our library is valuable to us in other ways. It is an effective traffic-builder. Most of our library members are good customers for other things, not only for sidelines such as personalized Christmas cards, but also for books. When a library customer discovers a book with a special appeal, he may well buy several copies as gifts for friends, or he may want to add it to his personal library. We try to encourage the ownership of books among our library readers by charging no rental fee for books they decide to buy. In this way we sell several books a day that otherwise probably wouldn't be sold. We do not regard the library in any sense as a sideline. It is so important and integrated a part of our bookstore that our store would lose part of its hold on the community without it.

We sometimes hear it said at bookseller meetings that the lending library is more trouble than it's worth, that it's harder to rent a book than to sell it, and that the space a library takes up can be used more profitably in other ways. Of course we can't agree. We don't think of the library as being much trouble at all. Its operation for us has become pretty mechanical and routine. No one clerk is assigned to the duties of the library, despite the fact that for statistical purposes we charge half the salary of a full-time clerk to library expense. We all have a hand in keeping the library going. If new books are to be added—and they are added practically every day—one of us will get to it when he has the time. But we never neglect it—even during the Christmas rush in December, which is actually the most profitable month of the year for the library as well as for the store generally, since there are so few new books published during that month that we can buy for circulation.

Personality of the Lending Library

We have found that there is really no conflict between the library and our paperback department of some 12,000 titles. In our experience the one complements the other. Every day we see any number of our library customers walking up to the cash desk with a rental book plus a paperback or two. Many of our paperback customers become library members when they discover that current titles unavailable in paperback are rentable at a very nominal fee.

What of the public library? Why should our people pay to rent books that they could get at our excellent local public library at no cost? There are two pretty good reasons. They can get the current books from us faster, and they have a considerably wider selection of new fiction, including mysteries. The public library buys one or two or three copies of a best-seller. We buy from ten to thirty. The public library must be selective in its purchase of fiction and mysteries. We buy at least one copy of almost every work of general fiction and one or more copies of every who-done-it published in America. We never think of the public library as being in competition with us, and the staff of the public library feels the same way about us. Practically every day they send people to us for books they do not have or for which there may be a waiting list of a month or more. Several members of their staff, including the head librarian, are active members of our library. They, too, come to us for books they do not have, sometimes to sample them with a view to possible acquisition for their shelves.

The library is the most personal department of our personal bookstore. All of us on the staff know practically all our regular readers by name. We know their likes and dislikes in novels and nonfiction, and even though we encourage self-service in the library, especially when we are all busy in other parts of the store, we are always willing to try to find the right book for anyone who asks our help. The comments we get from those we like to call our "good readers" are helpful to us in recommending books to others, both for sale and rent, and in reordering from publishers and jobbers.

We have about a thousand members on our library rolls. Some two hundred of these are regular readers who have one or more books out practically all the time. Of these there are six or seven who read, or at least take out, almost every book of fiction in the library, thus assuring us of some kind of activity and income even from the "turkeys." Then there are more than a dozen members who can be depended on to read every mystery published. Of the other eight hundred library members about three hundred are fairly regular readers, and the remaining five hundred rent books occasionally. About 75 per cent of our readers are women, 25 per cent men. Our library members come from the various economic, social, and educational strata of the community. We have readers who are well-to-do and others who must budget what they spend to rent books. Walter and Jean Kerr and Phyllis McGinley are regular library customers, as well as regular buyers of books. Among the best-read people in Larchmont are a house painter and a truck driver. Since our library offers such a complete selection of current books, some of our members come from a good many miles away, even from Connecticut and New York City, and we do a limited mail-order business with customers who have moved away and have found no comparable source of book supply in their new quarters. Though the teen-agers are among our best customers for paperbacks, there are practically no high school or college students using our library, and we do not encourage them for the practical reason that losses in books never returned by the youngsters are high. Now and then during vacation a student will rent a book on his parent's card with his parent, of course, responsible for its return.

Policies and Finances

About 65 per cent of the books we rent are novels, 20 per cent mysteries and suspense, and 15 per cent nonfiction. Our best renters are of course the best-sellers, both in fiction and nonfiction, and in mysteries the name authors, such as Christie, Gardner, and McBain. Since we have no reserves and do not notify customers when books they want are in, we try to have enough copies of the top books on the shelves so that no one need wait for them. Should the demand for a book increase, we add copies from stock as required. We feel that this is sound merchandising practice in the case of best-sellers, for we can always get top prices in our semi-annual used-book sale for these books when they are retired from the library.

We charge no deposit except for transients, who leave a dollar, which is refundable when they ask for it. If a book is lost or damaged beyond salvage, we ask the customer to pay the retail price of the book if it is a new book that we would have to replace. If it is an older book no longer in active demand, we settle generally for half list price. When books are taken out and not returned, we try by mail or telephone to persuade the customer to make what he considers a fair settlement. If the customer tells us he returned the books to our store, as is rather often the case, we take him at his word and charge the missing books to profit and loss. In this way we lose from thirty to fifty books a year, or less than a fraction of 1 per cent of our gross rental receipts. Most of our customers take out only one book at a time, yet many take out two or three when they find titles they want. There are a few customers who will take five, six, or even more books at a time. Sometimes a library member planning on a vacation will take along as many as ten or fifteen books, even though we do not offer a special vacation or "bulk" rate. The average ring of the cash register for the library is more than a dollar.

Our rates on books with a list price of $7 or less are 10¢ a day with a minimum rental of 50¢; on books that list between $7 and $9 there is a minimum rental of 75¢ for the first three days and 10¢ a day thereafter; on books that are $9 and more (mostly nonfiction), the rate is still 10¢ a day but the first three days are $1. Our rule of thumb is to have about 1,200 books in the library at one time, representing a capital investment of about $3,700 at our cost. Of these, about 800 to 900 books are on the shelves and between 300 and 400 on rental. If a book has not been rented in two to four months, we retire it to the used-book sale and mark it at whatever price we think we can get for it. If it doesn't sell, say, at 98¢, we'll reduce the price to 59¢ or 29¢. If nobody wants it at any price, we'll put it into a carton with other unsaleable books and when we've accumulated a carton or two, give the whole thing to a local charity, which is apparently grateful for our discards. We feel that we can't afford valuable store or storage space for books that we cannot sell or rent.

We try to keep bookkeeping to a minimum, but we like to know pretty accurately what the library is doing for us. The library has its special key on one of our two cash registers, so that we know exactly at the end of every day, week, and month what the gross receipts have been. It is equally important for us to know what we have spent on it. For this purpose we record in a loose-leaf 9"X12" notebook the title of every book that goes into the library, the date it is added, the number of copies of this title, and the list price. Additional expenses, such as the cost of plastic book covers, library cards, and paste, are recorded in a separate section of the same notebook. At the end of each month we add the list price of all the books for that month, and, to determine our net cost, take 60 per cent of this figure. Although we often do better than 40 per cent on some books, we feel that if we attempted to record the exact net price of every title it would complicate our bookkeeping and serve no particularly useful purpose, an idea with which our accountant agrees.

From 1968 to 1973, our library has had an increase each year in gross receipts of not less than 5 per cent. We must account for this annual increase not so much because we are circulating more books every year but rather because with the higher list prices of typical library books, we are renting fewer books at the minimum fee of 50¢ and more at 75¢ and $1.

Table 32.1 shows the income and outgo for the library in 1973.

TABLE 32.1

LENDING-LIBRARY PROFIT, 1973

Month	Receipts
January	$ 1,434
February	1,228
March	1,350
April	1,344
May	1,424
June	1,465
July	1,630
August	1,472
September	1,499
October	1,481
November	1,469
December	1,218
	$17,014
Used books	1,619
Gross receipts	$18,633
Cost of books	5,305
Other expenses	145
Gross profit	$13,183
Per cent gross profit*	70.7%

*We estimate that the library occupies about 6 per cent of our store area. Therefore if we charge 6 per cent of our store rental to the library and add to it half the salary of one of our clerks, we still come out with a net profit of more than 50 per cent. We spend no money on advertising, as we believe that word-of-mouth is the only effective advertising for a library, in addition, of course, to an attractive and orderly display in the store of the several hundred books available for rental.

Words of advice. There are always a few people around who expect super-treatment, and who sometimes demand more than we are able or willing to give. Sometimes it becomes necessary to have a heart-to-heart talk, as for example with a customer who can't understand why she may not take out a new art book on loan or perhaps the latest Newbery Medal winner to read to her children. We try to explain why this sort of rental is the proper function of the school or public library and not a commercial one like ours. But we try to be fair to all and not to play favorites. We don't, for instance, set aside books for some readers and not for others, for we feel that the word would surely get around to those excluded from the inner circle. Almost all of our library members, however, are understanding and appreciative, and some of them are among the biggest boosters in the community for our store.

All of us on the staff read as many books as we have time or inclination for, and we read the reviews in the newspapers and magazines that our customers are most likely to see, the most influential in our community being *The New York Times Book Review* on Sunday, the reviews and ads in the daily *Times,* and *New Yorker, Time,* and *Newsweek* magazines, pretty much in that order. When a customer asks for our opinion of a book, we don't attempt to give a literary review or a detailed summary of the plot. What they usually want to know is whether we think they will like it. The typical library customer is looking for escape literature.

Our attitude toward the library is not entirely commercial. We do not always remain passive and let demand alone determine what goes on the shelves. We work for a book that we consider important or neglected and urge our members to read it. If they agree with us, as they frequently do, they'll talk about it among their friends, who may come in to rent or buy it. By the simple power of word-of-mouth advertising we have often created a local best-seller of a book that has had little or no critical attention or publisher advertising. In the case of local authors, for whom we feel an obligation to do everything we can to bring their books—good or bad— to the attention of the community, we find the library most useful, more so than newspaper advertising, autograph parties, or posters and circulars. If we think that a book has no special merit except for having been written by a local author, we recommend it on this basis only. There are always library readers and book buyers who will want to read it or own it out of local pride or simple curiosity. We even put books of vanity publishers in the library if the authors are local. In short we feel that in the library we have an effective means of serving the cultural needs of our community.

Departments 2: Sidelines

Sidelines and the American Bookstore

33

JOSEPH A. DUFFY
Former Executive Director,
American Booksellers Association, Inc.

Diversification in retailing seems to have come naturally to the American merchant. The general store is just as home-grown as baseball. The large department store represents the full flowering of multiple merchandising in our country. The corner drugstore with its fantastic mix of divergent lines is the most commonplace example of the independent retailer's scramble for a share of the American consumer dollar and, therefore, survival.

Outside the large cities of the United States in the nineteenth and early twentieth centuries, books were sold predominantly as a sideline. Dry goods and books have been traditional allies. Stationery, school supplies, and books have a deep family relationship. Retailers in many fields from coast to coast have welcomed and fostered books as a sideline ever since the American community settled into place. For some odd and unexplained reason, even wallpaper hitched up with books as a team and there are signs reading "Wallpaper and Books" still hanging in the side streets of a few forgotten shopping areas of Midwestern towns. Some thirty years ago, the proprietor of one of these papermarts, unable to retire, staved off the depression and bankruptcy by becoming an insurance agent. He would lie in wait to sell an ordinary life policy to the unsuspecting book and wallpaper salesmen who came to the store to sell him their wares.

In the big cities of Boston, Philadelphia, and New York, the situation was somewhat different. Here the large bookstores were initially allied with book publishing itself. In fact they were either father to a publisher or the child of one. Which came first is left to the book-industry historians to say. To this day there are publishers with bookstores as a sideline and bookstores with book-publishing programs as moonlighting activities.

In these big towns, where buyer traffic is relatively heavy, special-ization among retail stores was to be expected and so the independent "books only" establishment was able to survive in normal times. How-ever, even these simon-pure purveyors of the printed word underwent a drastic change during the terrible days of the early thirties. They either succumbed to the depression or took on the money-making mer-chandise that spelled success. Today the average bookstore, whether in the East or West, in large city or in small, derives roughly 30 per cent of its income from non-book merchandise. There are a few exceptions. Perhaps three or four of the top twenty bookstores of the country can boast a 100 per cent offering of unalloyed literary fare, but only one out of two hundred smaller outlets can make the same claim. These figures are estimates developed from answers to a questionnaire sent to ABA members at the time of distribution of the 1965 *ABA Sidelines Direc-tory.*

One of the largest bookstore operations in the country is a chain group owned by a religious organization, and these outlets carry a heavy percentage of church goods and Sunday school supplies. They are true bookstores, however, carrying full-scale stocks of general trade books and they are recognized as centers for the most up-to-date and complete offering of the latest and best in town. Another chain of stores in a large near-Midwestern city is predominantly, that is to say 70 per cent, devoted to social and commercial stationery, but the remaining 30 per cent of its annual revenue is one of the country's largest dollar grosses in book volume.

Two of the best-known chain bookstore operations in the East admit to 80 per cent books. The remaining 20 per cent in one instance is made up largely of phonograph-record sales and ·a smattering of greeting cards. The other chain carries a large assortment of art objects, sculpture, and prints. But in both cases all sidelines are in harmony with books.

Smaller stores show a fairly uniform pattern of sidelines ranging from 50 per cent to 20 per cent. The very few stores reporting "books only" seem to be heavily committed to paperback sales. In fact there is evidence that paperbacks are elbowing into the background some sidelines that were formerly important to smaller dealers. To make space for the mass-market and trade variety of soft-cover books in response to popular demand, the dealer is balancing the added volume of paperback sales against the larger profits on sideline merchandise.

The question of space is terribly important. Some sidelines take up more than their share of shelf room, even though the markup is good. The space factor is, of course, of major concern to all who approach merchandising in the spirit of scientific analysis. The yield per square foot has driven many department store book departments upstairs and in some cases right out the door. This philosophy, however, seems not to discourage the store owner who is determined to wear the badge of Bookseller. Many concessions are needed to carry on and high book turnover may have to be sacrificed to a slower-moving but more complete inventory.

Let's stop and look at the situation. As much as he may want to lead the good life devoted to the noble cause of books alone, a good bookseller must adjust to the realities of successful marketing, to the stepped-up pace of this generation. To protect his first interest, books, the bookseller may have to bring up the reserves and surround his beloved book business with greeting cards, gifts, chessmen, ceramics, and, yes, even candy, a post office, or insurance, if fate decrees that this is the way to get a profitable turnover.

The average sideline carries a higher average markup than books. Many greeting cards, for instance, yield 100 per cent markups—with 50 per cent discount across the board, many sidelines put the book's average 37 per cent discount to shame.

Experience has shown that the inclusion of sidelines in his daily life does not necessarily dull the keen edge of a good bookselling talent.

Many sidelines are profitable in themselves but beyond that they can and do create traffic that leads to an increased sale of the main product, books, and they may attract customers who are not steady book buyers.

When the ABA came out with its first edition of the *Sidelines Directory,* it was issued with misgivings on the part of some ABA board members, who went along with the majority but adhered to the traditional view of bookselling as a sort of sacrosanct profession. Now even these and other idealists mix their merchandise a bit.

The reception of the *Sidelines Directory* was immediate and enthusiastic. It is revised frequently to keep up with the times. Rather than reach for every conceivable sideline and a listing of every possible supplier, the *Directory* has taken a qualitative approach. Congeniality is the key word. No sideline is listed unless it obviously fits into the "book" environment. If an off-beat product finds its way in, it does so only upon the introduction of some reputable bookseller who has experimented and found that sideline suitable.

There are a few do's and don't's to be observed by the knowledgeable bookman in his excursion into the land of new sidelines. The *Directory* points out a few of these. Some suggestions are pretty obvious, but all are essential to achieving a solid combination of saleable goods giving a healthy return and reasonable turnover. The foremost admonition is, of course, a reminder that sidelines are supplementary merchandise designed to build traffic, to increase the margin of profit, to add attractiveness to the store, to provide new services for existing book customers, and, it is hoped, to bring more potential book buyers into the shop.

The *Directory* admonishes limitation of the number of sidelines carried. It suggests avoidance of overcrowding, advocates the limitation of lines to items that fall fairly well within the bookseller's own interest and appeal to his own taste. He must, however, check the market for saleability even though a strong personal preference does exist. It is a mistake to go all-out and try to compete with full-time competitors. Remember, you are a bookseller first and only marginally a gift shop, card shop, stationer, or record dealer. Try to offer quality in all that you add to books. Keep space allocations under control—the store should continue to look like a bookstore, not like a random gift bazaar. Remember to preserve the bookstore image.

The bookseller's talent for personal salesmanship gives him an advantage in selling other merchandise. He has been trained by the very nature of books to probe into the personal likes and dislikes, the intellectual, social and economic capacities of his customers. The good bookman should be able to predict a sale of any harmonious sideline item. He should and usually does know his customers, and he therefore should be able to keep up with the things they want.

Generalities can go only part way in helping the interested bookseller make up his mind whether or not to embark upon a sidelines program. It may be useful to examine the reports of experienced bookmen now recognized as sidelines experts. Advice-laden essays will be found preceding the major sections of the *ABA Sidelines Directory*. These are filled with suggestions, facts, and the accumulated wisdom of ABA members in their varied contacts with goods that have successfully gone hand in hand with books in the past. Here one can learn to pick compatible merchandise that will give new impetus and profit to the business of selling books.

Snob Sidelines **34**

ELIZABETH C. LOWRY
Cannon's Book Store,
Oak Park, Illinois

There are many bookstores throughout the country that prefer, if it is economically feasible, to preserve a total identity as bookstores, and not be inundated by matches and paper napkins, and things. But—it is also a brutal fact that sidelines often carry a better markup than books, adding to the financial pleasures of life. I should like to report on three types of merchandise that are in complete harmony with books, bring in a nice penny, and, in two cases, are related to book sales: (1) chess sets, (2) jigsaw puzzles, and (3) literary dolls.

1. *Chess Sets*

First on the list of these profit-builders are chess sets. There is an intellectual alliance between books and chess. And speaking from personal experience, I can report that the sale of chess books leaps astonishingly whenever a chess set is displayed in our window or in the store. In the best stately homes, the best whodunits, and the best hippie pads, books and chess are go-togethers.

Of course, the Fischer-Spassky chess championship match was the greatest thing that ever happened to booksellers trying to turn an extra profit from chess books and chess sets. Chess has now become, if not exactly as popular as baseball, at least less forbidding than it used to be in the eyes of the public.

Variety of choice in styles of chess sets is endless, ranging from the simple, inexpensive, and conventional to elaborate, costly, and unique designs—everything from classic chess figures to the adaptation of musical comedy characters. Sets also come in an infinite variety of materials, inexpensive or costly: plastic, wood, metal, ivory, bone, ceramic, stone, semi-precious gem-stones, and even plaster, sometimes called "hydrostone."

For the shop first venturing into the field, I would recommend stocking the traditional Staunton pattern—the chessmen that look like chessmen—to try your market. We carry a line in this pattern which is inexpensive, but well made and attractive, and which is produced, in France, of handturned wood in a number of sizes and in either natural-tone wood or varnished wood. The chess pieces are felted and weighted, which means that the base of each piece is hollowed out, a weight added to decrease the possibility of tipping, and felt pasted over the weight. These French imports come in an inelegant but handy wooden box.

The size of a chess set is gauged by the height of the king; all other chessmen in the set are made in relation to it. The best sizes for the new chess-set outlet to handle (I speak both as a chess player and one who sells sets) are the two-inch and three-inch kings. These will give your stock enough variety for customers to choose from. I prefer the natural-finish to the varnished sets in this line, and the former are also a good deal less expensive. We do, however, carry a few varnished sets to round out our stock.

But if you are going into chess sets in a bigger way, the French import just discussed would be only the beginning. The excitement of handling this sophisticated bookstore sideline comes with selling the more unusual types. In a comparatively reasonable price range, you can get a reproduction of a twelfth-century Florentine set, in either red and white or black and white. It comes in a compartmented box, with its own board—not a very good board, but we'll discuss boards later. Going up the price ladder are chess sets in Limoges ware, alabaster, rosewood, ebony, gold and silver, as well as blown glass in brilliant colors, in either ultra-modern or portrait style. You can get small bone sets and elaborately carved ivory sets from Hong Kong. I have sold an unusual set, a reproduction of pre-Columbian figures, carved in stone, with a stone chess board. And a myriad of painted wood sets from all over Europe are available. These portray peasant groups, operetta casts, and goodness knows what all.

The prices of some of the more unusual chess sets may alarm you at first—they did me. But I found investing in one expensive set of unusual design and regarding it as part of my display budget was good business practice. A beautiful chess set is a striking display in either your window or in your store, along with the chess books. You will either sell it instantly, or hold it for awhile. But while you're holding it, it tells people interested in chess that you have a better-than-average stock of chess sets and chess books. And chess buffs are repeat customers.

In planning your chess department, don't overlook two other best-selling items—small pocket sets and separate chess boards. Small pocket sets, with either pegs or magnets to hold the moves in place after the set is folded up, vary in price. If you have a good selection of chess sets, the sale of separate boards will be excellent. Many sets do not come with a board; others have inadequate boards made of paper. A good separate folding board, made of linen over board, sells for $3 or $4, wears very well, and should not only be a plus sale for nearly all separate chessmen sales, but might also be suggested for those board-included sets that could be improved with a better board. More elegant and lasting boards of inlaid wood might be a welcome addition to your stock as your reputation for chess sets grows in your community. A fine chess set deserves a fine board.

When you set up your displays of chess sets, don't forget—*white, right;* that is, the white corner square is placed to the player's right.

2. *Jigsaw Puzzles*

Jigsaw puzzles—for grownups, not for kids—are another somewhat neglected bookstore sideline. The decline in this once highly popular merchandise is mainly the fault of the manufacturers of jigsaws. Cheap cardboard puzzles that hooked together in perfectly predictable strips, with subjects straight from the worst calendar art—hardly fare for the fairly sophisticated potential market for this adult pastime highly popular in the thirties—were all that were available for years. Now there are many interesting and challenging jigsaw puzzles to be had, and we are selling them to the grownup "kids" in our neighborhood at a satisfying rate.

A very fine line of jigsaw puzzles is made of cardboard, *heavy* cardboard, providing excellent interlocking for the pieces. Not only do they hold exceptionally well while they are being assembled, but when the puzzle is completed it can actually be picked up, no matter what its shape! One line is noted especially for its novel round and octagonal puzzles, in addition to more conventional square or rectangular ones.

Subject matter ranges from reproductions of both old and modern masters to novelty items such as Mickey Mouse, a silver dollar, and a pizza! Usually for the Christmas season, there are one or more Nativity scenes. There is quite a turnover in the subjects available, which is both an advantage and disadvantage.

There are now available miniature puzzles that are wonderful for hospital gifts and for stocking stuffers, and puzzles for children that come in two degrees of difficulty—48 pieces and 100 pieces—and in designs which should bridge the gap that exists between puzzles for the very young and 500-piece adult jobs.

If business is slow, and you have a little spare space in the shop, spread out a puzzle and start working it. Nine out of ten times, customers can't resist stopping for "just a minute" to add a couple of pieces.

And more than one will leave your shop a half-hour later with a jigsaw under his arm.

3. *And Now Dolls*

I'd be the last one to suggest you turn your bookshop into a doll shop. But I do ask you to consider one type of doll—the ones that go with certain books and therefore make eye-catching displays and natural plus sales.

Both adults and the young fry are partial to Charlie Brown, Snoopy, and others from the "Peanuts" cartoons and books by Charles Schulz. Raggedy Ann and Raggedy Andy are old-timers that should not be overlooked, both as books and dolls. They are just as suitable and saleable for little ones as they ever were. We have customers who report that the covers have been read off the Raggedy Ann and Andy books, and the dolls have taken on that protective coating of grime that makes Daddy reluctant to take the kids anywhere, because the dolls have to go along. And don't forget the Joan Walsh Anglund dolls to go with her delightful books—and the Babar dolls, too.

I've saved the best for last. Reproductions of the original Christopher Robin animal friends have long been available; they sell as well as ever. These include Pooh, Piglet, Kanga and Roo, Eeyore, and others. They are charming, they are authentic, they are moderately priced, and they go well with Pooh.

None of the merchandise I've mentioned is new. [The *ABA Sidelines Directory* lists names and addresses of suppliers of the principal bookstore sidelines.—ED.] Booksellers who have combined books and select sidelines profitably have often done so with these items. Of course, these things can be habit-forming. And this is the danger. Chess sets may lead to checkers, dominoes, cribbage boards, and Go. Jigsaws may coax you into the little puzzles like "15" and "Eight Men on a Log," as well as the kind in which seven balls must be led into seven holes in the right order. Dolls may persuade you into "snids" and "trolls." Only you know whether it is better to be stiff-spined or yield to temptation. Good luck—I'll be around any day for a chess game!

Greeting Cards **35**

HUGH BOWER
Vice President, Marketing,
Hallmark Cards, Inc.

Why sell greeting cards in a bookstore? An increasing number of book-sellers can provide a quick answer—profitability. With a little planning, a well-organized card department can bring high profits, almost automatically.

And there are other advantages. Greeting cards build traffic. Customers who stop in to get a card will become acquainted with the store and often buy a book on impulse. A woman buying a birthday card for her mother may decide that a new book would make a thoughtful gift. It's easy to suggest a card to a book purchaser, or a book to a card buyer. The promotional possibilities during such gift-buying seasons as Christmas, Valentine's Day, Mother's Day, and Father's Day are obvious.

It's not hard to get into the greeting-card business. All you have to do is to decide to give the go-ahead—the sales representatives of any of a number of greeting-card publishers will be delighted to work out the details of department layout, fixture recommendations, and establishment of a balanced display tailored to your marketing area. It's important to make certain your new department is visible from the street or mall. Since you're operating a bookstore primarily, potential customers will not know you feature cards unless they can see them as they walk by. Window or outside signing is also important when it's possible.

Before you open your department, you'll want to have a training session to acquaint employees with ordering procedures, display maintenance, and tips on selling greeting cards. It's also a good idea to plan a short orientation course for every new salesperson and a refresher session before major selling seasons, especially Christmas. Attentive, personal service to the customer is an important point to emphasize. One roving salesperson can give the card display constant surveillance, especially during busy seasons. Most customers will appreciate individual attention.

Capitalize on the fact that many books are bought as gifts by encouraging store personnel to use "suggestion" selling. It takes only a minute to ask a customer who selected a birthday card if she would like to look at gift books—but it's a technique that can bring add-on sales.

Merchandising. Successful greeting-card merchandising does not require technical knowledge so much as plenty of attention from those who work with the cards daily.

For the most profitable and best-looking department, responsibility for the card department should be assigned to one person who will then have a personal pride in the job. This will improve the department's performance. The person in charge should become intimately familiar with the inner workings of the department, and this can come only from working in it every day.

Supervising the day-to-day card operations is neither difficult nor time-consuming. Once the department is set up through the help of your salesman, reordering stock is fairly routine. Hallmark greeting cards, for example, are on the ticket reorder system—the first such system in the industry. For every card pocket in the display, there is a computer ticket along with back-up stock in a file drawer below that shows the stock number, price and caption, place in the fixture, and other store and account information.

When back-up stock in the file drawer is low, the salesperson will pull the ticket and send it in to the manufacturer for new stock. Envelopes are furnished for this purpose. This should be done at specified time intervals, usually every two weeks, depending on your own rate of sales.

Keeping records. An efficient record-keeping book, such as the Hallmark System-matic Reorder Record Book, contains a recap sheet that shows how many cards of each classification and price are in the department, plus a detailed list that gives a brief description of each card on display.

A sales-performance record sheet allows the salesperson to record each reorder by its file number. A quick glance then shows how many times that particular file number has been ordered and, consequently, how well it is selling. The Reorder Record Book thus serves as a guide for appropriate frequency of reordering.

Inventory control of greeting cards is relatively simple, since most of the back-up merchandise is filed right in the fixture drawers. Some related lines, such as wrapping paper, party goods, candles, or stationery, may require additional storage in the stockroom. Every store employee should know the stock location and the basics of restocking the fixtures.

Plan specific times for restocking, but remember that this schedule will need revision during peak selling periods. Assure that incoming merchandise is counted and checked against invoices before it's unpacked. Then dispose of all empty boxes and waste paper immediately —a clean, uncluttered stockroom is a must for successful retailing. Stock should also be sorted by fixture number. Once the new stock and invoice are checked, the stock is ready to put away in the fixture file drawers.

To keep disorganization to a minimum when bringing new stock on the sales floor, the salesperson should fill only one or two fixtures at a time. This prevents cluttered aisles, open file drawers, and disgruntled customers.

There is one additional point to remember in filling stock: Always put the new stock behind any remaining cards, so that older cards will sell out first.

Housekeeping. To maintain an appearance that is inviting to customers, the department should be dusted every day and pockets kept filled from the file drawers below. Missing or soiled cards, designs in wrong pockets, and general disarray can be taken care of before they cause lost sales and dissatisfied customers.

A complete cleaning is necessary at least every six months. The salesperson should take all cards out of the pockets, drop them into the file drawers, then disassemble and clean the pocket dividers. This major cleaning allows the salesperson to make a pocket-by-pocket inspection of each fixture and remedy any mixups in the cards or tickets.

Consistent housekeeping helps prevent an occasional greeting-card problem—missing or misplaced envelopes. When a customer can't find an envelope, she'll either decide not to buy the card, or take an envelope from another pocket, thus compounding the problem. The salesperson should arrange to have a reserve stock of extra envelopes, such as through Hallmark's extra-envelope system, to ensure that there is always a supply of all envelope sizes on hand. It's just one more way to gain customer satisfaction and maximum profits.

Seasonal merchandising. Season counter cards provide a way to maximize sales at peak times through the year. Many card publishers assist their accounts with a merchandising plan that illustrates model departments. These charts show how many pockets should be devoted to specific captions and where they should be located. Once the cards are in place, they need only the same basic care as everyday cards.

Another important part of seasonal merchandising is an end-of-season inventory. Conducted immediately after the season is over, it becomes a guide to reordering for the next year.

Promotional ideas. Once the department is running smoothly you can think about displays to encourage add-on sales. For example, you could build a display of books on a red background for Valentine's Day, scattering several valentines around the display or suspending them from strands of red ribbon.

About 30 per cent of annual everyday card sales come in the peak months of June, August, and September. Be sure to capitalize on these peak periods by featuring wedding, anniversary, religious, and travel cards in store displays. Many companies provide seasonal décor that can be especially effective in dressing up your store for every season. Colorful banners and signs will attract customers' attention and remind them of the coming holiday.

An attractive, efficiently merchandised greeting-card department can help create an environment that says, "Welcome to our store!" And with a minimum of fuss, greeting cards can bring maximum sales all through the year. Greeting cards and books are ideal go-togethers.

Personalized Christmas Cards

36

CHARLES B. ANDERSON
Anderson's Book Shop,
Larchmont, New York

At several ABA Conventions and also at ABA regional meetings, I have
described personalized Christmas cards as the most profitable of all
bookstore sidelines. In this chapter of the *Manual* are some of the
questions posed at meetings and by mail by my fellow booksellers together with my answers. It is suggested that those interested in starting
or expanding a business in personalized greeting cards ("PG's") refer to
the article on PG's in the current *ABA Sidelines Directory* and also to
the tabulation of the card lines which did best in our store during the
preceding Christmas season. The tabulation in mimeographed form is
available, free of charge, from the ABA office.

QUESTION. *Mr. Anderson, how do you define a PG?*
ANSWER. A PG is any Christmas card with or without name imprint
which is not carried in stock by the store but which is ordered from
sample albums. PG records and transactions should be kept separate and apart from those of counter cards. Even though the store
has a stamping machine and takes orders for imprinting cards
bought in the store, these orders, for purposes of systematic bookkeeping, should not be considered PG's. The percentage of profit
in PG's is higher than that in counter cards, because there are
practically no losses or markdowns in PG's.
QUESTION. *Why are you willing to give out so much information about
your business? Aren't you afraid of local competition stepping in
and giving you a clobbering? Does Macy's tell Gimbel's?*
ANSWER. I wouldn't know about Macy's and wouldn't care very much
either. I have found that the most successful booksellers have always been generous with me and with all their fellow booksellers
in supplying helpful information from their records. Doubleday,

Lauriat's of Boston, Johnson's of Springfield, and Kroch & Brentano's of Chicago, among others, have set an example that I have tried to follow in being willing and eager to share a good thing with the trade when they latch on to one.

Sales

QUESTION. *All the stores around are reporting lower sales in PG's this fall. We think we are doing well to stay about the same as last year, in spite of the extra effort we have put into them. Maybe this is going to be a mediocre year in PG's.*

ANSWER. In spite of stock market breaks, strikes, the weather, political upheaval, and other excuses the small merchant looks for to explain poor business, the nationwide business in PG's continues to increase and the Post Office handles additional billions of cards each year. Your store and the others may do a big business before the season is over. Don't worry too much about what the other dealers are saying or doing. The typical small dealer is normally gloomy about how bad his business is, no matter what. If his PG business is up, he may be unwilling to admit it to what he regards as his competition. More likely than not, he doesn't know what he's doing in PG's, for his PG's are probably all mixed up somewhere in his total sales. If you are working it right, you'll get your share of the additional money people are spending each year on Christmas cards.

QUESTION. *One of our greeting-card salesmen says we are better off with just a few good albums, because a great many just tend to confuse and discourage a customer. Shall we follow his advice?*

ANSWER. In my experience the most effective way the small store can compete successfully against the department stores and the house-to-house salesman (Fayette *et al.*) is by having a large selection of fine cards. Some of our customers groan and grouse about having to wade through so many albums, but whether they are quite aware of it or not, they come to us because we have the best selection of fine cards they are likely to find anywhere. Search for the small "personal" PG publisher. But watch their service!

QUESTION. *Do you take many orders in summer?*

ANSWER. We set up our album display in the store the day after Labor Day. During the summer there are generally three or four customers who order for early fall delivery from the albums that we have in our stockroom. Most companies do not print and ship before the first part of September. Some of our albums do not arrive until late August or September. I understand that some bookstores, especially those in resort towns and other tourist areas, do a lively PG business in summer, even though they work with a limited number of albums. These shops find that people frequently buy from them on the possibly mistaken assumption that they are less likely to be ordering the same cards as their friends and neighbors back home.

QUESTION. *Do you use commission agents who show the albums from house to house?*

ANSWER. No, all our cards are sold in the store. I have heard of stores that have used this method of building a PG business, but we are not interested.

QUESTION. *We lose many big orders to the Henri Fayette and Chryson saleswomen in our community. They start calling prospects in April and offer discounts for orders through the spring and summer. How can we compete against this kind of competition?*

ANSWER. I'll wager the Fayette and Chryson ladies and others are as active and aggressive in our community as they are in yours. They are at work among our customers in early spring and summer before we have even received our albums. Sometimes we can suggest to customers that they wait to see our selection before they decide on their cards. There is one story we use to beat off the Fayette competition, and it actually happened. One woman ordered a card from Fayette that she thought particularly lovely. It was indeed so lovely that it was Fayette's most popular card that year, and four of her friends sent her the same card. She and at least one of the friends have been ordering from us ever since.

QUESTION. *Do you do a big counter-card business in Christmas cards?*

ANSWER. No, our business in box cards and Christmas counter cards is less than a quarter of our PG business. If we lose counter-card business to PG's, we're glad it's that way.

QUESTION. *In years past we have had so many headaches with late orders that we decided this year to make it easy for ourselves and accept no PG orders after Thanksgiving. Do you go along with this?*

ANSWER. No, I certainly don't. We took 241 orders and did 28 per cent of our PG business after Thanksgiving last year. Not only is this kind of business too good to pass up, but we have found that our biggest headaches are caused by orders written before Thanksgiving that are still outstanding in December. At Thanksgiving we remove from display all albums except those of companies that have been giving us prompt and reliable service. After December 3 last year, we worked with only two companies, American Artists and Hallmark. We took our last order of the season on December 16, telephoned it to American Artists, and had the cards in two days.

QUESTION. *A friend of mine, impressed with the profits in the PG business, wants to rent a vacant store in a high-traffic street for the Christmas season and sell only PG's. Do you think this will work out?*

ANSWER. No. This is probably a good way to sell Christmas trees or even box cards but not PG's. The typical PG customer buys from a store where she does other shopping and in which she has confidence. This is why the fine department stores have built a big PG business.

QUESTION. *Our store makes extra profit by imprinting card orders on our electric stamping machine. When we take an order from the albums, we send for the cards without imprint and do the cards in the store. In this way we can offer our customers faster service with fewer errors in printing. Don't you think this is a good idea which could be used by other stores?*

ANSWER. No, I don't approve. I don't think you are playing fair with the customers, especially with the better cards. The fine card companies take great pains to match ink and type on the greeting page of their cards. No matter how varied a supply of tapes and types you have with your machine, you can't possibly do as good a job as most card companies. Occasionally, in the interest of quick service, you can do a job like this, provided you explain to the customer what you intend doing and have his or her approval. I don't like this as a way of making extra profits. You are getting top markup anyway. This is being greedy.

QUESTION. *A customer wants a card with a covered bridge. None of our albums this year has such a card. Is there any way we can accommodate this customer?*

ANSWER. Yes, write to several of your companies asking whether they have such a card in stock left over from previous years.

Pricing

QUESTION. *All the stores in our town offer a 10 per cent discount for cards ordered before October 15. Don't you think we should go along with this policy?*

ANSWER. It is possible, I suppose that in certain towns and neighborhoods, customers are so conditioned to receiving such a discount that they will insist on it or take their custom elsewhere. Although discounts in any form are anathema in our store, I can't presume to tell you it must be this way and no other. You know your customers, your town, and your store. From personal experience many times each season, I know how tough it is to see an order slip away because we will not allow a discount. Yet I am sure that we are better off in the long run sticking to our guns. There may be a certain distinction, a cachet, in being the only store around that offers no discount. In my experience, the best PG customers do not shop for discount. The fine stores in our area do not give discounts, either in PG's or books. This goes for Lord and Taylor, Altman's, Brentano's, Doubleday, and Scribner's, among others.

QUESTION. *Do you mean to say that you have never given a discount from list price to anybody?*

ANSWER. I wish I could claim that. Sure, we have weakened in times past. But I can say that every time that I recall making an exception and granting a discount, I have had occasion at a later date, for one reason or another, to regret it.

QUESTION. *We are considering the idea of offering a rebate at the year's end—provided we have a good year—to our customers who order cards from us. This would be something like the plan of some college cooperatives. We think our customers would be so overjoyed to receive a check or a gift certificate they didn't expect that they would all return to us next season. What do you think?*

ANSWER. I think this is discounting in another form, and I dislike it. I would like to see you spend your PG profits in new fixtures or new inventory that would make your shop a better bookstore. I suspect a lot of the customers entitled to such a rebate would agree.

Operation

QUESTION. *We are interested in having our own Christmas-card order books printed so that we can avoid the confusion of so many different order books from the various companies. What do you think?*

ANSWER. Don't do it. We looked into this several years ago and discovered that some of the card companies require the use of their own order blanks. They will accept orders on your blanks but because they transcribe them before processing your order, you may wait a day or two longer for your order with the additional chance for error in transcription. This is too great a penalty to pay for the convenience of having your own blanks. We find an accordion-type file reasonably satisfactory for containing the various order forms.

QUESTION. *Several customers each year report that they are several envelopes short on their order. We think they just spoiled the envelopes. What do you think?*

ANSWER. What's the difference what I think or what really happened? Write to the company for extra envelopes. Or better still, have a copious supply of envelopes on hand as an accommodation. No charge to the customer. He may recall the favor next fall.

QUESTION. *An order for cards came to us badly printed, and the customer refused to accept it. Are we obliged to pay the company for the cards?*

ANSWER. No, return the cards to the company and deduct from your payment to them. Sometimes a customer is unreasonable in finding fault with the cards he ordered or is even looking for an excuse to cancel the order. If this is the case, it would seem only fair that you should pay for the loss and not the company.

QUESTION. *A customer claims we ordered the wrong cards and she will not accept them. We happen to know that she is mistaken. This is a $30 order. What shall we do?*

ANSWER. Give the lady what she wants and accept the consequences. Unless she is a genuine deadbeat, which is unlikely among PG customers, she will be so disarmed by your offer to stand the loss that she will look for ways to make it up to you.

QUESTION. *We have waited a month for an order to come in and it is now December 10. The customer is frantic. What can we do?*

ANSWER. Telephone the company, whether it's in Boston or Los Angeles, preferably while the customer is in the store, and try to get a definite commitment as to when and how the cards were shipped or when delivery will be made. If the customer is still not satisfied, offer to cancel the order and help her find cards from one of the albums of a company that will get the cards out in a few days.

QUESTION. *A customer's cards have not arrived after more than a month. Though it is the company's fault and not ours, the customer blames us. Is this fair?*

ANSWER. Fair or not, the customer has to blame somebody, and you are there. This is one of the sad facts of life about the PG and book business. The card and book publishers will lose your orders, send them to the wrong store, pack them insecurely, or send what you didn't order, but you have to take the rap.

QUESTION. *A customer found a company invoice to our store packed with her card order. She is annoyed at us because she says we are making an inordinate profit on her cards. What can we do?*

ANSWER. Nothing, except to be more diligent in the future in ferreting out all invoices from card packages before they get to the customer. This is something that just shouldn't be allowed to happen. There is no use in trying to explain to the customer who has discovered this professional secret why you are entitled to the amount of profit you make on her card order. She won't understand.

QUESTION. *One PG company forces us to buy a lot of box cards that we don't want in order to get their album. Is there anything we can do to avoid being blackmailed like this?*

ANSWER. Yes, drop the company from your roster. Or it is usually possible to persuade the salesman to reduce the quantity of your box-card purchase by telling him you are chiefly interested in building a PG business and in converting box-card people to PG's.

QUESTION. *What do you do with your albums at the close of the season?*

ANSWER. Several companies request return of their albums. There is a children's hospital that likes to have a few of them each year. Mostly, however, they're consigned to the rubbish collector.

Sources of Supply

QUESTION. *Our store management prefers not to have Hallmark cards because they are to be found in cigar stores and newsstands almost anywhere and as a result add little or no distinction to our display. What do you think?*

ANSWER. I think this is shortsighted on the part of the management. When I am asked to name the one most valuable greeting-card franchise for any type of store, the answer has to be Hallmark. Each year they will come up with some of the most spectacular cards to be found anywhere, and they will help you sell them through their extensive TV and magazine advertising. Very few of the cigar stores and newsstands that carry Hallmark everyday cards even have the Christmas albums, because this type of store can't sell PG's in the Hallmark price range.

QUESTION. *Neither American Artists nor Hallmark will sell to us because they already have an outlet in a store down the street. What can we do about it?*

ANSWER. Keep after them. Try to convince the regional salesmen that you are building an important PG business and that they are passing up a good thing in not selling to you. If the salesmen remain indifferent, go over their heads and get in touch with the top men at company headquarters. It took our store three years to persuade Hallmark to sell to us and six years to win over American Artists. Our PG business increased even without the top PG producers.

QUESTION. *How can our store get the Henri Fayette cards?*

ANSWER. Your store can't get them, as they are sold only through their own agents, who work on a 25 per cent commission. Why would you want them with this kind of markup?

Promotion
and Advertising

Sales Promotion, Advertising, and Publicity

37

G. ROYSCE SMITH
Executive Director,
American Booksellers Association, Inc.

> *Advertise—or the sheriff will do it for you.*
> —P. T. Barnum

No matter how enticing you may think the books and sidelines in your store are, you will have no business unless you have customers, and there is no such thing as a store without some sales promotion. To be without any sales promotion, you would have to paint your windows and doors, remove all external signs, and cover the fixtures in your store with sheets. For sales promotion is anything you do to cause goods and services to move out of your store at a profit.

Putting an "Open for Business" sign in the window is sales promotion. Deciding on store merchandising policy, developing an image, selecting the titles you will carry, analyzing your community as a market place, deciding what you will push and what you will simply carry, scheduling your window displays with care, developing and directing yourself and your salespeople—these are all steps leading to a specific goal: the sale of a product or service. When they are supplemented by two other activities—advertising and publicity—they become a conscious sales promotion program.

Your Community and Your Image

In the beginning, even before you open the store, as you analyze your community you also develop your sales promotion program, consciously or not. You might as well do it consciously by asking yourself some simple but essential questions in five major areas:

1. *Who?* Who are the customers to whom I will cater? What are their characteristics, economic and social? What is their age, size of family, income? How do they earn it? What are their hobbies? Are they transient or permanent residents? What type of home?

What are their social interests and involvements? Who else caters to their needs in competition with me?

2. *What?* What do my customers want to buy today? What will they want to buy tomorrow? What is the size of the market over-all; for specific interest areas? What can I offer that is superior to what my competitor offers?

3. *When?* When do they need our product or service? At what times of the year will their demands for some of the things we offer be greatest and when least? When will they come to my store? When will they be most likely to buy?

4. *Where?* Where will they buy what we have to offer? Where do they come from? Are there geographic or psychological limitations which will prevent them from getting to my store from where they are? Where will they use it if we sell it to them? Outdoors or indoors? For work or leisure?

5. *Why?* Why will they buy what I am selling? Why will they come to me for it? Why won't people come to my store?

These are some basic areas of inquiry that are opened by the who-what-when-where-why approach. You will think of more. From this information you will make the "how" decisions on location, price range, assortment, quality, and service. Out of these decisions you can develop slogans that will define your image. They can be the corny cliché slogans we've all heard too many times. We are only using them to reach private decisions about our store. For public use, we would want to dress them up a bit if we used them at all.

Location:	"Opposite the Bus Terminal"
	"Next to the Library"
	"In [Our Town's] Smartest Mall"
	"At the University's Gates"
Price:	"The Bargain Bookstore"
	"Books for Every Wallet"
	"Books for the Discriminating"
Assortment:	"Paperbacks Only"
	"Exclusively Cloth"
	"The One-Stop Technical-Book Store"
	"Religious Books and Articles"
	"The Complete Bookstore"
Quality:	"The Best in Books"
	"Community Center"
	"Secondhand"
	"Satisfaction Guaranteed"

Service: "Special Orders Taken"
                    "Your Credit Is Good"
                    "We Mail Anywhere"
                    "Liberal Returns Policy"
                    "Check Cashing Service"
                    "Open Evenings"
                    "Adequate Parking"

Thinking about and establishing an image is important because that will influence everything else you do in sales promotion. If you want to develop a traditional literary image, your store must convey the feeling of literary tradition through its windows, wrapping, letterhead, salespeople, décor, lighting, advertising. Whatever image you develop, remember that the goal is to make a quick, permanent impression with your customer.

Surveys show that 70 per cent of all customers, for all kinds of merchandise, have a store of first choice even though they shop in many stores. If this is true for all kinds of stores, the percentage must be even higher for bookstores. To be on a customer's first-choice list, your store must stand for something concrete in that person's mind.

Analysis of your market can be aided by information from the Chamber of Commerce, local newspapers, community profiles, the U.S. Department of Commerce, publications of the Small Business Administration (SBA), and from other chapters in this book. Your best help will come from conversation—talking to your salespeople and your customers and the people in your community who are *not* your customers. But the final decision on image rests with you as store owner.

Advertising in Your Community

Some people regard retail advertising as a needless expense. The successful retailer knows it to be a necessary, profitable, vital investment. The difference in these points of view generally comes from experience.

If you think advertising is a needless expense, it may be because you have not yet mastered the techniques. This process involves an honest self-examination of your attitude about advertising, then deciding whom you want to reach with what and how, and then setting a sales goal, deciding how much advertising is needed to meet that goal, and scheduling your advertising program.

Let's find out about *you* first. Here's a ten-question quiz (Figure 37.1) based on one developed by the SBA for rating your attitude about advertising. Answer it honestly; if you don't, you won't be fooling anyone but yourself.

FIGURE 37.1.—CHECKLIST ON ATTITUDES ABOUT ADVERTISING

1. Has your business been growing each year?   Yes _____   No _____
2. Can you predict with reasonable accuracy what next year's sales will be?
                                                                Yes _____   No _____
3. Are you aware that advertising includes the coordination of *all* promotional and selling functions, such as window and in-store display?
                                                                Yes _____   No _____
4. Do you set aside time each month to make promotional plans?
                                                                Yes _____   No _____
5. Do you have figures at your fingertips on how much you invested in advertising in each month of last year?   Yes _____   No _____
6. If you answered the preceding question "Yes," did each month's percentage of the total year's advertising closely match each month's percentage of your total year's sales?   Yes _____   No _____
7. Do you have figures at your fingertips to show what percentage of each month's sales were made in each department (i.e., cloth, paper, remainders, greeting cards, etc.) of your store?   Yes _____   No _____
8. Did your advertising last month promote each department in relation to its contribution to total sales?   Yes _____   No _____
9. Do you know what percentage of sales is invested in advertising by other bookstores?   Yes _____   No _____
10. Do you know how to prepare a strong ad and to check on the results it brings?   Yes _____   No _____

Of course, if you are just getting started, you'll only be able to answer questions 3, 4, 9, and 10. Otherwise, three "Yes" answers or fewer means that you are not aware that a planned advertising program can help increase profits. Four to eight "Yes" answers means you are not immune to learning more. You have developed an understanding of what advertising can do for you.

The first step in a planned advertising program is to take into account your answers to the five questions in the first section of this article, "Your Community and Your Image." You must know who *you* are and who *your customers* are. If there are areas where uncertainty exists, the problems must be resolved before you can show your face in your advertising.

After that, you are ready to think about what to promote, basing your decision on your knowledge of your customers and your store. Every item to be advertised should be a wanted item. An item that no one wants cannot be sold simply by advertising it. Advertising informs consumers of availability and of what the product will do for them. Sometimes it triggers a latent impulse to buy. Only occasionally can advertising a book convince potential buyers that it will do whatever it does (entertain, enlighten, instruct, advise) better than any other book. Most often, such convincing comes about through word of mouth.

Your talent as a merchant will tell you what your customers want. These are the items that you will promote. Always promote the right merchandise at the right price at the right time in the right quantity.

- *The right merchandise,* as we have determined, conforms to the tastes, customs, and needs of the community and to the store's image.
- *The right price* is the price range that your customers are willing and able to pay.
- *The right time* is the time when your customers are ready to buy that particular item. Not garden books in October or mushroom books in February or skiing instructions in June.
- *The right quantity* is the quantity you'll need to satisfy your customers' demands but not so many that the cost of returns will negate profits.

Not all advertising need be product advertising. There is, as well, a nebulous thing called "institutional advertising," in which no specific merchandise appears. Such advertising may let people know that your store is the book center of your community and that books are O.K.

We would recommend that large ads be run just before and during the major shopping seasons rather than running small pointless box ads with your name and address every week. Consider running ten 15-inch or fifteen 10-inch ads, instead of 156 inches stretched over fifty-two weeks in 3-inch ads.

The best institutional advertising comes through offering special customer services and through active participation in community events: putting on special events away from the store (e.g., book fairs in schools), participating in outside-sponsored events, or holding demonstrations in the store.

How are you going to reach your customers? There are many methods of advertising. External advertising media include newspapers, radio, television, community shopping publications, direct mail, handbills, and outdoor signs. Internal advertising media include posted tear sheets and blowups of ads, manufacturers' literature, signs, posters, catalogs, window displays, dump bins, counter and table displays, and telephone solicitations.

Your choice of media will be dependent on many factors, such as the kind of book or other merchandise you're promoting, how much of it is available, how much money you can spend, and of course, the effectiveness of the medium, which is a product of the extent to which it reaches the particular people you wish to attract.

Each of these factors will vary in each advertising situation. In many communities, radio is a predominant means of advertising books today, while in others the newspaper proves more effective. Even where radio is best for new titles, the newspaper may still prove best for remainders. There are few hard and fast rules even within the same community. The retailer must develop the skill to evaluate the possibilities.

The newspaper offers low cost per reader, wide market coverage, family readership, quick public response, flexibility, and the greatest public acceptance. It is the medium the retailer knows best and can therefore learn to use most easily. It is effective in attracting new customers.

The limitations of newspaper advertising are those of competition and circulation. In newspapers the competition for the reader's attention is heavy. The circulation may involve a disproportionately large number of copies outside your shopping area, and the readership may not coincide with the portion of the community that you seek to attract.

The newspaper is purchased for the news. Books with news value, including TV appearances by the author, may stand the best chance in the main news section. If you can, place the ad where it will attract its natural audience. Cookbooks and etiquette on the society page and business books on the business page are obvious examples; a little imagination can result in other intriguing combinations.

What about the book page? If your newspaper has one, it is probably in a section of the paper where readership is limited and gets meager support from the paper's management. Its reviews may be unprofessional, ignored by book readers and non-readers alike. If you happen to be blessed with a good book page, one that stimulates conversation and generates respect, by all means support it to your utmost, for it is the rarest of the rare.

Consider also the want-ad columns for special books. Not only are these classified ads a relatively inexpensive means of advertising, they are highly selective and can be frequently effective. Career books in the help-wanted columns, dog care and training in the pet column, antiques under "Tag Sales" and "Articles for Sale," sailing under "Boats and Marine Equipment"—the possibilities are endless. Want-ad advertising is particularly adaptable to community shopping publications.

There is a routine involved in newspaper advertising. First, you make the decision to run the ad, based on the local appeal of the book as well as, frequently, the availability of cooperative advertising money from the publisher.

If your decision is influenced by the availability of "co-op" ad money, then you must contact either your publisher's rep or the publisher's sales manager (whose name will be found in the *ABA Book*

Buyer's Handbook) for details of that publisher's co-op ad schedule. Never proceed with a co-op ad without specific approval from the publisher. If you plan to spend only your own money (a rash decision, indeed, but one that may sometimes be justified), then this step is skipped. (More about co-op advertising later in this chapter.)

Next, schedule space in the paper. Generally, one person on the paper's advertising staff will be designated as your contact. His job as account executive is to sell what you are buying—display ads, as opposed to want ads—and it is to his interest to keep you happy by helping to make your ads as effective as possible. He can help with layout, type sizes and faces, and canned art, though he will not design your logo or photograph art work for you. Space should be booked two weeks in advance. He will tell you your local schedules, including the dates he needs copy and art work and the dates on which you will get proofs.

It is up to you to prepare your ad copy and arrange for any art work. Both will usually be available from the publisher if the only art work you want is a glossy photo of the book. But glossies may not be all you want, and the copy may not be to your taste or in your store's image. New art work may be required, and the copy most likely will have to be edited. If no one you know is talented in these areas, you will find free-lance artists and copywriters available. One goes to an ad agency seldom for a single ad but for a whole program, for agencies are frequently outside the budget of a small store. Allow time for this.

The copy, art work, and layout should all be checked before they leave the store. Are the authors' names spelled correctly, especially if they are local? Are the prices right? Have you included your store name (no joke!), address, business hours, and telephone? Keep a carbon of your copy for checking against the proof.

If the hour at which you expect a proof passes and you don't have it, call your account executive. Few papers today provide advertisers with two proofs of an ad, but you should ask for this service anyway. Generally, you get only one proof and that only a matter of hours before the paper hits the street. You may have less than an hour in which to telephone any corrections. If you check nothing else, be certain that all prices are correct.

Once the paper has appeared, you will normally receive two tear sheets (pages torn from the finished newspaper with your ad on them). Some papers do not furnish either proofs or tear sheets if an ad is under a certain size. One tear sheet should accompany your invoice to the publisher to collect any co-op money due you. The other should go into your "ad book," a scrapbook into which you place all advertising, along with costs and results, for future reference.

A periodic review of your ad book will reveal, if you are objective about it, your advertising strengths and weaknesses. Here are some pointers to keep in mind as you review what you have done:

- Your ads should be easily recognizable. The copy and layout should have a consistent personality and style. A repeated border such as the one used by Doubleday stores is an effective example.
- A simple layout is the most effective. The eye should travel through the message easily and in proper sequence. The final word in the message should be your signature, or logo.
- Tell your readers clearly what's in it for them. Will the book make them happier, richer, better fed, prettier, more desirable, brighter, more knowledgeable? Or will it simply entertain them? Let them know.
- Give complete information about the book succinctly but in a warm, sincere, enthusiastic tone.
- Be sure that you've always told who you are, where you are, when you are open, and how you may be reached by phone.

Tear sheets of ads may be used in your windows or mounted in sign-holders near your in-store display. They may be requested from your account executive in advance, over and above the normal two. There's no need for you to run to the newsstand to buy extra papers.

If you run ads with any frequency in your newspaper, you may be eligible for a discounted-contract, or "local," rate. The local rate is intended for use by local merchants. The higher national rate applies to national advertisers, such as tobacco, magazines, beverages, and other name brands, who do not advertise through local outlets.

Other advertising—radio and TV—are treated elsewhere in this book.

The Advertising Budget

How much should you spend on advertising? The most frequently quoted figures for bookstores are between 2 and 2½ per cent. But, as with all other average figures, these must be applied to the particular store.

- The new store needs more promotion than the well-established one.
- A neighborhood store needs more advertising than one in an airport.
- Strong competition between independently owned stores raises the budget.
- An expensive location is usually expensive because a part of the rent money, rather than advertising, is buying traffic.

But suppose you are average and doing annual retail sales of $50,-000. Would you look at 2 per cent of $50,000 and decide that you only had $1,000 to spend, so why bother? Not at all. You would use the publishers' co-op ad money, which we mentioned before, to increase the $1,000 to $2,000 or even $4,000.

Publishers offer cooperative money in a variety of ways: Some offer a percentage of annual net purchases; others offer a percentage of net purchases of a specific title or group of titles; some will pay 50 per cent of space costs; others will pay 75 per cent of space costs; some will share costs of radio or TV time as well as newspaper space; most will permit you to run the books of several publishers in one ad. The complexity and flexibility of ad policies make contact with the publisher's sales rep or sales manager essential even though these policies are required to be published, either by mail or in *PW.*

For example, suppose your annual net purchases from Friendly Publishers are $900. His policy is a 10 per cent of net on a 75/25 basis. This means that you have $90 of his money to spend to which you add $30 of your own. With $30 of your own money, you are able to buy $120 in advertising space.

Frequently, as with remainder houses, you are given a flat allowance—say, 10 per cent—of net purchases with no requirement that you add any of your own money. Equally, you are not limited in how much you may add.

Now suppose that Friendly Publishers has a new book called *Termites of the Great West,* which you want to promote. They allow 10 per cent of net purchases of a specific title on a 50/50 basis. *Termites* retails at $14.95. You order 30 copies at 41 per cent discount. The net amount of the invoice is $263.40, and 10 per cent of that is $26.34. Putting $26.34 of your own money with that, you have $52.68 to spend on your ad campaign for *Termites of the Great West.* But $52.68 will only buy one 15-inch 1-column ad in your newspaper at $3.50 per column inch. You want to run a 10-inch 2-column ad, or 20 column inches, which will cost $75.

You decide to spend more of your money, which is allowed. Being on a 50/50 basis means only that the publisher is limiting his participation in an ad (to which you are contributing at least 50 per cent) to 10 per cent of net purchases. In neither 50/50 nor 75/25 ads are you limited to spending 50 or 25 per cent.

The 20-column-inch ad then costs you $75 less the publisher's $26.-34, or $48.66. However, your ad is successful and you order and sell 20 more copies at 40 per cent discount from the publisher. The additional books cost you $179.40, giving you $17.94 more ad money from the publisher, or a total of $44.28. But the total cost to the publisher cannot exceed 50 per cent of $75, or $37.50. You may spend the excess $6.78 on another ad for *Termites of the Great West,* but not for any other book, if you match it with $6.78 of your own.

These are examples of the two most common methods of cooperative advertising. Obviously, the first is by far the simpler. The latter is more common. But both permit the bookseller to extend his advertising money considerably.

This money should be spent, generally speaking, to coincide with sales. So the first step in preparing an ad budget, once you have established how much of your own and the publisher's money you have to spend, is to allocate expenditures by month.

For purposes of planning an actual budget, since you won't know a year in advance how much co-op money you'll be using, it's best to be conservative and assume that all your ads will be on a 50/50 basis. Now let's make a table of last year's sales and this year's planned sales by month, percentage of month's sales to total, amount of advertising dollars by month, and percentage of monthly ad dollars to total. Figure 37.2 is a sample ad-budget work sheet for the first quarter of a year. It can be made just as easily for a half or full year.

FIGURE 37.2.—AD-BUDGET WORK SHEET

		Sales Dollars	Percent of Total	Ad Dollars	Percent of Total
January	Last Year	___	___	___	___
	This Year	___	___	___	___
February	Last Year	___	___	___	___
	This Year	___	___	___	___
March	Last Year	___	___	___	___
	This Year	___	___	___	___

It is best not to allocate all of a year's budget without leaving 5 per cent for taking advantage of unexpected promotional opportunities or for meeting competitive emergencies.

Once the budget has been established by month, decisions must be made as to the best time of the month to advertise, taking into account holidays, traditional sales days, heavy-traffic days, night openings, and perhaps the payroll days of important firms in the neighborhood from which you draw customers.

While the purpose of ad budgeting is to eliminate the waste that comes from advertising too early or too late, it can also be used to level out the normal peaks and valleys of retailing. Since expenses usually are about the same throughout the year, it is highly desirable to maintain sales at as nearly level a volume as possible. If you will plot out your sales by month on a sheet of graph paper, the peaks and valleys will be immediately apparent. By shifting a little bit of ad money from a couple of peak periods to a valley period, it may be possible to raise the valley without lowering the peaks. It's a goal you can't reach without planning and proper use of an advertising budget.

Publicity in Your Community

So far we have concentrated on spending money for advertising. But one of the most pleasant promotional efforts is getting publicity, which is free. Instead of money, it takes talent, imagination, and time, for nothing is ever entirely free.

Booksellers, of all retailers, have a unique opportunity to get publicity. Books are ideas, escape, information, culture, instruction, inspiration, and any number of things that are the subject matter of newspaper articles, radio and TV interviews and comment, and talks to luncheon and study groups.

Get to know the people who make your community tick and let them get to know you. Become a personality, unless you hate that kind of thing, in which case you should feed facts about books to the people who are personalities. Even the sheer number of books published each year, either in total or by category, is an interesting fact. The annual summary issue of *PW* is a gold mine for the fact-hungry personality.

Many booksellers have free time on radio in which to talk about books or news of books. Most such time is only about two minutes per spot, but they have remarkable impact. Some booksellers even have talk shows on TV for which they get paid a small fee. Almost anyone who can talk about books can be invited to speak at a study club or before a luncheon group.

The point is to recognize that you are dealing with a very exciting commodity. You can make it and yourself exciting to your community with a little effort. It's worth doing.

We have reviewed briefly for you the various aspects of image, advertising and publicity, prime elements in sales promotion. Other elements—among them display, developing a service-oriented staff, and stock selection—are covered elsewhere in this book. But you must look outside this *Manual* and other books, be constantly aware of what successful merchants of all kinds are doing, and apply what you see imaginatively to your own situation.

Store Windows and In-Store Display **38**

TRUMBULL HUNTINGTON
Huntington's Book Store,
Hartford, Connecticut

No merchandise lends itself more readily to display and point-of-sale techniques than books. Relatively small and thus easily handled and arranged, each title is decked out in the most saleable jacket its publisher can devise. Color, illustration, and design have been assembled with one purpose only—to delight the eye of the beholder. Jacket blurbs are written for one purpose only—to stimulate the potential reader's wish to buy.

It is essential, then, that booksellers take full advantage of these already built-in aids, using them to stop the hurried passer-by. And the first place to stop him is at your store window, for it is here that your most effective and least expensive advertising takes place.

Two Ways To Build a Window

Your window is not only your best advertisement but also very nearly the only one through which you can reach the non-book-buyer (a strange, double-hyphenated creature). This elusive individual is not on your mailing list; he is not influenced by book reviews; he does not read book advertising. But if you can make him stop and look at your window, if your window has something in it that will draw him into the store, then you may make a plus sale and gain a new customer.

Basically there are two ways of building a window. The first is to single out a book or a subject and try to pull the passer-by into your store by making him want that particular book or a book on that particular subject. Such a window might center around a novel by a local author, or it might usher in the fishing season with books devoted to the art of angling.

Booksellers with a real talent for display are able to create striking and effective windows of this type. By skillful use of appropriate props (tennis rackets, dolls, gardening tools, and so forth), they achieve heightened interest in the books displayed. What golfer, as the first soft spring breezes play about him on his way to a business lunch, will not stop to look at a bag of shiny new golf clubs? And nestled around it are new books on golf. Without the big bag of clubs, he might have walked solemnly on his way. But now he is stopped—and possibly he is induced to enter. What might Johnny Miller's book do for him? Local sports, garden-supply, and other stores are usually willing to lend the necessary props if proper credit is given.

The second method—and this is the real bread-and-butter window for year-in, year-out sales—employs the shotgun technique. This is not the kind of display that wins prizes at the ABA Convention or delights the hearts of publishers. Rather it is a display that has something in it for everybody, and it is arranged in such a manner that the passer-by is brought to a halt long enough to find the something that is for him. The books cover a wide variety of subject matter and yet the visual effect of the whole must have some sort of graphic design. The easiest design is, of course, balanced rows of books lying or standing in a straight line. It is a simple matter to break up this type of display by providing an emphasis here and there, a visual check point that will cause the viewer's eye to pause on a particularly important or newsworthy book.

Over the long haul, the shotgun display is not only the easiest to create, it is also the one that brings in the most people and sells the most books. While a window devoted to a single book is profitable only in extremely rare cases, displays built around related books, newsworthy events, or seasonal pastimes are definitely worth while. It is important, however, to remember the cardinal rule of all advertising—the effectiveness of your efforts is measured by the results obtained. In the case of your window, then, the effectiveness is *not* measured by the number of people who stop to admire the picture you have created, but rather by the number of people who are motivated to enter and to buy.

There is one more factor to be considered in window display. Without it, everything that has gone before has been wasted effort. Just as you would not look at paintings in the dark, your potential customers will not look at your window if it is not properly lighted. Strong even light, accentuated perhaps by spots, is essential.

Finally your window, the best single advertising medium you have, tells your sales story to every passing man, woman, and child. Make sure it reflects the story that you want told, and that it does so forcefully, invitingly, and clearly.

In-Store Display

When a person enters your store, whether motivated by your window or not, he usually has either a specific book or a subject in mind. It is important, then, that your arrangement and display of titles help him to find what he is looking for.

While fiction and general nonfiction are usually set out alphabetically by title or by author, too often the more specialized subjects (cooking, gardening, sports, nature, etc.) are not so carefully arranged. Each book in your store should be found in its correct place within its *subject classification,* and attractive signs in large bold type should make it possible for any person to find exactly what he wants.

There are two good reasons for this. First, regular bookstore customers are often rugged individualists who don't want salesmen hanging over their shoulders. Even those who are not regular buyers may wish to look around without the aid of a salesman. In either case if your customers find themselves in attractive surroundings where they can browse easily and find the subjects of their interest, they will quite possibly pick up an extra book or two. And they will be back.

Second—and this is particularly true during the Christmas season when you are operating at full blast and with extra untrained help—subject classification is also much easier for your salespeople. Looking for a book that you are sure you have—"it was right here yesterday"—is time-consuming and annoying to both your salesperson and the customer. It is doubly annoying when you run across the book an hour later on another counter.

So train your clerks to keep the books in your store in perfect order. A misplaced book is often the cause of a lost sale and a disappointed customer. Disappointed customers seldom come back.

Once everything in your store is in place and all your sections are suitably identified (and you have put the machinery in operation to assure yourself that they will stay that way), it is time to think about the frosting on the cake. Just as your window's prime function was to bring a customer into your store, so your in-store displays will be designed to bring a customer to a particular item, to emphasize the desirability of a particular title. Within the ranks of your fiction and general nonfiction this can be done by a broken-up display—i.e., some books face out interspersed with others spine out. Such an arrangement draws maximum attention to the face-out titles, which you have chosen for their saleability.

If all titles were set out with just the spines showing, your potential customer might as well be in the library stacks. This is all right if he has come for one particular book and no other. It is all wrong if you hope to interest him in other titles, encourage him to browse, give him a good time, and persuade him to return.

To have all the titles face out (besides being almost impossible due to limitations of space) is not a satisfactory solution either. The eye of the beholder is not caught, rather it is overwhelmed. There are neither high nor low points in your over-all display. Attention is not focused, instead it is dissipated.

Two categories of books demand all the special treatment you can give them: higher-priced juveniles and art books. While the former are not so expensive as the latter, a potential customer does want to see exactly what he is getting before parting with a large bill. Not only must these books be displayed face out, but, if you expect a reasonable turn-over, they should be given prominent store location. This is particularly true during the Christmas season. Many a customer who has already selected two or three books will pause over a large expensive gift book if that book is so placed that he cannot help seeing it. The result may be that his wife will find a new art book under the Christmas tree.

Single-title point-of-sale displays for autographing parties or other special events are seldom worth while. Subject-matter point-of-sale displays are something else again. Suppose your window to be full of fishing rods, creels, dry and wet flies, and many fishing books. Now make sure that your customer can get from outside the store to your inside display without having to ask the way. It will be best, of course, to have your fishing books up front while this window is in. If this is impracticable, handmade signs are excellent if your talents lie in that direction. "Izaak Waltons—This Way" may bring a smile and a gleam of anticipation to the eye of the beholder.

Make it easy for him to find the feast you have prepared, and then let him gorge himself. If he is a real *aficionado,* he will sell himself many more books than you could by standing at his elbow.

Just as in your window, in-store lighting is of prime importance. You can do everything else right, but if you do not make sure that everything you have done is clearly visible, you have worked to little effect. So make sure you have no dark corners in your store. Good electrical fixtures that will provide a strong, even light are absolutely essential to a modern bookstore.

Publisher display materials. A major problem confronting book-sellers is how to use effectively the mass of posters, counter displays and other materials that publishers send. Much of it is excellent, and considerable money, time, and effort have been expended in its creation. To a great extent, the use a bookseller can make of these display materials depends on the physical makeup and boundaries of his store. It is impossible to feature a large number of books in a small amount of space. To attempt it is both distracting to the customer and detracting from the effect each poster or display is designed to achieve. Choose publishers' display materials carefully. Then use the pieces you have selected with the books in question, for the customer whose interest is quickened by a poster does not want to wander about looking for the book it recommends. You have caught his interest for, perhaps, one second. You will hold it only if the book is immediately at hand.

Impulse sales. The best spot in your store to sell something a customer had not planned to buy is at the cash register. Supermarkets have developed these impulse sales to the nth degree, and it is a grim buyer indeed who can get through a supermarket checkout counter without making some small addition to his purchases. Bookstores can work this same magic. Choose your cash-register-counter displays with great care. They should be small and inexpensive. Keep changing your cash-register display so that your regular customers can see new items when they re-enter your store. It is fantastic to note, over the course of a week, now many of these items will have melted away. Ninety-nine per cent of these sales are pure impulse on the part of a customer who is standing there with money in his hand.

A final word. All promotion takes planning and none more so than window and in-store display. Holidays, special events, seasonal occupations and sports—all these call for special attention. Each must be anticipated and planned for. Keep a promotional calendar that will let you know in good time when to begin your plans for a window. This will save you from the embarrassment of learning about Father's Day by looking at the window of the card shop down the street.

"Currents from the Chinook"

39

JUDITH M. NOYES
Chinook Bookshop
Colorado Springs, Colorado

A customer walks into the bookshop and asks for *The Scarlet Pumpernickel.* The mother of a high school student comes in for *The Rejected Saurus;* another wants *The Taming of the Screw.* A young girl asks blushingly for *The Sinuous Woman.* And, our classic request, a student wonders where we keep the books by Ibid: "He must be an important writer since he's quoted in so many footnotes."

Such encounters brighten the day in every busy bookshop and help keep life livable in spite of overdue shipments, missing invoices, credit snarls, and leaks in the roof, and these incidents can be put to work selling books for you. At Chinook we keep mental and scribbled notes of things that happen in the shop which might add humor and the light touch to our promotional brochure, *Currents from the Chinook.* (A "chinook," we might explain, is a warm, dry wind blowing down the eastern slope of the Rockies, literally a "snow-eater" that dramatically raises temperatures and brings a promise of spring. We chose the word "currents" for its implication of flow and contemporary comment.)

Currents grew out of a brief monthly book column we wrote for a local FM radio guide when the bookshop was new; the opportunity for exposure cost us nothing except time and was welcome as a way of introducing ourselves to the book-buying public. When the little FM magazine folded, we decided to expand the column into a brochure of capsule reviews and commentary, and we sent out our first edition in October, 1962. To give an idea of how long ago that was, the new books we were discussing included Philip Roth's *Letting Go,* Joseph Heller's *Catch-22* in the paperback edition, *A Long and Happy Life* by Reynolds Price, William Golding's *The Inheritors,* and *Dr. Seuss's Sleep Book.* This initial effort was one page (one side), professionally printed, and mailed to several hundred customers. *Currents* is now six pages, goes to 6,000 customers (local, state, nation, and abroad), and is distributed in the shop. We consider it to be the most effective part of our advertising–public-relations program.

Although the attractive, mass-produced catalogs of Bowker and Booksellers Catalog Service, for example, are expertly done and readily available, they cannot achieve that personal touch or that this-is-written-for-*you* quality of the individual bookshop publication. The do-it-yourself newsletter has the advantages of: Allowing you to choose the books you plan to stock and promote—the titles you and your staff are most enthusiastic about, including certain odd-ball titles that might be overlooked in the mass-produced catalog; emphasizing books of particular local or regional interest; giving you one more chance to inform or remind your customers of the services you offer—and the opportunity of presenting your shop's own personality. The disadvantages to producing your own book newsletter are, let's face it, the time and money involved.

In Chinook's case, the actual writing of the brochure doesn't cost a cent since it is done by the shop's oldest living unpaid employee—me. I base the reviews on my own and my husband-partner's reading and on the critical opinions and comments of all the staff. Dick takes care of liaison work with the printer and the details of distribution. Writing is part of my background, and Dick is experienced in printing and publishing. But even if you lack specific experience, you, or someone on your staff, are probably capable of turning out some thoughtful, interesting, well-written paragraphs about the new books, geared to your own situation and customers.

Dick and I feel strongly that because *Currents* represents our shop, it must be quality in every respect. We don't try to scrimp on paper stock and ink, and we go over proofs meticulously. Typographical errors, grammatical mistakes, authors' names or titles misspelled, or other inaccuracies raise doubts about your knowledge of the books and your efficiency, and bespeak a sloppiness that your customer-readers could attribute to your whole operation.

For our first brochure, we hired a commercial-artist friend to design the masthead and advise on type and layout. We now do our own layout, working with the printer's representative. Each brochure features at least one illustration; the Christmas production, a six-page splurge, has several. These line drawings are taken from old magazines. (An old collection of the American humor magazine *Puck* has provided us with many interesting and appropriate cuts.) But be sure to use only material that is out of copyright. Such devices as fancy initial caps are also good for breaking the monotony of a solid page of type.

Your printer will be able to show you various types and grades of papers and inks. We've found a 75–80-pound stock the best for mailing purposes, and we prefer the appearance of a textured finish. We use what printers call an average higher-cost paper, primarily because this permits a greater variety of finishes and colors. For variety's sake we change colors with each issue. The fall issue may be a brown ink on gold paper; black on olive is good, and so is turquoise on white. For Christmas, red and white is an obvious choice, but other combinations (green and lavender, for instance) are sometimes more striking. We generally use 8- and 10-point Times Roman type. Make sure the ink is readable, as printed. See a sample run before you decide on a color. If the newsletter is difficult to read, you're defeating your entire purpose.

For size, we like an 8½"X14" sheet with a triple fold, printed by offset with linotype composition. The printer delivers 6,000 to us folded, ready to address (with our machine), and 1,000 unfolded for distribution in the shop. As of our last mailing, total creative-production-addressing cost was 12¢ each. This does not include postage. We used bulk-rate postage until recently when we learned that the mailing simply wasn't reaching our customers in time for Christmas ordering, and we switched to first-class postage. We felt it was worth the extra dollars to get the pieces to the customers promptly.

We cannot stress too strongly the importance of gearing your brochure to the particular interests of the people in your area, using the appealing qualities of the "soft sell" and personal touch—especially in contrast with the hucksterish prose of most direct-mail advertising. Here is where you can let yourself go creatively, and use limericks, rhymes, puns, or any other literary device you prefer, to make your point. Occasional caustic panning of a book or author (if you feel it is deserved) may come as a refreshing surprise to your customer-reader, who thereafter tends to respect you as a "critic."

References to regional and local authors, places, and events are quite acceptable and effective. Your out-of-state customers, who come to know you once on a trip or vacation, will enjoy the references and will learn of books that might not receive notice in their own region. We are often surprised by the number of mail orders we receive from people in Philadelphia, Chicago, Phoenix, and Santa Barbara, until we remind ourselves that a new book about Western history may not have received much attention in the press of these cities, and the customer respects our special knowledge of the subject and thinks of us as an obvious source. More and more people are learning that shopping by mail is easy, convenient, and painless, and your shop brochure can be a warm and personal invitation for them to use your services.

If you maintain a mailing list of both local and out-of-town names, this can be the main audience for your brochure. Our own list has been carefully developed and is constantly being enlarged, culled, and corrected. At first we mailed to out-of-town customers only. However, when we tried cutting down on other forms of local advertising and mailing the brochure to in-town customers, the results were overwhelming. It is impossible to know the exact total pull of *Currents,* but the measurable response (mail orders, customers specifying that they are buying titles mentioned in the brochure) is 7 per cent, which is extraordinarily good for direct mail. We estimate our total response at 15 per cent.

Doing your own book newsletter is time-consuming. It involves weeks of reviewing and selecting books to be discussed, hard hours at the typewriter, conferences with the printer, and putting up with publishers' whimsies. (They announce a grand-sounding book for Christmas, you include it in your promotion, and the darn book never does appear.) It is also expensive. But it's that something extra—that individual touch—that in this day of the mass, canned, powdered-pablum approach makes a refreshing personal appeal. And when the mail orders start arriving from fifty or five hundred miles away, and local customers come into the shop with their brochures earmarked and pencil-checked, and people from Wichita Falls to Winnetka ask, "How do I get on your mailing list?" and you begin to fancy yourself a member of Robert Cromie's or Gene Shalit's fraternity, then you know it's been worth it!

Direct Mail for Retail Bookstores   **40**

MORTON L. LEVIN
Executive Vice President,
The Viking Press, Inc.,
New York City

Each year more advertising money is being spent for direct mail. Today it is not unusual for large advertisers to make mailings of hundreds of thousands of pieces in an effort to sell a specific book. Addressing and mailing equipment, too, has had to become larger, faster, more sophisticated to handle these mass mailings. To the bookseller, particularly the owner of the smaller personal bookshop, it might seem as though direct mail is no longer a sales tool that he can use. Actually, nothing could be further from the truth.

The small store has two extremely important advantages that the mass mailer can never hope to have. The first is its mailing list. This is probably the most important ingredient in any sustained direct-mail program. Obviously the customer most likely to respond to a letter, card, or circular advising him of the availability of a new book would be one who is already a book buyer and has shown some previous interest in the type of book being offered. The bookseller's list of customers, showing whenever possible their interests, should be one of his most valuable assets. Certainly it would not be in the store's best interest to have a customer mailing list and not take advantage of it regularly —and it would be even worse to let customers walk out of the store without having the means to contact them until they decide to walk in again.

Once he can contact his customers, the bookseller's second advantage comes to his aid. Because he is a local merchant, his message is both more personal and more believable than one issued under the general signature of the mass mailer. Too, his customer has several ways of responding—by mail, by phone, or by stopping into the store so that the book or books may be examined.

Because direct mail is flexible and adaptable as a substitute for personal contact with customers, it would seem unwise for booksellers not to take advantage of it. Direct mail offers an effective, economical method of aiding in the year-to-year growth that is the normal objective of every business. It does this by developing new customers, keeping present customers, and helping the store get a larger share of each customer's book-buying dollar.

The Mailing List

The primary source of names for the bookseller's mailing list would be his current customers. If a sales slip is written up for each transaction, these names can easily be transferred to the mailing list. If transactions are rung on a register with no record of the customer's name and address, then an easy means must be available—easy both for the salesperson and the customer—for the name to be added to the bookstore's list. A padded form can be kept at the register, or a prepaid reply card can be placed in each book as it is sold. The text side of the card would point out the advantages of being advised of new publications and special offers by being on the store's mailing list and allow a space for the customer to fill in his name and address. The other side of the card would be preaddressed to the store so that the customer need only drop the card in the mail box.

An occasional double-postcard mailing to the store's list asking for the names and addresses of friends who might be interested in this service can be very effective in the development of your list. In addition, you will probably want to include the lists of people who belong to the same clubs and organizations you do, religious, fraternal, social, and business. Local garden clubs, art leagues, book-reading circles, educators, professional people, merchants, and civic leaders are all good possibilities.

Bear in mind that in direct-mail selling your most logical prospects are those who have bought by mail a product or a service closely allied in interest with the book or books you are selling.

Because there are so many different ways of maintaining a mailing list, the bookseller should familiarize himself with as many as possible before making his decision. The most common forms would be: (1) hand-addressing directly on the mailing piece or on labels; (2) the spirit-duplicator process; (3) fiber stencils; and (4) metal plates.

Each of these methods should be examined on the following bases:

   a) records no more information about a name than is necessary;
   b) can be broken down into the fewest divisions;
   c) holds duplication of names to a minimum;
   d) requires the minimum amount of clerical time to keep accurate and up-to-date;

e) makes addressing quick, easy, and inexpensive;
f) is flexible enough for unlimited growth.

One example of the spirit-duplicator process is the Keysort system offered by the Royal McBee Corporation. Information concerning the fiber-stencil process can be obtained from the Elliott Addressing Machine Company. For information on mailing from metal plates, contact the Addressograph-Multigraph Corporation about its Addressograph and Speedaumat systems. You might also contact Pitney-Bowes for information on its addresser-printer system, which also utilizes the metal plate and has been specially designed for the smaller mailing list. These systems can all be maintained through a mailing service, or through a local electronic data-processing service bureau for a computerized list.

One maxim of direct-mail selling that can never be repeated too often is that your mailing list is no better than its maintenance. People pass away, move, or for one reason or another cease to be prospects for your offers. Such names in your mailing list cost you money. You cannot build a list of so many hundred or so many thousand names and sit back. New names must constantly be added, old, inactive names removed, and addresses changed. It will pay you to go over your list regularly, separating the active from the inactive, prodding the latter until they are aroused to buy or proved to be worthless. By all means check with your local post office the ways in which the postal service can help you keep your list clean.

Further thoughts. The bookseller's direct-mail program begins with his mailing list and his ability to have these names placed on a mailing piece in as inexpensive and speedy a manner as possible. The next area of decision is what to mail. There are no rules and regulations governing what will or will not sell by mail. The only way you can be sure of what will affect customers in your community is to find out with the trial-and-error method. One thing you can be sure of, however, is that by using sound judgment in the selection of titles, good taste in describing them, and enthusiasm, your chances of success will be greatly enhanced. Don't expect a sell-out every time, but do expect that with regular mailings you can build up a steady flow of orders and thus help to fill the gaps between the seasonal peaks. In a very real and practical way, direct mail, when properly used, can spell for many booksellers the difference between a bare living and a thriving business.

In addition to single-postcard, double-postcard, and letter mailings that you might make up yourself, you should also take advantage of the mailing pieces prepared for booksellers by publishers, remainder houses, and syndicated catalog services. Try them. Test them for your store and your store's clientele. And bear in mind that direct-mail response is cumulative. The more you mail and the more regular your mailings are, the greater the response will be to your direct mail in total. After all, once your customers realize that they will be getting news of books from you, they will not be in such a hurry to respond to someone else's offer.

Also, it is rarely wise to do any mailings without sufficient stock on hand to fill orders at once. (The prepublication mailing is an obvious exception. However, be sure your mailing states when the book will be available.) One of the unchanging rules in mail selling is to get the merchandise to the customer as quickly as possible. A long interval between order receipt and order delivery slows up payments and increases the number of books returned.

Like most businesses, direct mail also has its ups and downs, its good seasons and bad. It is no get-rich-quick scheme. Don't expect too much at the beginning, but look for a steadily increasing volume of business. Use your best business judgment, be conscious of the costs involved, test wherever you can, and you will find that direct mail will reward you with greater sales and greater profit.

Successful Radio-TV Promotion   **41**

LEWIS MEYER
Lewis Meyer Book Store,
Tulsa, Oklahoma

WITH SOME GUIDELINES
FOR RADIO ADVERTISING
BY NICK CLEMENTE

Books are news. Books are entertainment. Both radio listeners and TV viewers like to know about new books. When such shows are pitched on an informal, chatty plane, they give the listener the illusion that he is reading these books just by hearing about them. He is improving himself—and no man, woman, or child can resist the urge to improve himself when doing so involves so little effort. The deadly exercise shows, the cooking shows, even guess-the-answer shows thrive because they flatter the listener's image of himself.

But book shows do more than please people. They sell books. A book sounds interesting. The listener wants to own it, whether or not he reads it. For years I reviewed a book a day on radio. I occasionally picked a book with an extremely limited appeal and featured it just to see what would happen. I discovered that every book has potential buyers—and the more buyers who hear about it, the more copies will be sold.

Most of this essay concerns free promotion, or publicity. But it's not *advertising.* Since books are news and entertainment, book shows are no more advertisements than are book reviews on a newspaper book page.

Radio

Let's begin with radio. There are so many radio stations in some cities that programing has become viciously competitive. This means that you have a good chance of getting your foot in the door with any new idea. It shouldn't be hard to convince at least one station that people want to hear more about books.

A do-it-yourself book show, fifteen minutes long, once a week, is good business for a station—particularly when the station can get the talent for the show (you) free and providing you have a personality that projects to the listening public. On this show you can name the top best-sellers in fiction and nonfiction, feature a children's book-of-the-week, and then give five or six minutes to your book-of-the-week. You work in an author interview now and then. The only commercial you need is the usual credit line to the store that supplies the books (yours), at the close of the show. More than one program like this has started as a sustaining, public-interest show, and actually picked up sponsors. I've sold everything from tires to nylons to home loans using books as my copy. But even the no-commercial program has its place. Radio and TV stations are constantly being goaded by the Federal Communications Commission to do more programs "in the public interest." Books count as "informational" public-interest shows. When the local library is plugged, particularly when the books mentioned are listed there, the show becomes "educational."

If a fifteen-minute show is too ambitious while getting your feet wet, start with less time. Many radio stations love the one-to-five-minute feature these days. A capsule of news followed by more music (the old "Monitor" format). Instead of taping one fifteen-minute program, tape several short fragments to be played at different times. "This is —— reporting on the ten best-sellers this week in ——." Everyone loves to hear the best-seller lists. In compiling yours, you can rely on *Publishers Weekly* or one of the Sunday book sections, or you can compile your own. Any bookseller knows that most prepared best-seller lists are about four weeks behind the times.

There are dozens of angles for these short features: "The How-to-Do-It Book of the Week"; "The Book Everyone Is Talking About"; and so on. In the beginning you will want to write out these programs, but you'll discover that in time you can ad lib easily. Dust-jacket copy may not influence browsers, but it is perfect for radio. Try to include in every radio review, however brief, at least one—preferably two—actual quotations from the book itself.

If you simply cannot do the show yourself, then select a local radio personality, a disc jockey probably, and work through him. He will present short book features along with his interviews, tidbits, and music. There was a time when "yak" was out. The radio stations insisted that no one wanted to listen to chatter. People must have music, music, music. The listeners rebelled against this dreary record-spot-record-spot programing. They *wanted* yak! Now the pendulum has swung almost completely the other way. Yak is back—and how! And books are fun yak! Once you get your radio performer interested in passing along book information, you can feed him a best-seller list each week, and you can give him books to talk about. Let him read the dust jackets. Chances are he'll do more than that, but dust-jacket reading is better than no mention at all.

Time out now to talk about how you can get books for radio (and TV) review without having to take them from your stock. *Ask* for them! I've yet to meet a publisher's publicity head who would not cooperate in a legitimate effort to get books mentioned. When I feel that a local columnist or lecturer or even a doctor or lawyer can help a book, I ask that he be sent a review copy. The easiest way to do it (after you line up your cooperative man at the station) is to write the publicity director a note requesting certain titles on his coming list (using suggestions from the traveler and the new catalog). Often those books will be sent to the personality with a little note saying they come with *your* compliments. Anyway, the performer will know the originating source of his free copies. Of course, press releases will be sent him, and many of these make excellent copy. Your job is to see that the personality does not become careless. I doubt if he will. Most radio and TV people are so delighted to receive free books that they go overboard to earn them through mentions on the shows. True, you can't expect a credit line every time, but the personality will get in a plug for you now and then in that carefree fashion peculiar to deejays.

Television

This method—feeding books to a personality—is especially recommended for TV. TV time is so costly, and TV stations are so few, it is harder to convince the program director that a book show will appeal to listeners. And most TV book shows are just not that interesting. But getting book mentions from established local personalities is another matter. TV is a great book-selling medium, yet less that 10 per cent of our TV stations have book shows.

I mentioned the program director. Of course, for a show of your own you must talk with him (or with the owner or manager who can cut all kinds of red tape). But if you are not contemplating a show of your own, try to avoid the program director and talk directly to the radio or TV personality you select. Call the cooking expert and ask if she'd like to review a cookbook now and then if you get them for her. There's a "women's page" on every TV station, a garden show, an early morning personalities-variety show. Talk to the people who do these shows. Sell them. They are hurting for live, entertaining material. They recognize the appeal of books and they like the prestige books lend their programs.

Here's a tip that may be the answer to your bookstore identity problems: Cultivate the TV (or radio) personality by seeing that he gets review copies, by taking him to lunch, by getting to know each other. Then sell the personality (*not* the program director) on his interviewing *you* once a week as a regular feature of the show. It's worth getting up at 6:00 A.M. to appear on the 7:00–8:00 sun-up show! You can bring your best-sellers, your book-of-the-week, your children's books with you. The camera catches the jackets of the books while you are talking about them. Directors like book plugs because they make for lively visual presentation.

Of course, the interview lends itself to radio, too. You can tape one or several short interviews with the performer that he can play on his show at any time. The beauty of an interview is that you are being mentioned or seen and *you* means your store. You will discover that all of the other bookstores are selling books from your plugs, and you might as well be a good sport about it. People react differently to book plugs than to furniture plugs or show plugs. They don't always go to the plugger for the merchandise, even though they take his advice.

Last words from our sponsor. So far we've talked about radio and television advertising for free. Can you profitably sponsor a radio or TV show plugging books from your store? Not TV: it costs too much. But you can on radio. A bookstore in Dallas purchased time on a radio station and presented its own book reviewer. After years of good reviewing, the show has a devoted following. Publishers have learned that the plugs sell books, and many now contribute modest amounts on a per-book-plugged basis to help defray the cost of the show.

In large metropolitan markets, publishers are discovering the effectiveness of thirty- and sixty-second spot commercials.

I have paid for newspaper advertising, and I have had the good luck to be on radio and TV for free, and I can honestly say that there is no comparison when it comes to results. I discovered that newspaper ads (even long personal ones, like chatty columns) not only did not pay for themselves, but seldom identified the books advertised with my store. The only newspaper ad that pulls is the sale ad. *And this is the one kind of ad that radio and TV cannot do effectively for the bookseller.* Remember this when you are selling your book-plug idea to radio or TV: The newspaper uses its valuable space to present book reviews on a book page. Radio and TV miss a bet in not doing the same to cater to the book-hungry public.

The publishers themselves are doing more now in radio and TV on the local level. I feel it would pay a publisher to send his publicity director on a tour of leading cities to meet the personalities in radio and TV who would be receptive to review copies. This eye-and-ear gold mine is practically untapped. The newspaper book-page editor is flooded with new books, 80 per cent of which never get a mention. Yet radio and TV people are practically ignored. If a smart publicity director, who has a really red-hot book, would spend two or three dollars on a long-distance phone call to the personality about a book he is going to receive, it would pay off better than an expensive newspaper ad.

This is an extremely frank and candid approach to radio and television promotion, perhaps too frank and too candid. But it is realistic—and it *will* work. Go after this publicity for your store and you will be richly rewarded for the time and effort expended. Do it *yourself.* You can!

EDITOR'S NOTE.—Nick Clemente, Pickwick Book Shops, Hollywood, California, has pioneered a massive kind of radio *advertising*—as opposed to Mr. Meyer's *publicity*—campaign. He aims at the "vast non-book-buying market. The people who never look at the book pages. The people who change the station when they hear, 'And now, what's new in books?'

"Be it on radio or TV," Mr. Clemente continues, "the average book review receives little reaction from the general public. The only people they reach are the same people who are already our customers, who won't be huckstered into buying a book.

"To reach the larger, non-reading market, we knew we had to bring a book to life—to present the book in a dramatic and exciting format, and literally surprise the listener. We also discovered that this new market had to hear the message a few times before it would begin to react."

For the average Pickwick radio commercial, "dramatic" is a mild word, "exciting" almost an understatement. The very successful format on which Mr. Clemente settled combines epochal pronouncements, riveting sound effects, cataclysmic announcers, and music straight out of Cecil B. De Mille trailers. A typical Pickwick commercial is not easy either to ignore or forget. But with equal effect, Mr. Clemente's forces can be channeled into quiet, gentle approaches for quiet, gentle books. His approach varies with the market each station commands. "To our delight," he says, "we found that each of the major stations has a well-defined listening audience. By picking certain stations, we are able to pinpoint the right market for a book promotion. And we are able to make the purchase of time pay off. Don't overlook the fact that a single station has many different kinds of audience at different times of the day."

Thus, to reach the non-book-buying public via radio, Mr. Clemente recommends that you give your presentations a dramatic and exciting format and understand the market each station reaches. In addition, he offers the following guidelines:

- Use sixty-second spots wherever possible.
- Use publishers' co-op ad money.
- Bargain for rates! Radio stations love having bookshops as advertisers. It's a prestige account, and they will negotiate.

- If possible, avoid running less than eighteen spots per week on a given
  title.

To this advice, we would have but one demurrer: Do not be fright-
ened off radio advertising if you cannot run eighteen spots on a given
title. In some markets, fewer exposures may well be desirable.

Authors Sell Books

42

SYLVIA SELIGMAN
*Department Manager, Book Department,
G. Fox & Co., Hartford, Connecticut*

Authors sell books. Everyone is aware that personal appearances on TV by authors with an appealing public image have done a great deal to start them on the way to becoming best-sellers. Similarly, live author programs around the country not only have been successful events but have strongly influenced the sale of their books. As a large department store, we have been able to use this to good advantage in promoting our book department. Perhaps a description of our activities will provide some useful suggestions even to those smaller stores that aren't able to call on as much assistance in author promotion as we are.

In undertaking any kind of promotion of authors, one must first establish rapport with the publicity people from all publishers, large and small. These people are absolutely wonderful to work with. If you give them a workable idea, they immediately latch on to it, and they provide quick answers to your queries. Sometimes they have to say no if their author is scheduled for elsewhere when you want him. Some authors work only with national media, but others are glad to cooperate with regional outlets. If the author lives in the vicinity, he will surely accept local invitations.

It's a time-consuming job to run a promotional event. The idea may come easily, but the execution can be very demanding. But book-author luncheons bring customers—the best—into the store. They come by the hundreds. If the store is large and the book manager can work with an in-store public relations (PR) person, as we do, it's possible to schedule more events than small stores can. Stores in smaller communities can't handle the events that are possible in a community of 650,000 people, but many of the basic principles are the same. And cooperation with other non-book stores in the immediate area can be fruitful.

Our PR man arranges the tie-ins with community events, week by week, season by season, and works at least six months in advance with various organizations to bring in nationally known and local authors. He's especially good at matching specific authors with specific organizations for celebrity fund-raising events.

Not everyone can be as lucky as we are at G. Fox & Co. Many authors live in Connecticut or close by in New York and can come up here for a day. As an illustration, let's look at a typical fall season.

In September, our store will have a week of cooking demonstrations with the housewares and book departments jointly participating. Recently we collected several thousand recipes in a statewide recipe contest. The winning recipes are scheduled to appear in an all-color housewares catalog. Contest winners, along with five cookbook authors and local chefs, are scheduled on a daily basis for personal appearances and demonstrations during "Gourmet Week." Such authors as the personable Perla Meyers, author of *The Seasonal Kitchen* (New York: Holt, Rinehart and Winston), and Ilka Chase, whose latest book is *The Care and Feeding of Friends* (New York: Doubleday Publishing Co.), will talk, cook, and demonstrate.

Then it will be "Career Week," with Governor Meskill and Dr. Joyce Brothers as speaking guests at a luncheon, and Caroline Bird, author of *Everything a Woman Needs To Know To Get Paid What She's Worth* (New York: David McKay Co.), will be featured at a seminar on "How To Improve Your Present Condition." Concurrently our gourmet and cheese and wine shops will have a wine-tasting party with appropriate books on display (a leftover of "Gourmet Week"?). During the same week (how to get tired!), by chance, Gina Lollobrigida, author of *Italia Mia*, will also be here. A champagne party sponsored by Boys' Towns of Italy will be followed the next day by a luncheon for five hundred in the store by the Connecticut Opera Guild. More than 1,500 people can be expected to attend the two events.

The next week we will have scheduled one of our three annual book-author luncheons. Each is cosponsored by a local group. The organization sells tickets and collects the profits for its own charity event. Our store provides the auditorium, ad, posters, and publicity. Organizations love these events and vie with each other to sponsor them. Often the same organization will come back year after year. At each event we follow a very close pattern that seldom varies. This makes for tight control. Expenses are not excessive.

We pay author's transportation and if necessary provide a hotel room. We never pay lecture fees. On the morning of a luncheon, the author appears on local TV or radio, followed by a press party arranged by the store, where the board members or hostesses of the sponsoring organization, the store executives, and the press can meet the celebrities. Four authors are maximum for a single program. Each is allocated fifteen minutes at the end of the luncheon, which itself should not exceed an hour.

After the two-hour program, an area within the auditorium will have been set up for selling and autographing. In twenty minutes, we may sell $500 to $1,000's worth of autographed books, after which the authors are free to leave. The authors' press coverage can be counted upon to generate interest and sales before and after the event.

We do not do straight autograph-only parties. We feel that, within our framework, these are non-productive. However, I would recommend them for smaller stores that need the community relations or where there is a strong local interest that calls for a small event with a more intimate approach.

Within its public relations framework our store also sponsors classes, lectures, and demonstrations on twenty-three different subjects, most of which involve books in some way. These classes run for a six-week period and are scheduled three times within a year. Such subjects as quilting, crewelwork, needle embroidery, creative rugcraft, early American decoration, gourmet cooking, sewing, terrarium-making, dinner-party entertaining, regional Chinese cooking, and others attract over ten thousand customers annually—a pretty healthy statistic! Local teachers of these classes all seem to be writing books or to be in the midst of having a book published. Financially, we just about break even on the classes, but they are great for community relations, and of course they sell books. Robert Bauer's book *Gardens in Glass Containers* (Great Neck, N.Y.: Hearthside Press) sold 150 copies in five days to a group enrolled in a class, and we expect to repeat the event again in the same year. All books for the classes are recommended by the instructors involved and are displayed and sold in the book department.

Many tailor-made events promote books in an individual or special way. An example was our champagne evening for Sir Rudolph Bing with the Connecticut Opera Guild. Events were also planned for Pearl Bailey, Shirley Chisholm, Helen Hayes and Anita Loos, Julia Child, and Gloria Vanderbilt.

Julia Child's cocktail evening (dress-up, of course) and a luncheon with a marvelous lecture and demonstration sold books and lots of cookware.

Gloria Vanderbilt's appearance involved these other departments: home furnishings, pillows, fabrics, collage kits, lithographs, loungewear, and of course her book. Store publicity covered every angle through newspaper stories, radio and TV interviews, and visits with feature editors of newspapers.

Success in events like this requires extensive planning at least three or four months in advance. Matching the right author with the right organization is essential. Local newspapers and radio and TV personalities must be interested in the celebrity. Imagination must be balanced by follow-through. Somewhere a light must go on—and then the arrangements start. If the media don't react positively, forget it! If they react positively, PR people can harness the mayor, religious groups, college clubs, Girl Scouts, service organizations, affluent musical groups, craft exhibitors, historical societies, and on and on.

It's important to get an organization interested and excited and to offer them a package that is strictly theirs from the start. The group must sell tickets with the understanding that the organization and the store will work together with biographical material and glossies provided by the publisher, work via the book department, the group, and the media. Then the public is alerted that a fabulous program is available to them. Don't try to palm off "little authors" to a big group. It simply won't work. Sometimes a local author has something worth while to say to your audience through his book—a local politician, a former senator, an architect, or even a good humorist, but be sure they're interesting.

Large programs require an auditorium. Our PR department issues an absolutely essential work schedule well in advance of the event so that each member of the store staff knows what to do and performs his function on schedule. Painters, electricians, hostesses, ticket-takers, and display people are all involved. Food services and adjacent press party facilities may well be, also. Publicity must be planned in advance to build the proper crescendo for the size of the group and the weight of the author.

All the pieces must fit. If everything isn't in writing and done early enough, it all falls apart.

It's always an asset if your city has a daily-talk-show personality who interviews authors—and loves them. In our area there is a female radio personality whose program covers Connecticut and a good part of two adjacent states. Woe betide us when we haven't been alerted who an author guest on her program will be, and we find ourselves without books. But on the whole, she sells books for us.

The *ABA Newswire* has helped recently. It gives us ideas, too, and sometimes we get jealous when we are not included in a particular publisher's promotion schedule. Many publishers' PR people today accompany their authors on tour and are on the road for weeks at a time. By the time they hit your store, they'll be tired and they are very grateful if you have arranged everything for their authors. Many times, poor planning causes embarrassment for them, the authors, and the audience.

You can always expect the unexpected, so be prepared. Be gracious, ready to change, and alert for an audience that may be losing interest. Veteran speakers realize that people may walk out during a speech because they have to get home, meet an appointment, or finish shopping. Smile and, above all, listen to the speaker! Don't serve "booze" to the public. It may be needed to soothe nervous authors at a press party, but don't let things get out of hand. If an author is more at home with a typewriter than a microphone, be prepared to open up a question-and-answer session that may be more personal, informal, and stimulating to a nervous author and the audience as well.

If you get a $150 bill for transportation, return it to the publisher. Don't let authors take advantage of you. Don't pussyfoot. Publishers will respect your forthrightness. And they know when you have done a good job. Thank them and they will thank you by giving you more of their hottest authors. Your reputation with publisher, author, and audience is worth feeding with great care.

Expert and specialist authors can be a challenge but very rewarding—black writers tied in with urban groups, or cooking and health writers. We ran a chess tournament for children last spring with eight hundred contestants and sold a raft of paperback chess books. The next time we will promote backgammon. Classes will lead to a celebrity appearance and a tournament. Jean Nidetch is great if you can ever get her. We have an equestrienne group that is dying to get William Steinkraus for a dinner with their three hundred members—and most will buy a book. Theatrical personalities are always good. And columnists; wine experts; notorious characters, if you can handle them; beauty experts go with exercise, diet, and health writers, male or female. We have antiquaries in fantastic numbers here in Connecticut and they are knowledgeable and lovely people to work with.

In other words, try to get anyone your imagination ties a string to, and make a neat package. Work closely with publishers' representatives. Keep pressing—their authors push them, too, to deliver this same package you have given them. Ask for cooperative money. Or get your store to give it to you in their budget. It all makes for wonderful community relations, measureable in-store traffic increases, and goes far beyond the "buck."

A Bookseller's
Continuing
Education

Trade Tools for the Bookshop **43**

ELIZABETH A. GEISER
Senior Vice President, Publisher,
R. R. Bowker Co.,
New York City

Booksellers from coast to coast have profited from the display in their windows of a decal that reads:

> *If you want a book, any book, ask us about it.*
> *Chances are we can give you immediate information*
> *as to price, exact title, and availability.*
> *If we don't have it, we can get it for you promptly.*
> *If it's out of print, we may still be able to get*
> *you a good secondhand copy.*

It was their way of saying, "We are here to serve all your book needs." Advertising yourself as the community know-it-all on books may seem presumptuous, unless you realize that this can be achieved with the aid of a few basic reference tools of the book trade.

The Annual Index: BIP

When the head of the local garden club comes in for *How to Prune a Hedge* and doesn't remember the author or the publisher, or a high school teacher asks for the least expensive edition of Mark Twain's *Life on the Mississippi*, or you want to order a deluxe edition of *A Child's Garden of Verses* for a doting grandmother, but don't know the publisher or current price—refer to *Books in Print. BIP* is an annually revised reference work including information on almost every *currently in print* book of more than 2,200 American publishers. Each listing includes author's name, title of book, publisher, price, ISBN, and, when known, date of publication. A complete list of publishers' mailing addresses is included in one of the volumes. For many years a two-volume publication, it was issued in four volumes in 1974.

With *Books in Print* at hand, you should rarely be stumped in searching for a book that is in print—if you know the author, but not the title, if you want to check the latest price, verify the publisher's name, see a listing of all books by an author, check the date of the latest edition, find out whether a book is illustrated, or is part of a series. Keep your set of *BIP* where both your clerks and your customers can use it. Some stores buy two copies—one for the customer area (to encourage customers to do some searching on their own) and a copy for the order desk. *BIP* is published in October by R. R. Bowker Co., 1180 Avenue of the Americas, New York, N.Y. 10036, and is sold with a money-back guarantee if it doesn't pay for itself the first month on the job.

And to keep your *Books in Print* up-to-date, there is a bimonthly periodical, *Forthcoming Books,* which provides author-title indexes to all books due to be published in the coming five-month season, plus a continuing, cumulative index to books published since the summer. With *Forthcoming Books,* you can research books months back as well as months ahead, a perfect supplement to *Books in Print.* Not only can you tell at a glance which books are scheduled for publication (5,000–7,000 forthcoming titles in each issue) and keep abreast of postponements, price changes, and so on, but you'll be able to locate recently published titles, issued since the last *Books in Print* appeared. These newly published titles will cumulate with every new issue, starting with 5,000 in November, and ending the cycle the following September with a listing of 30,000 titles. Information includes price, publisher, and publication date for nearly every kind of book—adult, juvenile, trade, text, technical, paperback, etc. Each issue's coverage overlaps and updates the preceding one. Also available: *Subject Guide to Forthcoming Books,* appearing every two months—on the same schedule as *Forthcoming Books*—and providing a subject index of books to come. Individual and combination subscriptions are available.

Books in Print Supplement, appearing in the spring, updates and closes the gap between the annual publications of *Books in Print.* New books published since July of the preceding year, back-list titles that have had price changes, and out-of-print books are all indexed by author and title; new books are also indexed by subject. Complete bibliographic data are provided for new and forthcoming books as well as those which registered price changes; sufficient details are given to identify those which are out of print.

The World List of Books in English: CBI

If you want to be able to track down specialized English-language material, *whether in print or not,* published in Rome, Athens, Copenhagen, Bombay, or Milan, or books in English on flower-arranging published in Tokyo, or literature from Australia, social-science theses from

Delhi, or cookbooks in English from Paris, you will need to use the famous *Cumulative Book Index.* While *Books in Print* covers only books published in the United States and only those in print, the *Cumulative Book Index,* subtitled *A World List of Books in the English Language,* lists all work in English from all over the world. It is a record of what has been published since 1898.

The *CBI* appears monthly (except in August) in paper covers, and at intervals the H. W. Wilson Co. publishes bound cumulations that recompile the information included in the monthly issues. Since 1957, permanent two-year cumulations have been issued; earlier permanent volumes cover four to six years. Since the compilation is chronological, you may have to consult a number of the cumulative volumes before finding the information you need. In a single alphabetical list, the *CBI* indexes all entries by author, editor, title, translator, and illustrator, and under as many subjects as contents demand. *CBI* is sold on a special service basis; rates will be supplied by the publisher, H. W. Wilson Co., 950 University Avenue, Bronx, N.Y. 10452.

Book Trade Magazines

Publishers Weekly: The American Book Industry Journal keeps you informed with its news of the industry and bookselling, editorials, articles, forecasts, and book lists. *PW*'s "Weekly Record" section gives a descriptive listing of books as they are published. Its "Forecasts" of paperbacks and of hardbound adult and children's titles alert you to forthcoming titles weeks in advance of publication. And three times a year, for spring, summer, and fall, giant announcement numbers tell you what will be published in the coming season, including annotations, publication date, price, and publisher.

Publishers Weekly also issues special numbers about children's books, scientific and technical books, religious books, and university press books, as well as an annual statistics issue. The three big announcement numbers, each with an index to books advertised in the issue, are available at a special rate.

Essential for college stores is the *College Store Journal,* published six times a year by the National Association of College Stores, 55 East College Street, Oberlin, Ohio 44074 (subscription included in NACS membership) and filled with details about college store operation, supplies, and stock. *Tartan Book News,* giving annotated listings of forthcoming adult books, is issued monthly by Tartan News of Books, 1609 Memorial Avenue, Williamsport, Pa. 11701.

Subject Guide *and Other Special-Order Aids*

If you have a bird enthusiast among your customers, a collector of Americana, a hamster fan, or a how-to buff, turn him loose on *Subject*

Guide to Books in Print, published every October by Bowker. In this volume, the titles in *Books in Print* have been reshuffled into subject categories, with the complete bibliographic information retained. The *Subject Guide,* in two volumes, classifies books under 63,000 Library of Congress subject headings, with thousands of cross-references to lead readers from one specific area of interest to all its related subjects. The how-to fan looking under "handicrafts" in the *Subject Guide* is reminded to look also under "basketmaking," "handweaving," and "leatherwork," to name a few. *Subject Guide* can help you satisfy a special request or provide a list on a specific subject.

American Book Publishing Record (*BPR* for short), also published by Bowker, is a subject listing of *PW's* "Weekly Record" section and includes the same book information: author, title, publication date, price, publisher, and a brief description. *BPR* keeps your *Subject Guide* up-to-date (*Books in Print Supplement* is also useful in this respect). Let your customers browse through the *BPR* sections on their favorite subjects. Annual cumulations of the *BPR* are also available.

When you want to order books, check on a discount (for a complete listing of publishers' trade policies consult the *ABA Book Buyer's Handbook*), study a publisher's list, or find a description of one of his books, you turn to the publisher's catalog. *Publishers' Trade List Annual* makes it easy for you to keep track of the catalogs and lists of 2,250 U.S. publishers. It consists of seven volumes of catalogs of these publishers, compiled in July of each year, and bound together in alphabetical order. Small publishers who do not have catalogs large enough to be bound into the book are listed in a supplementary section in front of the first volume. This trade tool has been in existence for a hundred years. Bowker publishes *PTLA* annually.

AB Bookman's Weekly, Box 1100, Newark, N.J. 07101, is a weekly magazine that lists books that are either "Books Wanted" or "Books for Sale" on the secondhand market—out-of-print books, particular editions, specialized books, and so on. For a small fee, you can list the item your customer wants you to find for him, and chances are you will get a bid from one of the many buyers or sellers who use *AB.* An annual subscription includes the *AB Bookman's Yearbook* of "permanent" wants and offerings.

Bowker's *Medical Books in Print* gives bibliographic information on medical books covering subject areas from psychiatry to veterinary medicine as well as paraprofessional areas, such as medical technology. Entries are indexed alphabetically by author, title, and subject.

Scientific and Technical Books in Print gives bibliographic information on more than 12,000 scientific and technical subject areas. Books are alphabetically arranged by author, subject, and title with the same information included for each listing. Available from Bowker.

El-Hi Textbooks in Print, an author, title, subject index to the available elementary and high school textbooks, provides information on price, grade level, and publisher. It is published annually by Bowker.

Paperbacks and Children's Books

Paperbound Books in Print is devoted to listing paperbacks published in the United States. In three issues a year, *PBIP* provides complete indexes of all available paperbacks, listed by author, title, and subject (averaging over 115,000 titles per volume). If you wish, for example, to choose from among all the available paper cookbooks, or select paperbound books on science, literature, history, mysteries, juveniles, or other major subjects, the subject section in *Paperbound Books in Print* lists all the titles, giving the price and publisher. You may want at least two copies, one for use by store personnel, the other for use by customers. *Paperbound Books in Print* appears in April, July, and November. Published by Bowker, annual subscription for *PBIP* is $32.50. A single copy costs $18.95, less 20 per cent discount on five or more copies.

Children's Books in Print provides author-title-illustrator indexes to children's books from kindergarten through twelfth grade and covers old favorites and recent publications in hardbound and paperbound editions. A directory of the publishers represented is also included. It is published by Bowker, as is *Subject Guide to Children's Books in Print,* which lists juvenile titles under more than 8,000 subject headings based on the Sears List of Subject Headings (H. W. Wilson Co.). Both books provide complete ordering information: author, title, publisher, year of publication, price, grade level, binding, edition, number of volumes, ISBN, and illustrator.

Other children's book lists that can be valuable to the bookseller: *Let's Read Together: Books for Family Enjoyment* (3d ed., 1969), American Library Association, 50 East Huron Street, Chicago, Ill. 60611; *A Parent's Guide to Children's Reading* (revised enlarged edition, 1969), Pocket Books, Inc., 630 Fifth Avenue, New York, N.Y. 10020; *AAAS Science Book List for Children,* American Association for the Advancement of Science, 1515 Massachusetts Avenue, N.W., Washington, D.C. 20005.

Foreign-Language Books

If you serve a Spanish-speaking community, or an area where more Spanish books could be sold, consider adding *Libros en Venta* to your reference shelf. *Libros en Venta* is the Spanish-language counterpart of *Books in Print* and *Subject Guide,* indexing by author, title, and subject the Spanish-language books available from nine hundred Latin American and Spanish publishers. The first edition was published April, 1964, by Bowker. Three supplements, published in 1969, 1972, and 1973, update the earlier volume. In addition, Bowker publishes *Fichero Bibliográfico Hispanoamericano,* a monthly record of the new Spanish-language books published in the Western Hemisphere.

British Books in Print is a record of all books in print and on sale in the United Kingdom; two volumes published annually in the fall and distributed in the United States by Bowker.

Whitaker's Five-Year Cumulative Book List, 1963–67, is a one-volume guide to books published in the United Kingdom in the period indicated; both author and title listings, with information on book size, number of pages, illustrations, binding, price, publishers, etc., available from Bowker.

Australian Books in Print indexes by author, title, and subject books published in Australia and also includes book trade associations, literary associations and societies, children's book councils, Australian publishers with representatives, and overseas publishers with their Australian agents. Approximately 1,600 Australian magazines are also listed. Available from Bowker.

German Books in Print (*Verzeichnis Lieferbarer Bücher*) lists books of all kinds currently available from some 1,700 West German, Austrian, and Swiss German-language publishers. Entries are indexed by key word as well as by author and title. The author volume provides full bibliographic data for each entry; the title volume contains the title and key-word index. The *Supplement* is arranged in the same format. A directory of publishers represented is also included. *German Books in Print* and its *Supplement* are both available from Bowker.

Répertoire des Livres Disponibles lists titles from France, Belgium, Switzerland, Canada, and virtually every other French-speaking country that are available in France today. Indexed by title and author in two separate volumes, the concise listings include every possible piece of necessary information and contain features that are in no other comparable bibliography. Available from Bowker.

Final Analysis

"Can you help me find a good book about Emily Dickinson?"

"My daughter is studying classical drama. Can you help me select a few books on the subject for her?"

"Which are the best of Paddy Chayefsky, Gore Vidal, Jean-Paul Sartre?"

The Reader's Adviser (the work of Winifred F. Courtney) can provide answers. It is a two-volume annotated guide to the best books of all times, covering drama, history, Bibles, travel, contemporary and classical poetry, American and English literature, Shakespeare, Russian and other foreign literature, science, philosophy, social sciences, and so on. A pithy introduction to each is followed by a list of selected titles in the field, with biographical facts about the authors, excerpts from reviews, and comments on the periods and works, all designed to help you choose among several editions, place the author within his period, and select additional titles in a field. *The Reader's Adviser* is published by Bowker—Volume I: *The Best in Literature;* Volume II: *Religions, Science, Philosophy, Social Sciences, History, and Other Subject Areas* —both volumes with full trade discount. Many stores stock several copies; one for their own use, others for resale as a home reference tool.

How To Get the Most Out **44**
of an ABA Convention

ROBERT D. HALE
Manager, Hathaway House Bookshop,
Wellesley, Massachusetts

Christmas comes early for booksellers. It begins in June at the American Booksellers Association Convention when hundreds of publishers present their new fall titles in a trade fair that encompasses the entire national publishing spectrum. Enthusiasm is rampant as the atmosphere crackles with predictions, promotions, and special offers. Major authors mingling with booksellers provide extra incentive and incidental bits of information that will help sell their books.

There are panels on every aspect of bookselling, including new ways to solve old problems and innovative techniques for increasing sales. There are breakfast meetings, author luncheons, dinner discussions, and cocktail parties at which the talk is all books. The ABA Convention is a once-a-year opportunity to engage in a crash course that will make one a better bookseller. It's a must for the professional.

Getting One's Feet Wet

Plunging into a mass gathering is never easy, even for the gregarious. For those who are shy or new in an association, the initial step can be almost traumatic. There are several ways to lessen the pain. If one is lucky, a familiar face, very often a known salesman, will happen by. These friends of booksellers have rescued many nervous first-timers from islands of isolation, but the convention is a strenuous work stint for them, so they can't be relied on totally for introductions and support.

ABA officials have long been aware of the difficulty for newcomers, so for many years there has been a first-night reception for first-timers, to introduce them to each other and to enough old-timers to create a few friendly landmarks. This very relaxed informal affair establishes contact between booksellers, old and new, and sets the tone for the days that are to follow. It launches the outgoing newcomer on his way with no trouble, and makes it easier for the introvert to introduce himself to other people.

Self-introduction is simple, as is knowing to whom one is speaking, because of the badges everyone wears. These identifying tags mean that booksellers with similar concerns, be they geographic or store size, can immediately spot each other and open a conversation. It doesn't matter whether one only talks to similar booksellers or very different booksellers, the important point is the great value derived from an exchange of ideas between practicing booksellers. Those who go to the convention, work the exhibits, attend the panels and parties, and then go home have missed much if they haven't also talked to as many other booksellers as possible. That overworked word, "communication," is essential and it exists only if someone makes real contact. This is as true for old-timers as for first-timers.

The convention has been described as having a spirit of helpfulness, not competition. All booksellers have common interests and there are few who aren't flattered when asked for advice. Most are eager to make new friends in the business and to share information.

The ABA Convention is also a market place. One should attend with that in mind and be prepared to buy. As in an *agora,* full participation includes purchase as well as acquisition of knowledge. It takes stamina to work the trade fair as it should be worked. Four days are barely enough to do it properly. Wandering through casually once or twice will not do it; constant concentrated effort is needed. No one succeeds completely the first time.

A proven method is to cover the entire exhibit once without buying anything, taking as much time as necessary to look at everything, to see what is there, to compare, to become aware that six publishers are doing fall books on the same subject, to get needed facts about authors (and perhaps editors, when that counts), and to find out about cooperative advertising budgets and special promotions. Listen to salesmen, learn from what they say about their companies' books, terms, and promotion plans.

Using the convention guidebook, mark the publishers to be revisited, note special offers, but keep moving. All along the way are brochures, samples, unbound copies, advertising agreements, and so forth, waiting to be picked up and taken back to the hotel room for quiet study. Solitary contemplation is necessary to digest what has been learned and to prepare carefully for the second, third, and fourth trips, during which the real business of buying and bargaining will take place. Only alone, with careful consideration, can wise decisions be made, special convention discounts be dispassionately figured, and awareness that more information is needed be developed. (A word about those special convention discounts: There are booksellers who feel they save enough money on those offers to offset the expense of attending the convention.)

Working and reworking the trade fair for three full days with a part of the last day for mopping up is just that, work, but it may be the most productive work a bookseller accomplishes during a twelve-month period. It is an annual opportunity to find out what is going on and where the action is going to be in the fall—the booksellers' major selling season. More vital information can be acquired in four convention days than in a year of salesmen's visits.

Panels and Special Events

Educational opportunities more formal than the exhibition exchange are available in the planned panels of the convention program, usually held mornings, sometimes with two or three running consecutively. Subjects discussed cover the areas of greatest current concern to booksellers, such as distribution, advertising and display, ways to build profits, new kinds of publishing, beginning booksellers, and so on. From these panels and the discussions that follow, some of the most effective services of ABA are developed.

Wise booksellers have learned that attending these panels with an open mind is the only way to acquire anything of value. Those with small stores can listen to those with large, and scale down. Conversely, some of the most creative thinking is of necessity done in the small personal bookstore, so large-volume booksellers pick up ideas by listening to modest independents. Sometimes the really fruitful aspect of these panels is not what the panelists say, but the way they nudge listeners into thinking for themselves.

Each ABA Convention includes an evening session of open confrontation between booksellers and publishers. Sometimes it appears that the two are deadly enemies rather than partners in a complicated business, but out of arguments come new perspectives with combatants leaving the fray revitalized. Results can be positive.

One morning there is a business session, usually more sparsely attended than it should be. This is the time for members to ask officers and directors questions about the association—to challenge policies, seek clarification of clouded issues, to suggest changes. Not the place to air individual problems about order fulfillment, nor to discuss discounts, it is the place to talk about bookselling in general and how the ABA can more effectively serve booksellers. The strength of any organization is derived from the active involvement of the members. ABA isn't just its board of directors, it is every bookseller who belongs, and more of these should attend their association's business session.

Book-and-author luncheons at the convention are a hallowed tradition. Most of the greats of the literary world as well as many celebrity authors have appeared at one time or another. Listening to authors can give booksellers tidbits to take home and share with customers who might be interested in buying the author's book. Open a conversation with the browsing customer by saying, "He wrote that while tied to a tree in Taiwan. He told me all about it at lunch." Name-dropping is perfectly honorable when it's in a good cause, such as selling a book.

Perhaps more discussed than any other phase of the ABA Conventions are the parties given by publishers. To some, these are a monstrous waste of time, but they need not be. They provide an opportunity to continue the communication with other booksellers, with salesmen, publishers, editors, and authors on a very informal level. While always festive, they can also be educational.

The ABA Convention is exactly the same as any other experience: The more one gives to it, the more one gets out of it. There is much to receive. To close channels, shut one's eyes and ears, ignoring ideas, belittling conversation, is a real waste of time. With an open mind, receptive and eager, the convention can be an exciting, invigorating experience. To any bookseller, new or old, it can be of inestimable value.

The Booksellers School   **45**

ROBERT D. HALE
Manager, Hathaway House Bookshop,
Wellesley, Massachusetts

How to sell books most efficiently for maximum profit and greatest personal satisfaction is a proposition discussed formally and informally in all its aspects each year in late February and early March at two sessions of the Booksellers School, jointly sponsored by the American Booksellers Association and the National Association of College Stores. Until 1966 there was no structured training in the United States for booksellers or potential booksellers. The only way to learn was by doing, either by working for an established bookseller or by jumping in cold turkey with one's own investment, opening or buying a bookshop, and hoping the answers would come in time to avoid catastrophe.

NACS, long concerned with training its membership for greater professionalism and recognizing the need for improvement in the trade book departments of college stores, charged two noted booksellers— Marjorie Goodman, of the University of California at Riverside, and Roysce Smith, then of the Yale Co-op—with the task of designing a curriculum that would provide enough information in a three-day seminar to give the novice bookseller a fighting chance and the experienced bookseller an opportunity for growth. The first Booksellers School was held in Oberlin, Ohio, and met with such positive response that it was immediately expanded into two sessions, one held each year in the East and one in the West.

In 1969, ABA joined NACS in sponsoring the school, which then became a five-day seminar covering subjects of vital concern to the personal bookseller and the chain-store department head, as well as the college-store book buyer.

While the scope of subjects taught at the school has grown, and continues to grow and change, the basics are not forgotten. Those essentials that every bookseller must know and understand continue to make up a major portion of the schedule. For instance, tools of the trade are discussed, such as *Books in Print, Publishers' Trade List Annual, Publishers Weekly,* and *Cumulative Book Index,* as well as some items not always thought of as tools: reviews in all the media, *ABA Book Buyer's Handbook,* and *NACS Trade-Text Manual* (Oberlin, Ohio: National Association of College Stores). How to use each of these to greatest advantage is something even experienced booksellers do not always know.

The basics of buying books, whether to use a jobber or buy directly from the publishers, how to order, how to receive, how to find out-of-print books, how to import books, how to purchase government publications—all receive attention. All are subjects of importance to a bookseller. As are: how to meet a salesman and how to assess the information he provides, how to decide on quantities, and even how to choose titles taking into account the varying needs of different kinds of bookstores.

Once books are on the shelves—as well as the sidelines needed to provide a balanced stock—the merchandise must be sold. All aspects of selling are discussed at the school, from personal contact with customers to advertising and display, promotions and store layout. Self-service stores may not provide as much personal contact as old-fashioned clerk service, but the need for customer recognition is still there. How to do it most effectively can be taught, and is.

Small stores, brand-new stores, any store with few funds needs to know about simple means of advertising, free if possible. A session is devoted to this. More sophisticated operations need to know how to achieve the greatest return on cooperative advertising in more complicated arrangements. This, too, is discussed. It's all part of selling.

Buying and selling are not all there is to the retail business. Records must be kept. The smallest store has to know what sales tax it has collected, what money it has taken in, where that money is to go, whether expenses are exceeding income. Several sessions are devoted to record-keeping, with suggestions as to forms and methods. Budgeting is discussed, with workshop periods in which problems are solved. Projections and planning for the future, immediate and long range, are adjuncts of the budget.

One of the most revealing sessions is always "Practical Details for Improving Profits," which is nothing more than an examination of the importance of details, all of which affect profit, with examples of specific small reductions in expenses and equally small increases in sales that can result in substantial increases in final profit. Every bookseller can adapt the information given in this session to his or her own store.

Bookselling is details, and throughout the course of the Booksellers School, details are discussed, whether the subject is customer service, staffing, specialization, or any other topic of concern. Throughout these discussions, in formal classes and in casual conversations, there is a vital exchange between those who are already booksellers and those who wish to become booksellers, those who are on the faculty and those who are students.

Because the students come to the school from all over the nation and from Canada, and because they bring widely divergent experiences, the opportunity for productive brain-storming is endless. The talk goes on almost twenty-four hours a day, and it is all about bookselling. Those who are giants in the profession share ideas with those who are owners of small bookshops. Those who are just starting or thinking of starting talk with those who have been at it for decades.

The faculty is equally and purposely diverse, with representatives from every kind of bookshop and every level of experience. Because of the great number of potential booksellers attending the school, there is on the faculty a bookseller who has been in business a very short time, to provide an experience sufficiently immediate to be valid for those who are just beginning. Because department stores and chain stores are often most adept at promotion, booksellers from these stores frequently teach that subject.

While each faculty member is selected as a kind of expert in the subjects he or she is teaching, each one is also a practicing bookseller in search of new information, so dialogue between the teacher and the taught is welcomed. This creates an atmosphere that is most conducive to learning for everyone. Rather than pedantic instruction with an only-one-way-to-do-it approach, all views are aired so the bookseller can choose the method best suited to his store.

The Booksellers School graduated in its first seven years almost 1,300 students, most of whom have gone on to bigger and better things in their profession. Some have learned at the school that bookselling is not for them, and even they have been served. It would be impossible for it to meet the needs of all who attend, but it strives to change to reflect the needs of its students.

The school intends to give the basics to the beginner, to introduce the experienced to new methods, and to stimulate through association the creation of new ideas, new ways to solve old problems, and new suggestions for selling not yet considered. It is meant to make better booksellers of us all. It is truly a forum where the constant topic of discussion is how to sell books most efficiently for maximum profit and greatest personal satisfaction.

Bookseller-Publisher Relations

46

MORTIN L. LEVIN
Executive Vice President,
The Viking Press, Inc.,
New York City

Both the need and the practicality of a close bookseller-publisher relationship can be understood by anyone familiar with the history of both functions. The early printer-publisher-bookseller was a one-man band to today's symphony. The technologies of producing books have changed. The needs and desires of readers have grown and diversified. The complexities of operating any kind of business have multiplied many times over. Now most of us tend to specialize in one or the other function. But, the interdependence continues.

A publisher who selects, edits, and produces a book fulfills his obligation to the author only after he has made his best effort to get the book into the hands of interested readers. The publisher's success or failure with any book is the measure of how well he has been able to sell it to its *potential* readership. Considering that the potential sale may range from a few hundred copies of a book of poetry to a hundred thousand or more copies of a best-selling novel, success can have many faces. While most publishers recognize that it might not be impossible for a book to reach its full potential readership without the cooperation of booksellers, they realize that it's highly improbable.

Most booksellers, too, feel a dual obligation. First to their store and the ability to sustain it, and second to the book-buying community they serve. We live in a society that is producing acceptable book manuscripts at a rate never before experienced. We also have a tremendous diversity of interest that brings one person inside looking for a book on comparative religion, while the next asks for a guide to fixing a car, and the third will be satisfied only with the novel mentioned in last week's book review. Without clear, concise information from publishers, and without prompt, efficient service from publishers and wholesalers, the problems of satisfying customer demand not only seem insurmountable, but might even *be* insurmountable—at least in an economic sense.

So the mutuality of need and interest is obvious. It is the implementation that has often led to frustration on the part of both publishers and booksellers. Probably the most important single contributor to frustration is, and has been, the lack of understanding publishers have tended to show toward the pressures, problems, and economics of bookselling, and the same lack of understanding on the part of booksellers of what happens in a publishing house. How many publishers will read through this *Manual* to get a better understanding of bookselling? How many booksellers would be willing to wade through the annual statistics report of the Association of American Publishers to get a better idea of the economics of publishing?

To sort out the real—from the unreal—requests and demands that booksellers and publishers tend to press on each other takes knowledge and understanding. One of our best hopes for the future, at least in this regard, comes from the concern and patience shown by the members of the ABA-AAP Liaison Committee and the similar one between NACS and AAP. Both groups merit much more attention than they have received from the members of the associations they represent. Here, in small groups of concerned people who are as willing to listen as they are to talk, minds and methods can be changed, new ideas can be tried, and frustrations can be reduced when one knows that the problem is understood and that kindred souls are trying to help solve it.

We all know the problems created by "too many books" and "too few bookstores"—inventory control problems, returns problems, and the flow of pieces of paper that threatens to drown us all. How many publishers know or care about the number of individual packages to be opened, invoices to be checked, statements to be analyzed, and checks issued by even the smaller bookstores—much less how the problems involved might be ameliorated? How many booksellers recognize how often, by not being sure of author or title or publisher, their order form or note or postcard creates the same consternation on the part of a publisher's order-editor that a similar request from a customer brings to the face of the clerk in their store? In both cases, overhead and tempers rise. But there are ways of consolidating orders and consolidating billing—through individual publishing houses, service bureaus, multi-publisher warehouses, and better use of wholesalers and depositories. Orders can be processed faster and more accurately when current information is supplied, as on microfiche, and when such tools as the ISBN are utilized for identification.

Even this is an oversimplification of the problems. Any solutions must concern both the $75,000-a-year bookstore and the multi-million-dollar chain of bookstores. Further, these solutions must relate to the one-man publishing enterprise that is dependent on the sale of its twelve published books each year, just as much as to the highly departmentalized and computerized house that publishes hundreds of titles each year.

So, we go on coping and groping, realizing that it takes more than just a love of books to sustain a bookstore, and that it takes more than the editorial process to sustain a publishing house. And because we are so dependent on each other, we'd better keep on trying to be more responsive to each other's problems.

Obscenity and the Law 47

NANCY F. WECHSLER
Member, Greenbaum, Wolff & Ernst,
New York City

In June of 1973, the United States Supreme Court handed down rulings in a number of obscenity cases. As a result, the law of obscenity, which had achieved a degree of relative stability, has entered a phase of uncertainty and confusion that is not likely to end for years to come.*

Background

Until 1973, the law of obscenity, though hardly a model of precision, had settled down into a pattern most writers, publishers, and booksellers could live and cope with, in practice. Starting with the first major Supreme Court obscenity case, *Roth* v. *United States,* which was decided in 1957, and following a series of cases that culminated in *Memoirs* v. *Massachusetts* in 1966 (the case that cleared Fanny Hill), the Court had worked out standards for application of obscenity laws that seemed to leave enough leeway for the printed word to satisfy all but the most exacting proponents of First Amendment freedoms—at least so far as works for sale to adults were concerned.

Indeed, an outstanding lawyer in this field, Charles Rembar, who successfully defended *Lady Chatterley's Lover* and *The Memoirs of Fanny Hill,* as well as the Henry Miller books, concluded that books (as distinguished from motion pictures) had become virtually free of legal restraint on obscenity grounds, and wrote a book called *The End of Obscenity.* Until June of 1973 he was right, for the standards developed between 1957 and 1966 were generally thought to require the government to establish that a book was "utterly without redeeming social value" in order to punish its publishers or stop its publication, and not many publications could be proved so lacking in justification.

*This article was written before the Supreme Court announced decisions in two obscenity cases on June 25, 1974. Reference to these cases will be found in footnotes added as the book went to press.

The government was also required to prove that the predominant appeal of the book was to a prurient interest in sex and—even if such was its appeal—that the book was "patently offensive" under prevailing community standards.

Certain kinds of works were specially vulnerable—material deemed obscene for minors, material promoted by "pandering" (i.e., soliciting the trade of those seeking pornographic material), and material that invaded the privacy of the community. Neither the "minors" nor the "pandering" concept had been very clearly defined, but these limits on the underlying liberality of the pre-1973 law were not serious obstacles to most writers, publishers, and booksellers, and the matter of invasion of privacy had limited application to the publishing world. Few publishers and booksellers had difficulty avoiding pandering or invasion of privacy in the ordinary course of things.

The courts had also sustained federal laws aimed at securing privacy by various restrictions on use of the mails to distribute unsolicited "sexually oriented" materials, but these laws have little if any impact on publication and distribution of general books, or on sales through usual trade channels.

In addition to the liberal definition of obscenity that appeared to have been established, in 1959 the Supreme Court enunciated an important principle relating specifically to booksellers in *Smith* v. *California*. In that case, the Court held unconstitutional a Los Angeles city ordinance that made it unlawful for any person to have in his possession an "obscene" or "indecent" book in any place where books were sold or kept for sale. The ordinance permitted conviction of a bookseller for merely having an obscene book on the premises, because it required no proof of what the law calls "scienter," i.e., knowledge by the defendant of the contents of the book. It was this aspect of the ordinance that the Court held to be a violation of the First Amendment.

The Court did not rule that a bookseller could never be prosecuted for possession of an obscene book. At present, there is no clear decision on whether or not a state law (such as exists in New York) can constitutionally establish a presumption that a bookseller is aware of the obscene character of books he sells, putting on the bookseller the burden of proving his lack of knowledge. The Court's holding in *Smith* v. *California*—that mere possession of an obscene book was not in and of itself punishable—freed booksellers to a considerable extent from fear of prosecution under state obscenity laws; but if the Court of Chief Justice Warren Earl Burger were to sustain the validity of laws establishing a presumption of knowledge, that freedom would, of course, be considerably eroded; and the 1973 decisions reflect a spirit that might just lead to that result.

I have given the foregoing brief description of pre-1973 obscenity law because what happened in June of 1973 is necessarily discussable only by reference to what had gone before.

The 1973 Decisions

There is considerable difference of opinion among lawyers about what the 1973 decisions portend. Some predict severe inhibition of open writing on sexual or sex-related matters, and even possibly a return to the pre-*Roth* days when obscenity laws were used to suppress books such as *An American Tragedy* and *Strange Fruit* because they expressed unpopular ideas. Others are less pessimistic and believe that under the reasoning of the majority opinion written by Chief Justice Burger in the 1973 cases, only publishers of "hard-core pornography" need be concerned. Few, however, dispute the likelihood that the 1973 decisions will encourage the censorious or that we will see new efforts to repress works of literary value. Clearly there will be years of litigation and many attacks on particular publications and visual media before the impact of the 1973 decisions becomes clear. Reports of actions against motion pictures like *Paper Moon* suggest how the atmosphere has been changed—hopefully only temporarily. But there has been an upsurge of community pressures seeking to ban from public and school libraries books like *Catch-22, The Catcher in the Rye, The Learning Tree,* and *Grapes of Wrath.* Efforts have been made to bar *Ms. Magazine* from the high school in Bennington, Vermont.

The 1973 decision which restated the basic constitutional definition of obscenity was *Miller* v. *California,* a five-to-four decision. The majority of the Court rejected the *Memoirs of Fanny Hill* test under which it had been widely assumed that the prosecution must prove a work is utterly without redeeming social value (and, indeed, argued that this standard had never been adopted by a clear majority of the Court). Relying on the 1957 decision in the Roth case to the effect that obscenity is not protected by the First Amendment, the majority opinion (written by Chief Justice Burger and joined by all of the Nixon appointees plus Justice Byron R. White) undertook to "formulate standards more concrete than those in the past." The "more concrete" standards refer to those specified in the Miller case. The Court stated:

> *State statutes designed to regulate obscene materials must be carefully limited ... to works which depict or describe sexual conduct. That conduct must be specifically defined by the applicable state law, as written or authoritatively construed. A state offense must also be limited to works which, taken as a whole, appeal to the prurient interest in sex, which portray sexual conduct in a patently offensive way, and which, taken as a whole, do not have serious literary, artistic, political or scientific value.*

The majority has thus substituted the standard of "serious literary, artistic, political or scientific value" for "utterly without redeeming social value." It is anything but clear what is meant by "serious" value, or how courts or juries will make concrete decisions under this rule. The Chief Justice seeks to get around this by including the requirement that a state must "specifically" define the sexual conduct that may not be depicted or described (note that "described" is given equal importance to "depicted"). The Court gave a "few plain examples of what a state statute could define" as follows:

a) Patently offensive representations or descriptions of ultimate sexual acts, normal or perverted, actual or simulated.

b) Patently offensive representations or descriptions of masturbation, excretory functions, and lewd exhibition of the genitals.

Justice William J. Brennan, Jr., in a major dissenting opinion (written in a companion case, *Paris Adult Theatre I* v. *Slaton*), argued that the constitutional justification in the Roth case for putting obscenity outside of the protection of the First Amendment was "precisely *because* it lacks even the slightest redeeming social value" and asserted that:

the court's approach necessarily assumes that some works will be deemed obscene—even though they clearly have some social value—because the state was able to prove that the value, measured by some unspecified standard, was not sufficiently "serious" to warrant constitutional protection.

The Chief Justice's opinion in the Miller case appears to confine "obscenity" to sexual matters, and thus exclude application of state or federal obscenity laws to unpopular expression unrelated to sex. The Miller opinion is, indeed, replete with references to "hard-core pornography," "the public portrayal of hard-core sexual conduct," and "patently offensive hard-core materials." Yet there is no insight into what is "hard-core" material, and the "plain examples" of permissible statutory definition quoted above seem to equate "hard core" with "patently offensive."*

This leads to consideration of another major departure of the 1973 decisions, the explicit rejections of a national standard for judging what is "patently offensive." The Burger Court has not relieved the prosecu-

---

*On June 25, 1974, the Court held in *Jenkins* v. *Georgia* that the film *Carnal Knowledge* did not involve "public portrayal of hard-core sexual conduct for its own sake and for ensuing gain," that it could not be found to "depict sexual conduct in a patently offensive way," and thus could not be held obscene. The Court said: "While ... there are scenes in which sexual conduct including 'ultimate sexual acts' is to be understood to be taking place, the camera does not focus on the bodies of the actors at such times. There is no exhibition whatever of the actors' genitals, lewd or otherwise during these scenes. There are occasional scenes of nudity, but nudity alone is not enough to make material legally obscene."

tion of the necessity to prove that a book is patently offensive as well as lacking in "serious" value. But the decision permits application of different tests of offensiveness in different parts of the country, so that a book, magazine, or film might be deemed patently offensive in one place and not in another.

A majority of the Court had not before this adopted the requirement of a national standard, but neither had the Court explicitly sanctioned banning a work acceptable in most places if it runs afoul of a low threshold for patent offensiveness somewhere else. In *Miller,* the Court approved submission to the jury whether the material involved in that case "*affronted contemporary community standards of decency in the State of California* [italics supplied]." But it is not clear from the opinion whether courts must apply a statewide standard, or whether local community standards—county or city standards—will suffice. The Miller opinion says: "It is neither realistic nor constitutionally sound to read the First Amendment as requiring that the people of Maine or Mississippi accept public depiction of conduct found tolerable in Las Vegas or New York City." The reference to Las Vegas and New York City has led some to conclude that it will now be possible to ban publications on the basis of local, rather than statewide, notions of patent offensiveness. Only future litigation will clarify this problem.

As of the date of writing this report (June, 1974), the Supreme Court had under consideration a case involving the film *Carnal Knowledge.* The Georgia courts had found the film obscene on the basis of the standards of a local community. It is uncertain, however, whether the Court's disposition of this case will clarify the question of whether the standards of a "community" smaller than a state may be invoked.*

As a practical matter, once an obscenity case is presented to a judge or jury for determination of whether the publication is "patently offensive," the trier of fact is fairly free to decide the issue with reference to its own notions of patent offensiveness, as has been the case in New York State, where the film *Deep Throat* was convicted in New York City and cleared in Binghamton. Obviously the concept "contemporary community standards of decency" is elusive at best, whether the "community" is city, state, or nation. The thrust of the Miller case is toward permitting states, at the least, to insulate themselves from materials emanating from or acceptable to more sophisticated or "permissive" centers. By emphasizing state or, perhaps, local option in obscenity

---

*The Court's decision (*see* note, page 303) was that *Carnal Knowledge* was not obscene. Language in that decision, and the decision in a case decided the same day (*Hamling* v. *United States*), makes it clear that the Court will *not* require juries to decide on the basis of statewide standards. Justice Rehnquist's opinion in the Hamling case says: "A juror is entitled to draw on his own knowledge of the views of the average person in the community or vicinage from which he comes." The Court acknowledged that this permits a distributor of allegedly obscene material to be "subjected to varying community standards" in the states and in "various Federal judicial districts."

cases, the Court has thus opened the way to possible severe restriction on national distribution of films or books. This presents serious problems for publishers and motion picture producers, who may choose to avoid trouble by avoiding all dubious material. The community-standards aspect of the Miller case may have less-immediate impact on local booksellers, at least to the extent that even in the past they tended to conduct themselves in accordance with their perception of what would be unacceptable to the local community.

The Court did not decide in the 1973 cases that states could ban any work containing a description of sexual conduct simply by banning a particular category of sexual conduct and labeling it an impermissible subject for writing. Much of the pre-1973 definition of obscenity appears still to be in effect. A work must be judged as a whole; it cannot be condemned as obscene unless as a whole it appeals to "the prurient interest in sex," a fuzzy concept, at best, but apparently meant to be something other than a "healthy" or "normal" interest in sex. Also, although the Miller opinion is not entirely clear in this respect, it does not seem to overturn the earlier doctrine that required three findings before a work could be banned. Probably, therefore, in addition to finding that the work as a whole appeals to "prurient interest," it must *also* be found that the work is "patently offensive" and *also* that the work taken as a whole is without "serious literary, artistic, political or scientific value." It may be, therefore, that even books that juries find prurient and patently offensive under contemporary community standards will be protected if courts find serious value in them. Thus, while "serious" value is a standard permitting more repression than "utterly without redeeming social value," the Miller case may be interpreted as protecting any work of "serious" value no matter how "offensive" it may be to the "community," and it is this aspect of the Miller case that some observers believe will ultimately confound those who predict a new era of repression.

Yet there are many ambiguities and uncertainties in the present situation, and as the lower courts begin the process of clarification by ruling on new cases they may tend to be guided by an apparent turning away of the majority of the Court from expansion of First Amendment protections toward preference for what the Chief Justice referred to, in *Paris Adult Theatre I* v. *Slaton,* as the right of government to "maintain a decent society."

"The interest of the public in the quality of life and the total community environment, the tone of commerce in the great city centers, and possibly the public safety itself," said the Chief Justice, justifies the new rules laid down in the Miller case. The First Amendment, under this approach, does not prohibit states from concluding that "a sensitive, key relationship to human existence, central to family life, community welfare, and the development of human personality can be debased and destroyed by crass commercial exploitation of sex" and therefore banning "depiction" or "description" of sexual conduct. The Chief Justice insisted that the courts could "distinguish commerce in ideas, protected by the First Amendment, from commercial exploitation of obscene material." But the vagueness of the definition of obscenity in terms of "prurience," "patent offensiveness," and "serious" value permit wide scope for suppression if the courts apply these concepts repressively. Justice Brennan, dissenting in the Paris Adult Theatre case, said:

> *After fifteen years of experimentation and debate I am reluctantly forced to the conclusion that none of the available formulas, including the one announced today, can reduce the vagueness [of the tests of obscenity] to a tolerable level while at the same time striking an acceptable balance between the protection of the First and Fourteenth Amendments on the one hand and on the other the asserted state interest in regulating the dissemination of certain sexually oriented materials.*

He argued that, if a state can ban sexually oriented materials on the basis of a state interest in protecting "morality," serious erosion of the First Amendment may take place.

The Media Coalition

The 1973 decisions have led to the formation of a Media Coalition representing a number of organizations, including the Association of American Publishers, the American Booksellers Association, the Motion Picture Association, the National Association of College Stores, the Periodical & Book Association of America, and others.

The Coalition unsuccessfully sought reargument of the 1973 cases, hoping to obtain clarification that might avoid the painful and time-consuming process that will otherwise ensue if all of the present uncertainty must be resolved by litigation on a case-by-case basis. It is working as a clearing house to keep the industry informed of developments in state legislatures and to support model bills designed to protect the industries involved from regressive implementation of the decisions, as well as to aid those who may become involved in litigation. The Coalition has warned against panic overreaction to the decisions, stating:

> *The decisions have the potential for a great deal of haphazard local mischief, but we want to warn against overreaction. Whereas ten years ago the Supreme Court was way out ahead of the country in suggesting what might be permissible, on the whole today the Supreme Court is way behind. There has been an enormous maturation of public opinion and we believe that, when it gets to determining what is patently offensive,*

juries are going to surprise prosecutors all over the country. At the same time, we recognize there will be ridiculous things done by some local prosecutors under the terms of these decisions and that is why we make emphatic that the industry will stand on the principles of the Bill of Rights, which ensures that freedom of speech and press are guaranteed under the First Amendment.

Yet, in April of 1974, the ABA reported that "new censorship legislation is pending or has been passed in twenty-nine of the fifty states," and noted that "though the court rulings were aimed at hard-core pornography, most of the legislation that is resulting from them can have disastrous effects on all booksellers, not just those that carry 'smut.' "

The only conclusion about the present state of the law is that there are many more unanswered questions about obscenity than there were before. What happens next will depend on whether local authorities and lower courts perceive the recent decisions as a go-ahead signal to attack unpopular or unconventional writing under the guise of controlling "obscenity" and whether there is forceful action toward limiting frank and open discussion or description of sexual matters. Possibly these cases will be seen primarily as a vehicle for controlling "hard-core pornography," and thus affect only fringe publications. I think it is fair to assume that, in the long run, the courts will not sanction suppression of primarily non-sexual material by misapplication of the obscenity laws. But until states have "defined" the kind of sexual conduct that is not to be described or pictured and those definitions have been tested in the courts, there seems no way of knowing how far the law of obscenity will go, or how much writing that is not "hard-core pornography" will fall by the wayside. In the meantime, local community groups that think they have a mission to decide what others may read will be encouraged to continue their efforts to suppress publications they don't like by applying extra-legal pressure on schools, libraries, and bookstores.

Bibliography

Books About Books: A Bookman's Library

CHARLES B. ANDERSON
Anderson's Book Shop,
Larchmont, New York

In Chapter 43 of this *Manual,* Elizabeth Geiser, an expert in the field of books for the industry, names the essential reference books for the bookstore and tells how they may be used most effectively in the daily regimen of bookselling. These are the basics, the books that no bookstore deserving the name can afford to be without. Besides these, there are hundreds of other books that have to do directly or indirectly with bookselling, books that would be consulted only occasionally for reference but that may be read for pleasure and for information about our bookselling craft. The annotated bibliography that follows is a selected list of currently available books about the history of bookselling, bookmaking, and publishing from the beginnings to the present day, as well as books on other subjects of interest to booksellers. Several are about bookselling and publishing in England, a few are in paperback only, but all are in print and available from American publishers as this edition goes to press. Many booksellers I know, like myself, own most of these books and many others that are now out of print. For the dedicated bookseller, there is no hobby more appropriate or rewarding than collecting a personal library of books about books.

ADLER, MORTIMER J. *How To Read a Book.* New York: Simon and Schuster. In paper and cloth. Practical information about how to become a better reader.

ARBUTHNOT, MAY HILL. *Children and Books.* New York: Lothrop, Lee & Shepard Co. A discussion by a children's book specialist of the importance of books for children.

BAILEY, HERBERT S., JR. *The Art and Science of Book Publishing.* New York: Harper & Row. ("Torch Book.") Book publishing from the point of view of a prominent university press publisher.

BENNETT, JAMES O. *Much Loved Books.* New York: Liveright. A lively discussion about many books, classic and modern.

BENNETT, P. A. (ed.). *Books and Printing: A Treasury for Typophiles.* Gloucester, Mass., and New York: Peter Smith/World Publishing Co. A collection of essays about fine printing by one of America's best-known typophiles.

BINGLEY, CLIVE. *The Business of Book Publishing.* Elmsford, N.Y.: Pergamon Publishing Co. How books get published in England.

BLAND, DAVID. *A History of Book Illustration: The Illuminated Manuscript and the Printed Book.* Berkeley, Calif.: University of California Press. An account of book illustration beginning with the illuminated manuscript.

CANFIELD, CASS. *Up and Down and Around: A Publisher Recollects the Time of His Life.* New York: Harper's Magazine Press. An esteemed publisher and editor tells of his life with books and the people who write them.

CHARVAT, WILLIAM. *Literary Publishing in America, 1790–1850.* Philadelphia: University of Pennsylvania Press. A scholarly account of book publishing of an earlier day.

COLBY, JEAN POINDEXTER. *Writing, Illustrating and Editing Children's Books.* New York: Hastings House. An author, illustrator, and editor writes about producing children's books.

COURTNEY, WINIFRED F. *The Reader's Adviser.* 2 vols. New York: R. R. Bowker Co. A standard reference about authors and books, revised and updated every few years.

DOWNS, ROBERT B. *Books That Changed the World.* New York: New American Library. Cloth ed., American Library Association. Evidence that the pen is mightier than the sword.

DUFF, ANNIS. *Bequest of Wings: A Family's Pleasures with Books.* New York: Viking Press. An eminent children's book editor talks about books in her home.

——. *Longer Flight: A Family Grows Up with Books.* New York: Viking Press. A companion volume to *Bequest of Wings.*

FOSTER, JOANNA. *Pages, Pictures and Print: A Book in the Making.* New York: Harcourt Brace Jovanovich. A specialist in children's books writes entertainingly about how a book is put together.

GRANNIS, CHANDLER B. (ed.). *The Heritage of the Graphic Arts.* New York: R. R. Bowker Co. A collection of articles about prominent typographers, selected and edited by a devoted typophile and amateur typographer.

_____. *What Happens in Book Publishing*. New York: Columbia University Press. Articles by specialists about various aspects of the book trade, edited by the former editor-in-chief of *Publishers Weekly*.

GROSS, SIDNEY, and STECKLER, PHYLLIS B. (eds.). *How To Run a Paperback Bookshop*. New York: R. R. Bowker Co. (Paper only.) Contains useful information about running any kind of bookshop.

GUINZBURG, HAROLD K., *et al*. *Books and the Mass Market*. Urbana, Ill.: University of Illinois Press. The late president of Viking Press writes about the marketing of books in America.

HACKETT, ALICE PAYNE. *Seventy Years of Best Sellers*. New York: R. R. Bowker Co. A fascinating account of book sales and reading habits in America from 1895 to 1965.

HAIGHT, ANNE LYON. *Banned Books*. New York: R. R. Bowker Co. An account of more than three hundred books that have been banned during the last twenty-five centuries.

HAINES, Helen E. *Living with Books: The Art of Book Selection*. New York: Columbia University Press. Choosing books for a home library.

HART, JAMES D. *The Popular Book: A History of America's Literary Taste*. Berkeley, Calif.: University of California Press. (Paper only.) American best-sellers from early colonial times to the twentieth century.

HENDERSON, BILL (ed.). *The Publish-It-Yourself Handbook: Literary Tradition and How-To*. Yonkers, N.Y.: Pushcart Book Press. Practical information about publishing a book on your own.

HIGHET, GILBERT. *People, Places and Books*. New York: Oxford University Press. A distinguished author and classical scholar writes with enthusiasm and charm about the literary world.

JOVANOVICH, WILLIAM. *Now, Barabbas*. New York: Harcourt Brace Jovanovich. (Now in paper only.) An autobiography by one of our leading publishers.

KERR, CHESTER. *American University as Publisher*. Norman, Okla.: University of Oklahoma Press. A digest of a report on American university presses.

KNOPF, ALFRED A. *Publishing Then and Now: 1912–1964*. New York: New York Public Library. (Paper only.) Reminiscences by one who is regarded as the dean of American publishers.

KUNITZ, STANLEY J., AND HAYCRAFT, HOWARD (eds.). *American Authors (1600–1900)*. New York: H. W. Wilson Co. A standard reference about American literary history.

_____. *Twentieth Century Authors*. New York: H. W. Wilson Co. A companion volume to the one preceding.

LARRICK, NANCY. *A Parent's Guide to Children's Reading.* New York: Pocket Books. A useful book for buyers of children's books.

LEHMANN-HAUPT, HELLMUT, *et al. The Book in America.* New York: R. R. Bowker Co. A history of the making and selling of books in the United States.

MCMURTRIE, DOUGLAS C. *The Book: The Story of Printing and Bookmaking.* New York: Oxford University Press. An excellent account of how a book is produced.

MADISON, CHARLES A. *Book Publishing in American Culture.* New York: McGraw-Hill Book Co. A prominent book editor discusses the influence of book publishing on the cultural scene.

MALKIN, SOL M. *ABC of the Book Trade: New and Used, Old and Rare, Out-of-Print and Specialist.* Newark, N.J.: Antiquarian Bookman. (Paper only.) The founder and publisher of *Antiquarian Bookman* talks about the antiquarian field.

MANSFIELD, KATHERINE. *Novels and Novelists.* New York: Somerset Publishers. An informal and informative book by one of the great writers of the short story.

MEIGS, CORNELIA, *et al. A Critical History of Children's Literature.* New York: Macmillan Publishing Co. A survey of children's books in English from the earliest times to the mid-1950's.

MORLEY, CHRISTOPHER. *The Haunted Bookshop.* Philadelphia: J. B. Lippincott Co. A classic American novel about an antiquarian bookstore.

———. *Parnassus on Wheels.* Philadelphia: J. B. Lippincott Co. A companion volume to *The Haunted Bookshop.*

MOTT, FRANK L. *Golden Multitudes.* New York: R. R. Bowker Co. America's favorite books from 1662 to 1945.

MUMBY, FRANK A., AND NORRIE, IAN. *Publishing and Bookselling: A History from the Earliest Times to the Present Day.* New York: R. R. Bowker Co. The standard British work on the subject, revised and updated in 1973.

NEMEYER, CAROL A. *Scholarly Reprint Publishing in the United States.* New York: R. R. Bowker Co. A guide to the selection, acquisition, and use of scholarly books.

RANDALL, DAVID A. *Dukedom Large Enough: Reminiscences of a Rare Book Dealer.* New York: Random House. The former head of the rare books department at Scribner's Bookstore writes about his life with books.

SMITH, DATUS C., JR. *A Guide to Book Publishing.* New York: R. R. Bowker Co. A basic guide to the general principles of book publishing.

SMITH, ROGER H. *The American Reading Public: What It Reads—Why It Reads.* New York: R. R. Bowker Co. The publishing industry and its relationship to the reading public.

SPILLER, ROBERT E., *et al. Literary History of the United States.* New York: Macmillan Publishing Co. Revised edition in one volume, originally published in three volumes.

STEINBERG, S. H. (ed.). *Cassell's Encyclopedia of World Literature.* 2 vols. Funk & Wagnalls Publishing Co. A standard reference work.

TARG, WILLIAM (ed.). *Bibliophile in the Nursery: A Bookman's Treasury of Collectors' Lore on Old and Rare Children's Books.* Metuchen, N.J.: Scarecrow Press. Informative articles on collecting old and rare children's books.

TAUBERT, SIGFRED. *Bibliopola: Pictures and Texts About the Book Trade.* 2 vols. New York: R. R. Bowker Co. A breath-taking set of books in three languages—English, French, and German—about world bookselling from its beginnings to the present. Many spectacular illustrations in full color.

TAUBERT, SIGFRED (ed.). *The Book Trade of the World.* 3 vols. (to be completed in the mid-1970's). New York: R. R. Bowker Co. A country-by-country survey of bookselling and publishing today.

TEBBEL, JOHN. *A History of Book Publishing in the United States.* 3 vols. (to be completed in the mid-1970's). New York: R. R. Bowker Co. On the publication of the first volume in 1973, it was immediately hailed as the definitive history of American book publishing.

UHLAN, EDWARD. *The Rogue of Publishers' Row.* Jericho, N.Y.: Exposition Press. A "vanity" publisher defends "vanity" publishing.

UNWIN, SIR STANLEY. *The Truth About a Publisher.* New York: R. R. Bowker Co. The autobiography of a renowned British publisher.

———. *The Truth About Publishing.* New York: R. R. Bowker Co. The eminent British publisher discusses his profession.

VERVLIET, HENDRIK D. L. (ed.). *The Book Through Five Thousand Years.* London: Phaidon Press. A bulky, handsome, and expensive book with lavish illustrations, mostly about the book before Gutenberg and Caxton.

WHEELOCK, JOHN HALL (ed.). *Editor to Author: The Letters of Maxwell E. Perkins.* New York: Charles Scribner's Sons. An eminent American poet edits the letters of an eminent American editor.

WOLFE, THOMAS. *The Story of a Novel.* New York: Charles Scribner's Sons. The author of *Look Homeward, Angel* talks about his craft.

A Bookseller's Glossary

Expressions, Abbreviations, and Financial Terms of the Trade

CHARLES B. ANDERSON
Anderson's Book Shop,
Larchmont, New York

AAP   Association of American Publishers.

AAUP   Association of American University Presses.

AB   Actually, *Antiquarian Bookman,* but accepted as abbreviation of the merged publication *AB Bookman's Weekly,* a journal of the antiquarian book trade, published by AB Bookman Publications, Inc.

ABA   American Booksellers Association.

academic reprints   New printings of scholarly works issued by a publisher other than the original; generally reproduced by a photographic process and intended to satisfy a relatively small, specialized academic market.

accounts receivable   An asset account in a balance sheet, showing amounts due from a store's customers.

addenda   Material added to the original text of a book, usually printed on a slip of paper, a *tip-in* (q.v.), that is pasted in the finished book at the time of binding.

adult bookshop   A store that makes a specialty of selling sexually explicit literature.

advance copies   *See* Review copies.

advance order   An order placed for titles in advance of publication, frequently through the publisher's salesman.

advance royalty   A sum paid an author by a publisher in advance of the receipt of a finished manuscript or of publication, to be deducted later from earned royalties.

agate line   A space one column wide and a fourteenth of an inch deep, used as a measurement in newspaper advertising. There are fourteen agate lines in one *column inch* (q.v.).

ALA   American Library Association.

allowance *(advertising)*   A sum of money or quantity of merchandise committed by a publisher to assist a bookseller in advertising or promoting a single title or group of titles.

allowance *(freight)*   Partial payment by a publisher of the cost of transporting books to a bookseller.

Americana   Books of American history, geography, biography, etc.

-ana   A suffix added to the names of persons or places, denoting a collection of assorted material: Americana, Shaviana (about Shaw), etc.

anthology   A collection of writings around a central theme, usually by a variety of authors. *The Oxford Book of English Verse,* for example, is an anthology.

antiquarian bookseller   A dealer in old and rare books.

anonymous (anon.)   Of unknown authorship.

anticipation *or* **anticipation discount**   A discount, usually ½ per cent a month, sometimes offered by sidelines suppliers for payment in advance of the due date on an invoice.

apocryphal   Of questionable authorship or authenticity.

appendix   Supplementary material at the end of a book. The plural is "appendixes" or "appendices."

asterisk   A star-shaped symbol (*) commonly used to indicate a footnote.

author's copies   Complimentary copies of the first edition of a book given to the author by his publisher, usually six in number.

autograph   The signature of an author, usually on the title page or flyleaf of a book. Authors sometimes make public appearances in bookstores to autograph books for purchasers.

avant-garde   Literally "vanguard," from the French. Literature that is experimental or unorthodox, as avant-garde fiction or poetry.

backbone   *See* Spine.

back list   A publisher's list of older titles kept in print because of continued demand.

back order   The unfilled portion of an order, promised for future delivery.

backstrap   *See* Spine.

basic stock   The titles from various publishers' back lists that the bookseller decides to carry continuously in stock.

best-seller   A term coined in 1895 by the *American Bookman,* which published each month a list of six best-sellers in the stores. The expression is now common in all the principal European languages.

Bible paper   A thin but sturdy paper used for Bibles and certain other lengthy books to reduce bulk. *See* India paper.

biblio-   A prefix from the Greek meaning "book." A "*biblio*graphy" is a listing of books; a "*biblio*phile," a lover of books; a "*biblio*pole," a bookseller. The Bible, also from the same root, is "the book."

BIP   *Books in Print,* an annual publication issued by R. R. Bowker Co. listing all American books in print.

blurb   A term coined by American humorist Gelett Burgess which now denotes the promotional copy of a book that appears either on the book's jacket or in its advertising, but which was once defined (by *Webster's Sixth Collegiate*) as "a fulsome commendation," and by both the *Second* and *Third International* as a brief, often extravagant, commendatory notice of a book.

boards   The stiff material used for the front and back of a book, usually covered by cloth, leather, or other material.

boldface   A heavy-faced type, in which the key words in this glossary are set.

book   By origin from the Germanic *beech,* the bark of which was used for runic inscriptions. A book may now be defined as "material printed in page form and bound between covers." In order to qualify today for *book rate* (q.v.), the U.S. Post Office requires that a book be at least twenty-four pages, permanently bound.

book club edition   Books distributed by the various book clubs are usually, but not always, printed on cheaper paper and given a cheaper binding than the original edition. The publisher's list price may not appear on the jacket. Customers, sometimes unknowingly if the book is a gift, will present these editions for return. It behooves the bookseller to be able to recognize them.

book fair   An exhibition for the display and sale of books that developed in Europe as the printing of books became widespread. Although several countries in the world sponsor book fairs today, the largest by far is the International Book Fair held each fall in Frankfurt, West Germany. Its nearest American equivalent is the book exhibit at the annual ABA Convention. Book fairs at the local level, sponsored by schools or other groups, are fairly common in various parts of the United States. Booksellers often work with the sponsors by providing the books to be displayed and sold.

book paper   Paper used for books and periodicals as distinct from newsprint.

book rate   Special fourth-class postage rate, a flat, unzoned rate applicable to books and other educational materials, which allows national distribution of books to libraries and booksellers without penalty for geographical location.

book sizes   The terms *folio, quarto, octavo,* and *duodecimo* (q.v.) derive from the page size resulting from the number of times a standard-sized printed sheet was folded. They now indicate the approximate size of a book. See individual terms.

Book Token   A book certificate sold and redeemed by participating booksellers throughout Great Britain. In 1947, the ABA, in the hope of emulating the success of the British Book Tokens, developed for its membership what were known as Give-a-Book Certificates. The plan was abandoned after a few years because of lack of interest on the part of many booksellers.

bowdlerized   A text altered to remove passages offensive to the editor or the era. The word derives from Thomas *Bowdler,* an English editor of the nineteenth century, who published expurgated editions of Shakespeare and others.

brochure   A small pamphlet or booklet. The last syllable is accented and pronounced like *"sure."*

budget   *See* Chapter 14.

calligraphy   Fine penmanship.

cap(s)   Capital letter(s). Also called *upper-case* (q.v.) letters.

carriage   Transportation from publisher to bookseller.

case binding   In everyday parlance, a *case-bound* book is any hardback as contrasted with a paperback. *See also* Clothbound

Caxton, William (1422?–91)   The printer and publisher of the first books in the English language, the most famous of which was Chaucer's *Canterbury Tales.*

CBA   Christian Booksellers Association, an organization of booksellers dealing in religious books. Also Canadian Booksellers Association.

CBI   *Cumulative Book Index.* A comprehensive index of all books published in English anywhere in the world. Published by H. W. Wilson Co.

clothbound   Bound in genuine or imitation cloth over stiff boards. Almost all "hardbacks" ("hard-cover," or "hardbound," publications) are *clothbound* books.

colophon   From the Greek meaning "finishing stroke." An inscription, usually at the end of a book, giving facts about its publication. Also a publisher's emblem or trademark, usually placed on the title page.

column inch   A space one inch deep and one column wide in newspaper advertising. While column width can vary, it is usually about two inches. *See* Agate line.

concordance   An alphabetical index of the words in a text showing where each may be found. In frequent use with Bibles.

conglomerate   A holding company, usually listed on the New York Stock Exchange, which has acquired ownership of other companies. In recent years, a number of publishing companies have been bought by conglomerates.

consignment   Stock which remains the property of the publisher but which is shipped (or *consigned*) to a dealer, usually for promotional purposes, payment to be made only after the sale is accomplished.

converting from cost to retail   *See* Chapter 14.

cooperative advertising   A formal plan through which the bookseller and publisher share a specified percentage of the cost for local advertising of a book or group of books. Also called "co-op money."

copyright   The right, granted by Federal law, to the creator or distributor of literary or artistic material, for exclusive publication, distribution or sale of such property. To secure a copyright to a book, the author must deposit two copies with the Copyright Office in the Library of Congress in Washington, together with a registration fee. The copyright is presently in effect for twenty-eight years and may be renewed for another twenty-eight years if applied for by the author or his heirs. After this time, the work is regarded as being in the "public domain"—it may be reprinted or published without permission or payment of royalty. Pending legislation would change the term of copyright in the United States to a period extending fifty years after the death of the author.

cost of sales   *See* Chapter 14.

counter display   A small rack or a poster with a pocket for display and for impulse sales at a checkout counter or on a sales table.

cut   Any printed illustration or the engraving from which it is printed. *See* Line cut.

c.w.o.   "Cash with order."

dating   An extension of credit offered by a publisher. For example, books may be purchased in the summer with the invoice bearing a December or January due date.

Dewey Decimal System   A classification of books into ten major categories with many subdivisions. Used by most public and institutional libraries in classifying and shelving their books, it was devised by librarian Melvil Dewey in 1876, at the age of twenty-five.

direct mail   Advertising material mailed to a specific list of potential customers, soliciting orders directly by mail.

discount   A percentage of the retail price of a book or books allowed by the publisher to the wholesaler or retailer as compensation for acting as distributor. To determine discount, divide the difference between the cost and retail price of an item by its retail price. $2 *(Retail Price)* – $1.20 *(Cost)* = $.80 ÷ $2 = .40, or 40%.

Douay Bible (D.V.)   An English translation of the Latin Vulgate Bible by Roman Catholic scholars.

drop ship   Delivery to an address other than the one to which the invoice is sent. In the interest of saving time and additional postal charges, a bookseller, for example, may direct a publisher to *drop-ship* a special order to his customer.

duodecimo *or* **12mo**   A book approximately seven and three-quarter inches high. *See* Book sizes.

dummy   A mockup of a forthcoming *title* (q.v.), a *dummy* book with blank pages surrounded by the cover and jacket actually designed for it. Often used by publishers' salesmen when taking advance orders for a book in which format and appearance are important.

dust jacket (d.j.)   The paper cover placed around a bound book. Also called "dust wrapper" (d.w.).

el-hi   A term used to indicate books intended for elementary and high school use.

embossing   Raised ornamentation or printing made with a blank die.

end papers   Paper at the beginning and end of a book, half of which is pasted to the inside of the case binding to conceal the raw boards and the binding tape. The other half becomes the first or last leaf of a book and is normally an unnumbered page.

engraving   *See* Halftone and Linecut.

e.o.m.   "End of the month," an invoice symbol. Often *2/10 e.o.m.:* 2 per cent discount may be deducted by the tenth of the month following date of the invoice; later payment is net. If the invoice is dated on the twenty-fifty or later, it is generally accepted that it will become due a month later. Taking 2 per cent is equivalent to an annual interest rate of 36 per cent; 1 per cent, to 18 per cent on a yearly basis. Since many publishers prepare and date invoices at times when their computers would otherwise be idle, the actual shipping date appears only on the publisher's statement, which is valid for discount purposes.

erotica   Literature that deals with sexual acts.

errata   Errors found in a book after it has been printed, usually noted on a page, or slip (*tip-in*, q.v.) inserted into the volume. The singular is "erratum."

ex libris   "From the books of," a Latin phrase used on bookplates followed by the owner's name.

expenses   *See* Chapter 14.

fiscal year   *See* Chapter 14.

fixtures   Shelves, tables, and other devices on which books are displayed in a store.

flat display   A display of books with jackets or front covers facing the customer as contrasted with "spine-out" display.

flyleaf (flyleaves)   The unprinted page or pages at the beginning and end of a book that are not the *end papers* (q.v.).

f.o.b.   "Free on board," an invoice symbol. Delivery from the warehouse to the carrier is free, but the rest of the trip is at the buyer's expense. Originally it referred to the transport of goods from the warehouse to the railroad terminal in the days before truck freight, now it means simply that the buyer pays the freight from the shipping point.

folio   A book approximately fifteen inches high. *See* Book sizes. It also means "page number," as: "Even *folios* are on the left-hand pages and odd *folios* on the right-hand."

fore edge   The edge of a book opposite its *spine* (q.v.).

fore-edge painting   A picture hand-painted on the fore edge of a book which becomes visible only when the leaves are fanned. This form of book decoration flourished in the late eighteenth century. Books with these paintings are collectors' items today. It is not unusual, however, to find counterfeit, recent paintings on older books.

format   The shape, size, design, and general makeup of a book.

frontispiece   An illustration facing the title page.

galley proof   Printer's proof taken from type before it has been arranged in page form. A *galley* is a printer's storage drawer that holds a column of type about twenty-two inches long.

goffered *or* **gauffered edges**   Indented or embossed edges to add decorative effect to a book. Books that are *goffered* are sometimes collectors' items in the antiquarian trade.

gothic novel   A romantic-historical novel of suspense. Daphne du Maurier, Victoria Holt, and Mary Stewart are among the most popular writers of *gothics* today.

gross profit   The difference between total receipts and actual cost of goods sold.

gutter   The margin or white space between the facing pages of a book.

Gutenberg, Johann (1398?–1468?)   Printer of the Gutenberg Bible, one of the earliest and certainly the most famous of large books printed from movable type.

halftone   Reproduction of a photograph or painting using a series of dots so tiny as to be almost invisible. The dots are incorporated by photographing the original through a screen, the "screened" photograph then is used to make a printing plate. Fine reproductions require paper of high quality and make use of 150 and more dots to the square inch. The screen size is indicated by the number of dots per square inch. *See* Line cut.

hardback   *See* Clothbound.

hardbound   *See* Clothbound.

hard cover   *See* Clothbound.

hornbook   A primer, usually in the shape of a paddle protected by a sheet of transparent horn, having on it the alphabet and other rudiments, such as the Lord's Prayer, and used in Colonial America and England to teach children to read. Though hornbooks were common at one time, authentic examples are very rare today.

hurt book   A damaged or shopworn book that is still readable with all the pages intact. Some publishers make hurt books available to booksellers at greatly reduced prices.

ICBA   International Community of Booksellers Associations, a world group with headquarters in Vienna.

imprimatur   From the Latin meaning "let it be printed." Official approval of the Roman Catholic Church to print and publish a book.

imprint   The publisher's name, or the name of a subsidiary or special series, placed on the title page of a book.

incunabula   The plural of a Latin word meaning "cradle." Books issued before A.D. 1500, in the earliest days of printing. More than 35,000 examples are known to exist.

India paper   A thin, sturdy, opaque paper often used in Bibles and dictionaries. Less brittle than ordinary paper, it will not eventually break if accidentally folded or creased.

inserts   Illustrations or other material added to a book before it is bound.

inventory   The total stock-in-trade in the possession of a retailer. *Taking inventory* is the process of determining the value of goods on hand. *See also* Chapter 14.

invoice   A detailed list, with prices, terms of payment, and other information, of an individual shipment from a publisher or other supplier. The publisher's bill.

ISBN   International Standard Book Number. A numbering system designed to identify by publisher and title every book published in any country using the system.

italics (ital.)   A slanted type as distinct from "roman." *This sentence is set in italics.* This sentence is in roman.

jacket   The removable paper cover placed around a bound book. Also called "dust jacket" (d.j.) or "dust wrapper" (d.w.).

Jiffy bag   A padded paper bag used to mail books, commonly available from wholesale paper companies in six different sizes.

jobber A wholesale distributor of books, usually stocking books of all major publishers.

job lots Groups of books, usually discontinued, offered by publishers at reduced prices.

King James Bible An English translation of the Bible from Hebrew and Greek published in 1611 under the auspices of King James I of England. Despite numerous modern translations, the King James Bible, or Authorized Version (A.V.), is still widely used.

kraft paper From the German for "strength." A sturdy brown paper used for wrapping books and other packages.

laminate Literally "in layers." Book jackets are commonly *laminated,* that is, covered with a clear plastic sheeting that provides them with a glossy effect and adds to their durability.

l.c. *See* Lower case.

lending library A library from which books, mostly current fiction, may be rented for a fee. In the early 1930's and early 1940's, there were well over 30,000 lending libraries in stores of all kinds throughout the country, many stocked and serviced by chain distributors. There are far fewer today because of the easy availability of paperbacks and also because of more generous allocations of funds for public libraries. Called also "rental library" or "circulating library."

letterpress *See* Offset.

library binding A specially reinforced binding for library use. Because of the higher cost of manufacture, books with library bindings usually carry a lower discount. Some books are available only in library binding.

limited edition A special printing of a book limited to a stated number of copies, usually numbered consecutively and signed by the author.

line cut An unscreened photoengraving on metal, usually zinc, for reproducing black-and-white drawings. Known also as "line etching." *See* Halftone.

list price The price set by the publisher as the recommended retail price of a book. The bookseller's discount is based on the list price.

literary agent An intermediary between author and publisher, paid on a commission basis by the author. It is often as difficult for an unpublished author to find a competent literary agent willing to work with him as it is to find a publisher.

LJ *Library Journal,* published semi-monthly (monthly in July and August) for public and private libraries by R. R. Bowker Co.

loss leader A book or other merchandise advertised and sold below or near actual cost to attract customers into a store. Because they have an established list price, books have long been regarded as being among the most effective merchandise for such promotion.

lower case (l.c.)   Small letters as distinguished from *upper-case* (q.v.), or capital, letters.

markdowns   Unsold or shopworn books reduced in price for clearance.

markup   The difference, expressed as a percentage, between what the bookseller pays for a book and what he sells it for.

mass-market paperbacks   Books, frequently reprints of previously published hard-cover titles, on less expensive paper and bound in flexible paper covers, for wide distribution in many types of outlets, such as newsstands, variety stores, and supermarkets, as well as in bookstores. These books are sold today in more than 100,000 outlets. (The latest edition of the *American Book Trade Directory* lists about 16,000 stores and shops that compose the regular "book trade.")

microfiche, microfilm   A *microfilm* is a strip of film, often 16mm or 35mm wide, on which the pages of books and documents are photographed in greatly reduced size. A *microfiche* is another photographic method of storing information, with the advantage of being extremely compact and easy to store. An entire book may be accommodated on a 4"X6" card, as may large portions of a wholesaler's inventory. A disadvantage of both microfilm and microfiche is that they require special equipment to be read.

mint *or* **mint condition**   A book so described is like new.

Morris, William (1834–96)   English poet, artist, and craftsman, founder of the Kelmscott Press, which produced many books that are still regarded as among the finest ever printed.

morocco   A durable leather made from goatskin commonly used for bookbinding.

ms.   "Manuscript." Plural, "mss."

NACS   National Association of College Stores, originally a splinter group from ABA. Today many members of NACS are also members of ABA, and there is close cooperation between the two organizations.

NBC   National Book Committee, a national organization made up of prominent individuals interested in the support of books and reading. In addition to bestowing the National Medal for Literature and conducting the National Book Awards and National Library Week, the NBC has undertaken other important projects designed to stimulate the wide distribution and use of books.

net profit   The actual profit made by a store after all costs, such as merchandise, rent, and wages, have been deducted from gross receipts. *See* Gross profit.

nihil obstat   From the Latin, "nothing hinders." Approval by a Roman Catholic censor for the publication of a book. *See also* Imprimatur.

NLW   National Library Week, a promotion under the direction of the National Book Committee to encourage reading in general. Many booksellers also participate in NLW.

non-book   A book of small literary value frequently composed of pictures, press clippings, or speeches.

n.o.p.   "Not our publication," an invoice symbol.

n.y.p.   "Not yet published," an invoice symbol.

o.c.   "Order canceled," an invoice symbol.

occult   *Occult* books are those that relate to mysticism, magic, clairvoyance, etc.

octavo   A book approximately nine and three-quarter inches high. *See* Book sizes.

offset *or* **photo-offset**   A method of printing that involves the indirect transfer of an impression from a printing plate to paper as contrasted with "letterpress," which involves a direct impression from type or a printing plate made from type. Offset printing, once used mainly for large editions, is now used for printing most books.

on consignment, on sale   *See* Consignment.

opacity, opaque   *Opaque* paper is not transparent. It is important that India paper or any thin paper have a high quality of *opacity,* so that the printing on one page does not show through on the other side.

open to buy   That amount in a store's budget available for new purchases in a given period of time.

option   The right to buy or sell a property, as a manuscript or a book, within a specified time at a specified price. Not a retailing term, it refers most often to subsidiary rights.

out of print (o.p.)   When a book is out of print, the publisher has no more copies for sale and does not intend to reprint.

out of stock (o.s.)   The publisher or distributor has no copies in stock and is, usually, awaiting delivery of a new printing. Other abbreviations commonly used: *o.s.i.,* "out of stock indefinitely"; *t.o.s.,* "temporarily out of stock," copies should be available in the near future.

overhead   The cost of running a business, including rent, wages, utilities, etc. *See also* Gross profit, Net profit.

packing slip   A list, enclosed with a shipment, indicating its contents. Frequently a partial copy of the invoice, it generally shows the list price of the titles shipped but not the discount or net price.

page proof   After the *galley proof* (q.v.) has been read and corrected, the type is then arranged by pages and new proof is pulled and resubmitted for final correcting.

paperback   A book bound in flexible paper covers without boards. *See also* Mass-market paperbacks.

perfect binding   A glued binding using newly developed, strong adhesives, not sewn or stitched, employed for most paperbacks and occasionally, in order to cut costs, for hard-cover books.

PG (PG's)   "Personalized greeting" card(s). Imprinted Christmas cards, one of the most profitable bookstore sidelines.

photo-offset   *See* Offset.

pied type   Type that is completely mixed up and must be re-sorted before it can be used. This is a very old printing term, originating in the idea that the type was "knocked into pie."

pirated edition   A book reproduced and sold without legal authorization or permission of the copyright owner. *See also* Unauthorized edition.

plates   Illustrations inserted in a book at the time it is bound.

plug   A slow-selling book. Also called "stiff," "dog," "turkey," or "bomb."

plus sale   The sale of a second or third book by recommendation of the salesperson to a customer who has requested a specific title.

pocket book   Frequently misused as a synonym for "paperbacks." Actually Pocket Books is the imprint of Simon and Schuster's mass-market subsidiary. The confusion is understandable since Pocket Books was the first of the American companies to produce mass-market paperbacks and was a pioneer in what is often called the "paperback revolution."

point   The measurement of type, a *point* is approximately 1/72 of an inch in height. This sentence is set in nine-point type; the chapter essays are set in ten-point type. The smallest type in general use for books is six point; the largest, fourteen point.

pre-pub   A special price for a new (usually expensive) book offered for orders in advance of the publication date. Often such prices are in effect through the Christmas season until the new year.

process engraving   *See* Thermographing.

pro forma   From the Latin meaning "for the sake of form." A *pro forma* invoice from a publisher requires payment in advance of shipment.

protected, fully protected   Books so designated by a publisher may be returned, if unsold, for full credit.

PTLA   *Publishers' Trade List Annual,* a collection in seven volumes of the trade lists of all the principal American publishers, published each year in September by R. R. Bowker Co.

public domain *See* Copyright.

publisher's rep. A publisher's *representative* who travels to make calls on booksellers in a defined region. Also, *traveler* (q.v.).

pulps *See* Slicks.

PW *Publishers Weekly,* a publication for the entire book trade, publishers, booksellers, and book manufacturers. Officially, the name of the journal is now spelled without an apostrophe.

quality paperbacks *See* Trade paperbacks.

quarto A book approximately twelve inches high. *See* Book sizes.

quire A measure of paper consisting of twenty-four sheets. *See* Ream.

q.v. "Which see."

rag paper Paper that is made from cotton or linen rags rather than from chemical pulp. Fine stationery or fine book paper has a high degree of rag content. Because it is thought to have a maximum durability, all U.S. paper currency and most stock and bond certificates are made of 100 per cent rag.

ream A ream of paper is now usually 500 sheets. Formerly it was 20 quires, or 480 sheets.

recto The right-hand page of a book. The left-hand page or the reverse of a printed sheet is the "verso."

remainders Publishers' overstock offered to booksellers usually through "remainder houses" at reduced prices. When a book is *remaindered,* it is generally declared out of print. Sometimes a publisher will sell part of his stock of a title as a remainder and retain the rest to be sold at list price. Such books are known as "partial remainders." Remainders are also referred to as "promotional books," "sale books," "bargain books," and *reprints* (q.v.).

rental library *See* Lending library.

reprints A new printing of a book or an edition, usually in cheaper form than the original. *See also* Academic reprints.

review copies Complimentary copies of a newly published title sent out by publishers to the book review media. Sometimes booksellers may buy from reviewers a quantity of newly published books for which they have no further use at substantial discounts off the list price.

roman *See* Italics.

royalty The commission paid by a publisher to an author, usually a percentage of the list price of all copies of the book sold.

RSV Revised Standard Version (of the Bible).

sales per capita *See* Chapter 14.

sales per square foot *See* Chapter 14.

SCOP   Single Copy Order Plan. A system worked out by ABA and most of the larger publishers through which booksellers, by sending payment with order, may buy a single copy of a book at a favorable discount.

Second International   *See Webster III.*

signature   A printed sheet that when folded forms one section of a book.

silk screen   A process of printing in which ink is forced through a screen of silk or other fine fabric into a printing surface, which may be paper, plastics, or textured material. A few of the smaller greeting card companies use the silk-screen process to produce Christmas cards and everyday cards intended to look different from the mass-produced kind.

skid   A wooden platform on which paper or books are delivered. A skid of paper or books weighs about 3,000 pounds.

sleeper   A book for which there is little demand when first published but for which a market develops over a period of several months or a year. *Jonathan Livingston Seagull,* one of the best sellers of all time, was a sleeper.

slicks   Magazines printed on slick, or coated, paper. Those printed on cheaper paper, similar to newsprint, are known as "pulps."

slipcase   A protective container with one open end into which a book or books can be inserted.

slit-card   A card that is slit so that it may fit into or around a book for purposes of display.

spine   The back of a book connecting the two covers. Also known as the "backbone," or "backstrap."

standing order   An order that holds good until it is filled. Also an order for succeeding issues of a publication. Most booksellers, for example, leave a standing order with the R. R. Bowker Co. for *Books in Print* and other reference works.

statement stuffers   Publishers' advertising designed to be mailed to booksellers with the publisher's monthly statements.

stet   From the Latin meaning "let it stand." A common printers' and proofreaders' mark denoting that a word or passage previously deleted is to be retained.

subsidiary   A publishing company owned by a parent company. *See* Conglomerate.

text edition   A book intended for the classroom, usually without a jacket and carrying a discount lower than that for a *trade edition* (q.v.).

thermographing, thermography   A process of raised printing that makes use of a powder sprinkled on a freshly printed sheet or card and heated to make the lettering rise. Wedding invitations and social stationery that are thermographed have been considered inferior in quality to those engraved from a copper plate, yet in the past few years some of the leading thermographers have become so expert in their craft that it is difficult to tell a thermographed sheet from one engraved by plate. Thermographing is also known as "process engraving."

thesaurus   From the Latin meaning "treasure." A collection of words or concepts relating to a particular field, as a thesaurus of medical terminology. Also, specifically, a book of synonyms and antonyms, as *Roget's Thesaurus.*

Third International   *See Webster III.*

tip-in   An illustration or leaf pasted, or *tipped,* into a book, often by hand. Illustrations in the more expensive art books are usually *tipped-in.*

title   A book, its physical and metaphysical aspects, as: "Booksellers could stand fewer *titles* from publishers."

tooling   Impressions made on the cover of a book using gold leaf or other decorative material.

t.o.s.   "Temporarily out of stock," an invoice symbol.

trade edition   An edition of a book intended for general distribution through the bookstores, as contrasted with text, library, paperback, and book club editions. Books so designated are entitled to full bookseller discount.

trade paperbacks   Those not intended or suitable for the mass market but chiefly for sale in bookstores, such as Doubleday's Anchor Books or the Scribner Library. *See also* Mass-market paperbacks.

traveler *or* **book traveler**   A publisher's salesman. Also, *publisher's representative* (q.v.).

turnover   *See* Chapter 14.

typo   An informal expression for "typographical error."

typographer   A typsetter, printer, or printing designer.

typophile   A lover of printing or typography.

unauthorized edition   An edition published without the permission of the author or the original publisher. *See also* Pirated edition.

upper case (u.c.)   Capital letters, as distinguished from *lower-case* (q.v.), or small, letters. *See also* Cap.

vanity publisher   A publisher who issues books at the author's risk and expense.

verso   The left-hand page of a book or the reverse of a printed sheet. The right-hand page is called the "recto."

watermark   The design in paper that may be seen when held to the light. Paper for a fine book edition is sometimes *watermarked* with a design to show that the paper was made expressly for that edition.

Webster III   The third edition of *Webster's New International Dictionary*, published by G. & C. Merriam Co. in 1961. The first edition was published in 1909; the second (*Webster II*), in 1934.

zinc etching   *See* Line cut.

Index

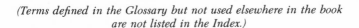

*(Terms defined in the Glossary but not used elsewhere in the book
are not listed in the Index.)*